D0144211

List of Annotated Sample Student Papers

FIFTH EDITION

POCKET
KEYS FOR
WRITERS

Ann Raimes

Susan K. Miller-Cochran
North Carolina State University

CENGAGE
Learning·

Australia • Brazil • Mexico • Singapore • United Kingdom • United States

CENGAGE Learning®

Pocket Keys for Writers, **Fifth Edition, Ann Raimes and Susan K. Miller-Cochran**

Product Director: Monica Eckman
Product Manager: Christopher Bennem
Managing Developer: Leslie Taggart
Content Developer: Stephanie P. Carpenter
Associate Content Developer: Rachel L. Smith
Product Assistant: Kerry DeVito
Media Developer: Cara Douglass-Graff
Senior Marketing Manager: Erin Parkins
Content Project Manager: Rosemary Winfield
Art Director: Marissa Falco
Manufacturing Planner: Betsy Donaghey
IP Analyst: Ann Hoffman
IP Project Manager: Farah Faud
Production Service: Thistle Hill Publishing Services
Text Designer: Cenveo® Publisher Services/Alisha Webber
Cover Designer: Roycroft Design
Compositor: Cenveo® Publisher Services

Library of Congress Control Number: 2014951116

ISBN: 978-1-305-09213-6

Cengage Learning
20 Channel Center Street
Boston, MA 02210
USA

Cengage Learning is a leading provider of customized learning solutions with office locations around the globe, including Singapore, the United Kingdom, Australia, Mexico, Brazil, and Japan. Locate your local office at **international.cengage.com/region**.

Cengage Learning products are represented in Canada by Nelson Education, Ltd. For your course and learning solutions, visit **www.cengage.com**. Purchase any of our products at your local college store or at our preferred online store **www.cengagebrain.com**.

Instructors: Please visit **login.cengage.com** and log in to access instructor-specific resources.

Printed in the United States of America
Print Number: 01   Print Year: 2014

Acknowledgments

This new edition of *Pocket Keys for Writers* has benefited from the wisdom, experience, and critical thinking of many dedicated composition teachers around the country. We are grateful to all of the following for their help:

Patricia Barnes, Delaware County Community College
Lisa Beckelhimer, University of Cincinnati
Ann Bliss, University of California, Merced
Amy Burtner, Monroe Community College
Beth Capo, Illinois College
Marian Carcache, Auburn University
Tim Carens, College of Charleston
Allan Carter, College of Dupage
Stephen Criswell, University of South Carolina,
    Lancaster
Linda Cullum, Kutztown University
Susan Garrett, Goucher College
Forrest Greenwood, The College of St. Scholastica
Betsy Hall, Illinois College
Jane Hammons, University of California, Berkeley
Jackie Herbers, Viterbo University
Nancy Hull, Calvin College
Patti Kurtz, Minot State University
Terri LaRocco, University of Findlay
Angela Laflen, Marist College
Gregory Lattanzio, Monroe Community College
Lea Masiello, Indiana University of Pennsylvania
Diane Matza, Utica College
Leanne Maunu, Palomar College
Kevin McKelvey, University of Indianapolis
Christy Newman, University of San Francisco
Laurie Olson-Horswill, North Idaho College
Gerald Richman, Suffolk University
Matthew Schmeer, Johnson County Community College
Tracy Schrems, St. Bonaventure University
William Schuh, Erie Community College
Nathan Shepley, Ohio University
Mark Spencer, Southeastern Oklahoma State University
Lillian Taylor, Highland Community College

Special thanks go to editors Stephanie Carpenter and Leslie Taggart, who made many valuable suggestions for this new edition, especially on what and how to revise and where to include new material in the text. This edition has benefited greatly from their input, and we are grateful to them for their dedication to this handbook and their insights into what teachers and students need.

PART ONE

Writing in College

CREATE

PURPOSE

- What is/was the text meant to accomplish? Is that purpose explicit or implied?
- What possibilities are there for creating a text that could meet that purpose?
- Are there specific expectations the text must meet to achieve its intended purpose? If so, what are they?

AUDIENCE

- Who is the audience for this piece of writing? Is there more than one audience? If so, are their interests similar or competing?
- What does the audience expect in terms of content, language use, tone, style, format, and delivery method?
- If expectations are not met, what is the impact on the audience?

VOICE

- What unique perspective does the author bring to this piece of writing? How is that unique perspective communicated?
- How explicitly should the author make reference to his or her perspective? Should the author use *I*, and if so, when and why?
- What is the author's tone in the piece of writing? For example, is it playful, serious, accusing, encouraging, hopeful, factual? What effect does that tone have on the piece of writing?

MEDIUM

- How could the writing be delivered to its intended audience to meet its purpose? A blog posting? A printed essay? A website? A newspaper article? An academic journal article? An mp3 file? A YouTube video?
- What formatting rules should the text follow in that medium?
- What would the impact be of delivering the text in another medium?

1 The Writing Process in Context

Starting on a writing project can be hard if you think of a piece of writing only as a permanent document that others will judge. A blank page or an empty screen can be daunting, but the act of writing generally offers an advantage over speaking: You can go back and make changes.

In fact, the activities of writing overlap and recur; the writer loops back, revisits, rethinks, reconsiders, and refines. A writer (you!) continually revisits the steps of the process, adjusting and improving all along the way. Always remember, writing is a process of creation that involves planning, prewriting, drafting, reading, revising, editing, proofreading, and presenting (not necessarily in linear order)—all guided by critical thinking.

As you get started on a writing project, remember that writing is a conversation. When you write, you write for someone. With some writing tasks, you write only for yourself, and other times you write for another individual (for example, a teacher, a supervisor, a friend) or for a group of people (such as a class, a work group, an admissions committee). How and what you write are influenced by your purpose in writing, by your knowledge, by your reading and thinking about a subject, and by the expectations of the audience for which you are writing.

1a Your purpose

Ask yourself: What is my main purpose for writing in a particular situation? Here are some possibilities that are common in academic writing:

- explain an idea or theory or explore a question (expository writing)
- analyze the structure or content of a text (analytical writing)
- report on a process, an experiment, or lab results (technical or scientific writing)
- provide a status update on a project at work (business writing)
- persuade readers to understand your point of view, change their minds, or take action (persuasive or argumentative writing)
- record and reflect on your own experiences and feelings (expressive writing)
- tell a story (narrative writing)

The purpose of your writing will determine your options for presenting your final text.

1b Your audience

A good writer keeps readers in mind at all times. Achieving this connection, however, often proves challenging because not all readers have the same characteristics. Readers come from different regions, communities, ethnic groups, organizations, and academic disciplines, all with their own linguistic and rhetorical conventions. This means that you as a writer have several shifting selves, depending on your audience. In other words, you write differently when you text a friend, post a message on *Facebook*, post a blog, write an essay for a college instructor, or apply for a grant, an internship, or a job.

KEY POINTS
Know Your Audience

- What readers do you envision for your writing? What do those readers expect in terms of length, format, date of delivery, use of technical terms, and formality of language?

- Which characteristics do you share with your readers? How might their nationality, culture, race, class, ethnicity, gender, profession, interests, and opinions affect their reception of your message? What common ground do you share that might influence your style, tone, dialect, words, and the details you include?

- Is your instructor your main reader? If so, find out about the expectations of readers in his or her academic discipline. In most cases, regard your instructor as a stand-in for an audience of general readers, and ask yourself what background information you need to include for a general reader. Ask to see a model paper.

1c Your voice

Your voice in writing is the way you come across to readers. What impression do you want them to form of you as a person—of your values and opinions? One of the first considerations is whether you want to draw attention to your opinions as the writer by using the first person pronoun *I* or whether you want to use the more neutral approach of keeping that *I* at a distance. Many academic disciplines have specific expectations for when and how to use *I*. It is always useful to consult your instructor when you are unsure.

Regardless of whether or not you use the word *I* in a particular piece of writing, beware of the leaden effect of using *I*-avoiding phrases such as "it would seem" or "it is to be expected that" and of overusing the pronoun *one*. William Zinsser in *On Writing Well* points out that "good writers are visible just behind their words," conveying as they write "a sense of I-ness." He advises at least thinking of *I* as you write your first draft, maybe even writing it and then editing it out later.

1d   Your use of media

What are you working toward? A print document? A document with embedded images or other media? A multimedia presentation? An online document with hyperlinks, images, sound, or video? As you work through the process of choosing and developing a topic for a defined purpose and audience, consider simultaneously the communication means that are available to you, especially if you are presenting your work online or with the help of presentation software. Always bear in mind how you can enhance your ideas with the design of your document and the use of images, graphs, or multimedia tools.

1e   Revising and editing

In your everyday communications with friends and family using *Instagram, Facebook, Twitter,* and such, you may be used to writing often and writing fast. In the academic and business worlds, almost everything is drafted, circulated, and revised. Revising is a common practice for a good reason. A first draft gives you a road map of what to do next, but it is not a polished work that you can hand in as a final version. You need to build in time for analyzing and reworking a draft, using your own thoughts on how to improve the draft, as well as getting feedback from other readers. After you have improved the ideas, flow, logic, clarity, and completeness, you can then do another reading specifically to check that the sentences, grammar, and punctuation are accurate and graceful. Chapters 12–37 will help you revise and edit your papers to free them of the glitches or errors that may annoy readers.

As you probably know, a certain type of language—called Standard Academic English—is preferred by academic audiences. It is vastly different from the language used in informal writing. It avoids slang and abbreviations and adheres to a largely agreed-upon set of conventions for spelling, grammar, punctuation, and style. Yes, times change, and language changes. Disputes do inevitably arise, such as over the use of *who* or *whom, they* or *he or she.* Still, there exists enough agreement over what is "correct" for this preferred language to be labeled "standard."

You may wonder who sets this standard. No one person, committee, or professional organization determines it. Rather, Standard Academic English is a set of conventions used by educated speakers and writers. Despite some local variations, areas of dispute, and shifts over time, Standard Academic English remains politically and sociologically branded as the language of those in power. No matter how insightful and original your ideas may be, readers will soon become impatient if those ideas are not expressed in language that follows the conventions of Standard Academic English. Readers who keep coming across what they see as errors in words and sentences may simply dismiss your writing. Rather than charitably overlooking grammatical problems and sentence snarls, they will perceive you, the writer, as careless or simply not aware of what readers expect. Using the version of Standard Academic English presented in this book, along with the editing guide in 33b, will help you avoid being perceived in this way.

2 A Framework for Critical Thinking

Texts in academic, personal, and professional settings all have contexts that influence how we interpret, respond to, use, or ignore them. Understanding that context, both when reading and when writing, is a key to critical thinking. The word *critical* is not negative and does not indicate that you are finding fault with something. Instead, *critical thinking* refers to the careful, reflective consideration that writers give to a text when they are reading closely and writing deliberately. In this sense, the ability to understand the context of a piece of writing (either one you are reading or one you are writing) and to consider the ways the purpose, audience, voice, and medium shape the text is a key component of critical thinking.

KEY POINTS
A Framework for Critical Thinking

As you read and write, especially for academic purposes, you may find the following framework useful for critically considering the relationship between context and writing:

PURPOSE	AUDIENCE
• What is/was the text meant to accomplish? Is that purpose explicit or implied? • What possibilities are there for creating a text that could meet that purpose? • Are there specific expectations the text must meet to achieve its intended purpose? If so, what are they?	• Who is the audience for this piece of writing? Is there more than one audience? If so, are their interests similar or competing? • What does the audience expect in terms of content, language use, tone, style, format, and delivery method? • If expectations are not met, what is the impact on the audience?
VOICE	MEDIUM
• What unique perspective does the author bring to this piece of writing? How is that unique perspective communicated? • How explicitly should the author make reference to his or her perspective? Should the author use *I*, and if so, when and why? • What is the author's tone in the piece of writing? For example, is it playful, serious, accusing, encouraging, hopeful, factual? What effect does that tone have on the piece of writing?	• How could the writing be delivered to its intended audience to meet its purpose? A blog posting? A printed essay? A website? A newspaper article? An academic journal article? An mp3 file? A YouTube video? • What formatting rules should the text follow in that medium? • What would the impact be of delivering the text in another medium?

You can use these questions as a guide for understanding and interpreting the text you are reading. When you write, you can use these questions to help you make decisions at important points in the writing process. These questions can be useful for writing that you do in many contexts, including professional settings and college courses.

3 Reading and Writing Arguments

It is a good habit to step back and read a piece of writing critically, whether it is your own or somebody else's, in order to identify its merits and faults. One type of writing you will encounter often in college is argument. We often associate the word *argument* with combat and confrontation, but the Latin root of the word *argue* means "to make clear." The goal of an argument, then, is to win over your audience with clear explanation and persuasion. In the end, the good argument is the one that presents its position on a claim in a measured, logical way. It marshals evidence and reasons, acknowledges assumptions, and considers exceptions.

To think critically about an argument, keep an open mind and ask probing questions while you consider the context of the argument. Readers will use the same care when they read an argument that *you* write.

Do not assume that something you read is accurate or unbiased. Here are questions to ask yourself as you read an argument, either your own or someone else's:

QUESTIONS ABOUT CONTEXT

1. **What is the writer's purpose?** Is the writer expressing an opinion, arguing for a course of action, making an evaluation, or arguing against another claim?

2. **Who is the writer's audience?** Are there choices the writer has made to present the argument most persuasively to the intended audience?

3. **Who is the writer, and how credible is his or her voice?** What is the writer's background and credentials? What is the writer's bias? Is the writer credible?

4. **What medium has the writer chosen to deliver the argument?** Is the choice of medium appropriate for the argument? Does it constrain the argument in any way? Would another medium be more appropriate or accessible?

QUESTIONS ABOUT ARGUMENT

5. **Is the argument built around a debatable claim (thesis)?** Has the author made a conclusion about a topic rather than just stating a fact?

6. **How reliable are the writer's statements?** Are the writer's statements measured, accurate, fair, and to the point? Do readers feel the need to interject a challenge, using "but…"?

7. **What assumptions does the writer make?** If a writer argues for a college education for everyone, is the underlying assumption that a college education automatically leads to happiness and success?

8. **Does the writer support claims with evidence?** Is the writer relying on extreme language or name-calling rather than on presentation of evidence? Does the writer fail to support any part of the claim?

9. **Where does the evidence come from?** Can the reader trust the sources? Is the evidence persuasive to the writer's intended audience?

3a Is the argument built around a debatable claim (thesis)?

The position a writer takes on a topic constitutes the argument's claim or thesis. If you are writing an argument, keep a working thesis in mind as you write your first draft, but be flexible. You are the boss as you write. You can change and narrow your thesis whenever you like. Sometimes a clear thesis may not emerge for you until the end of your first draft, pointing the way to the focus and organization of your next draft.

KEY POINTS
A Good Working Thesis

- narrows your topic to a single main idea that you want to communicate
- makes your point clearly and firmly in one sentence or two
- states not simply a fact but rather an opinion or a summary conclusion from your observation
- makes a generalization that can be supported by details, facts, and examples within the assigned limitations of time and space
- stimulates curiosity and interest in readers and prompts them to wonder, "Why do you think that?" and then read on

An effective claim is focused, specific, and debatable. In other words, it should not be an overly broad statement; a statement of fact; a bland, self-evident truism; or a personal feeling.

Too broad	This paper is about violence in video games.
Revised	The violence in video games can have negative effects on children's behavior in school.
Fact	*Plessy v. Ferguson,* a Supreme Court case that supported racial segregation, was overturned in 1954 by *Brown v. Board of Education.*
Revised	The overturning of *Plessy v. Ferguson* by *Brown v. Board of Education* has not led to rapid or widespread advances in integrated education.
Truism	Bilingual education has advantages and disadvantages.
Revised	A bilingual program is more effective than an immersion program at helping high school students grasp the basics of science and mathematics.
Personal opinion relying on feelings	I think jet-skiing is a dumb sport.
Revised to a specific proposal	Jet-skiing should be banned from public beaches.

3b Is the argument supported by reasons and evidence?

Supporting your claim Think of an argument as a structure of building blocks. A main idea, the claim (or thesis), is supported by reasons, each of which is supported by the main pieces of evidence. Each piece of evidence, in turn, is supported by specific and concrete details. Some writers make a rough, numbered outline of thesis, main points, and supporting examples before they work on their first draft. Others prefer to write a draft and then examine it for what has emerged. Formal outlines can be useful here, too. To write an outline, begin with writing down the thesis, and then list the sentences, making the points that provide support for the thesis and numbering them I, II, and so forth. Indicate the different levels of the points and examples that provide evidence for each point by using A, B, and so on, and then 1, 2, and so on, differentiating levels of supporting evidence. Making such an outline will focus your attention on structure and organization, revealing the sequence and logic of what is on the page as well as any gaps and redundancies.

You can support a claim by telling and showing readers what reasons, statistics, facts, examples, and expert testimony bolster and explain your point of view.

Reasons Imagine a reader asking you for reasons for your claim. Think of a reason as something that can be attached to a claim by the word *because*.

Thesis (claim)	**Colleges should stop using SAT scores to determine admissions.**
Reasons	1. (because) SAT scores are biased toward certain demographic groups.
	2. (because) There is not a strong correlation between SAT scores and student success in college.
	3. (because) Other factors are more important to consider in the admissions process.

Evidence An argument needs reasons, but reasons are not enough. Specific evidence that supports, illustrates, and explains the reasons is also needed. Imagine a reader saying, after you give one of your reasons, "Tell me why I should believe that." Your evidence will make your argument more persuasive by supporting your reasons.

Add to the outline any items of concrete evidence you will include to illustrate and explain your reasoning. What counts as evidence? Facts, statistics, stories, examples, and testimony from experts can all be used as evidence in support of your reasons. Consider using visual evidence, too: tables, graphs, images, and—for both oral and online presentations—multimedia (see 4c–4e).

3c Does the argument find points of common ground?

When you discuss views that you oppose, try to establish some common ground so that you do not offend readers who hold those opposing views. After all, you want them to continue reading and to be receptive to learning your point of view.

> **KEY POINTS**
> Establishing Common Ground
>
> 1. **Avoid extreme views or language.** Do not [ ] someone's views as *ridiculous, ignorant, immoral, [ra]cist,* or *crooked,* for example.
> 2. **Write to convince, not to confront.** Recognize shared concerns, and consider the inclusive use of *we.*
> 3. **Steer clear of sarcastic remarks** such as, "Suspending kids for fighting surely won't lead to additional problems."
> 4. **Use clear, everyday words** that sound as if you are speaking directly to your readers.
> 5. **Acknowledge valid arguments from your opponents,** and work to show why the arguments on your side carry more weight.
> 6. **If possible, propose a solution** with long-term benefits for everyone.

3d Can the argument be strengthened by using visuals?

Because of their immediacy and subtle appeal to a viewer's reason, emotions, and morals, visual arguments can be as persuasive as written arguments, if not more so. Whether their purpose is to strengthen an argument or to illustrate an argument in its complexity, writers often choose to supplement their essays with visuals. When you write an argument, consider adding to the impact of your thesis by including visual support. Vivid images such as maps, superimposed images, photographs, charts and graphs, political cartoons may say more than many words can to your readers.

Analyzing a visual for its unspoken argument or point of view is also part of the critical thinking process that underlies good reading and writing. Consider an advertisement

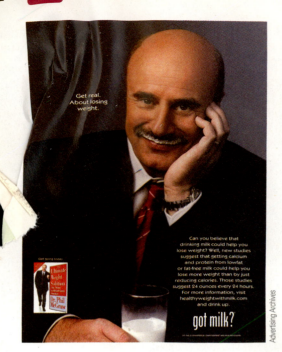

Advertising Archives

from the popular "Got Milk?" campaign. The advertisement features Dr. Phil McGraw, a mental health professional and former clinical psychologist who hosts the television talk show, *Dr. Phil*. The text to the left of Dr. Phil's image uses his catchphrase, "Get real," to make a claim about milk's potential for helping people lose weight above a thumbnail picture in the lower left-hand corner of an advertisement of Dr. Phil's just-published book, *The Ultimate Weight Solution*. Are the connections among Dr. Phil's credibility, milk, and book logical ones? Just as written arguments challenge readers to question assumptions and implications, visual arguments push viewers to think critically about the implications and intended effects of images.

Creating multimedia arguments   Present-day technology allows for a new way to express ideas. No longer limited to using type on a page, writers now can use screens to present an interaction of words, color, music, sound, images, and movies to tell a story and make a point. In preparing a presentation, consider the effectiveness of conveying emotion and meaning through colors and pictures as well as through words. If you use media imaginatively, you can do what writing teachers have long advised: Show, and don't just tell.

In Model Paper 1, which follows, visuals serve to illustrate and reinforce the writer's claim that family photographs, now accessible on the Web, go beyond private moments and show a variety of events, opening up pictures of family life to one and all.

KEY POINTS
The Features of a Good Argument

If you are writing an argument, examine your draft for the following features. You may also use this list to evaluate someone else's argument, such as the one shown in Model Paper 1:

- Your argument deals with a debatable issue.
- You use careful analysis of experiences, readings, or sources.
- You avoid an emphasis on strong personal feelings or beliefs, unsubstantiated by evidence.
- You take a position on and make a clear claim about your chosen topic.
- You support that position with detailed and specific evidence (such as reasons, facts, examples, descriptions, and stories).
- You establish common ground with listeners or readers.
- You take diverse viewpoints into account and discuss opposing views logically.

Model Paper 1: A student's argument essay (MLA)

Here is a draft of Amy Rae Dong's paper responding to an assignment to make a claim about a chosen topic of interest and support it with evidence. Dong is herself a keen photographer and is planning to become a moblogger, which is what attracted her to pursue this topic. She follows MLA 2009 guidelines for undergraduates. See chapter 9.

NOTE: Annotations have been added here to point out features of the paper that may be useful to you when you write your own argument essay in MLA style. **Blue** annotations point out issues of content and organization; red annotations point out MLA format issues.

MLA no longer recommends the inclusion of URLs (Web addresses) in the works-cited entries. However, you should include URLs when the reader probably cannot find the sources without them or if your instructor requires them.

**Name,
instructor,
course,
and date**

Amy Rae Dong

Professor Mahard

English 120, section 039

8 October 2014

**Title
centered**

The Family Photograph:

About More Than Just the Good Times

↔
1"

Many people hold one basic idea about the

phenomenon of family snapshots: that families *take*

pictures of good times to create a story for themselves

that says "unified, happy family." While this idea

remains partly true, it does not tell the whole story

any more. Today, ordinary family photographs are

often posted online and viewed there by strangers,

distant "friends" on social networking sites, or fellow

photo bloggers. Photographers with small, easy-to-use

digital cameras and large, relatively anonymous online

audiences are blurring the lines between private and

public, shifting what the family photograph means and

looks like. Putting our photos online for public scrutiny

is doing more than moving with the technological times;

it is changing our sense of why we take, save, and view

family photographs. Family snapshots are now less

**Claim
(thesis)**

about the private nuclear family and more about the

extended online human family. When posted online,

they become a means of self-expression, notoriety, and

**No extra
space
between
paragraphs**

connection with an online community.

Those who study traditional family snapshots and

albums conclude that people take and keep these

images to tell a proud message to themselves and

**Cites
author and
credentials**

others in their immediate circle. The essayist Susan

Sontag comments on this self-affirming way that

Dong 2

families preserve good memories: "[E]ach family constructs a portrait chronicle of itself—a portable kit of images that bears witness to its connectedness" (9). Vacation snapshots serve a distinct purpose, too: "Photographs will offer indisputable evidence that the trip was made, that the program was carried out, that fun was had" (9). In other words, family photographs make a type of equation between good times and enduring family bonds. These photos "bear witness" and "offer . . . evidence"—almost as if in a court of law. Conversely, not having a photographic record of troubled, disturbing, bad, or boring times allows negative experiences to slip away, deemphasized or even forgotten. While people may know that weathering rough times together can bring a family together, somehow they don't want a detailed photo reminder of those down times.

Capital added: 8c, p. 56

Other scholars have written about how valued family photographs have a positive theme and purpose. Art historian David Halle studies the clustered way that people display photos in their homes and finds there "the wish to repeat, again and again, one motif—the closeness of the nuclear family" (222). Anthropologist Richard Chalfen, in his book *Snapshot Versions of Life,* sees the positive purpose from a somewhat different angle: "Snapshot collections manifest a pride-filled movement toward adult life" (99). From firsthand experience, many people can confirm that the camera indeed comes out mainly on special happy family occasions (such as snowstorms, Halloween, a new puppy, a reunion, a holiday meal) and milestone events

Purpose of family photos

Page number

Dong 3

(a birthday, a prom, a move, leaving the military or returning from military service, an anniversary). The family photographic record often tapers off as people get older, but even if incomplete, this record of loved ones—and of being near to or surrounded by loved ones—can be deeply satisfying and meaningful.

Supporting evidence of change from photo albums

Today, however, we rarely make a physical photo album to show family and friends. Instead, many or most of us now take and store thousands of tiny photos on cell phones or digital cameras. In an article about Polaroid's plant closings and other changes in the photo industry, Ron Glaz, a digital imaging specialist, says, "Today's consumers prefer to look at photos on their computer screens and are more likely to say, 'E-mail that to me' rather than 'Give me a hard copy'" (qtd. in Bray C5). In addition to e-mailing photos, we can post

Bray, not Glaz, is in works-cited list

images to *Facebook, Twitter,* or *Instagram.* On *Look at Me,* a site that New Media professor Julian Gallo discusses, we can see and contribute to a large and wonderful gallery of miscellaneous family photographs that were found on the street, in the trash, or at flea markets. On *Flickr,* we can post old and new family photos, write some accompanying commentary about them or not, and tag them with search terms like *siblings, feasts,* or *hikes.* Figure 1 shows a typical family

Source of image from personal collection

photo (one of my family's Thanksgiving gatherings) that is now posted online and thus viewable by more than its original intended audience of just the family.

The "come one, come all" nature of these photo-sharing sites leads people to post photos not just of good times or big events but of everyday activities, even

Blue = content issues   Red = format issues

Dong 4

Stacey Dong Miskell

Fig. 1. Dong family photo.

tooth brushing. Figure 2 shows an atypical family photo: not dressed up for the occasion, not a special event, with nobody looking at the camera, but with an interest and a story all its own. These sites are like a family photo album but faster, bigger, cheaper, less filtered, more about everything, and more open to the world. The sites usually offer some gate-keeping mechanism to control access and contents, but in general, the world can now see an almost infinite number of family photographs, as opposed to a few when old family albums sat quietly on a shelf in the home.

> **Reference to Figures 1 and 2 as showing change in events recorded**

    In the past, we might not have wanted to look at strangers' family photos, considering them boring, and we might not have wanted people to look at our family photos, considering it an invasion of privacy. But now such postings and viewings are common online. Why

> **Use of *we* to establish common ground**

Dong 5

Roxanne Paris

Fig. 2. Toothbrushing party, 10 Dec. 2005.
<http://www.flickr.com/photos/mistersix/72237270/>.

Supports idea of online community

look at images of unknown people—faces we've never met and never will meet? The collection online is so big and varied that it can give a pleasant, reassuring feeling of being connected with all humanity, not stuck in a small particular circle or place. We see an endless array of snapshots of beauty, average looks, cuteness, human interest, day-to-day normalcy, and varied faces, and we inevitably realize that we are all quite similar.

Anticipates opposing views and seeks common ground

Why enter photos of ourselves and our own family into this huge mix? Posting photos can be a gateway for connection, creating an online community where people communicate with each other, give feedback, offer compliments, ask questions, compare notes, or appreciate the artistry or humor of an image. While the danger is that posted digital family photos will devalue the traditional old form—taking it out of context, commercializing or trivializing it, or adding a voyeuristic or exhibitionistic element—the meanings and purposes

Blue = content issues   Red = format issues

Dong 6

of family photographs keep shifting and expanding
beyond anyone's control.

   Photobloggers (or mobloggers, for "mobile
web bloggers"), for example, show how the family
photograph form is, for better or for worse, doing more
now than creating and saving a record for the family
of its own good times. Photobloggers take numerous
snapshots of their own and their families' daily lives
and post them regularly for their online audiences to
respond to. Döring and Gundolf describe the three-step
moblog process simply as "seen—snapped—posted"
(85), while journalist Sarah Boxer sees "something
touching but also appalling about so much global
attention focused on such mundane stuff":

> I clicked my way through site after site:
> here was an old picture of someone's
> friend's grandmother as a young woman
> on the beach. There was a little white dog
> with a chew toy in its mouth. Here was
> a picture of the curtains in a hotel room
> where one blogger was staying.

   Asked about his motivation, one moblogger, Adam
Seifer, says he likes the attention, communication,
creative outlet, and fact that in this world, "Anybody
can be famous" (Boxer). Others say they do it "for
experimentation, to relieve boredom, to kill time, or
to make use of pictures already shot on their camera
phones" (Döring and Gundolf 87). Many mobloggers,
realizing "the revelatory, intimate aspect of the
medium," keep "a degree of separation between
themselves and their viewers" (Badger). But in other

Marginal notes (blue = content issues):
Examples provide evidence of change

Marginal notes (red = format issues):
Long quotation indented one inch, not in quotation marks

No page numbers for online source

Blue = content issues   Red = format issues

cases, moblogs can "take on the character of a lonely hearts service" (Döring and Gundolf 88). So the evolving, extended family photo album serves ever-new functions, as what was once private now becomes public.

Reiterates claim

Visual artist and literature professor Michelle Shawn Smith looks at some strangers' family photographs, and they inspire her to ask, "Do we simply play a part in an already scripted narrative? What is the story that keeps being told? And what does that story cover over, stitch together, hide?" (99). With the family photograph being opened up to freer and wider uses, perhaps everyone can save him- or herself the trouble of having to pretend everything is picture perfect in life. We can still enjoy taking and looking at pictures of loved ones and good times and see these pictures as a window into what's rock-solid important in life. But perhaps we can also see these photographs as telling shifting, complicated, and ambiguous stories, too, and see that we now inhabit a giant new freeform photo album together.

Looks to future advantages to the change

Blue = content issues   Red = format issues

Dong 8

New page

Works Cited

Heading centered

Badger, Meredith. "Visual Blogs." *Into the Blogosphere: Rhetoric, Community, and Culture of Weblogs.* Ed. Laura J. Gurak, Smiljana Antonijevic, Laurie Johnson, Clancy Ratliff, and Jessica Reyman. U of Minnesota, 2004. Web. 16 Sept. 2014. **Organized alphabetically by last names**

Boxer, Sandra. "Prospecting for Gold among the Photo Blogs." *New York Times.* New York Times, 25 May 2003. Web. 15 Sept. 2014.

Bray, Hiawatha. "Polaroid Shutting Two Mass. Facilities, Laying off 150." *Boston.com.* New York Times, 8 Feb. 2008. Web. 14 Sept. 2014.

Chalfen, Richard. *Snapshot Versions of Life.* Bowling Green: Popular-Bowling Green State UP, 1987. Print.

Döring, Nicola, and Axel Gundolf. "Your Life in Snapshots: Mobile Weblogs." *Knowledge, Technology, and Policy* 19:1 (2006): 80–90. *MasterFILE Premier.* Web. 16 Sept. 2014.

Gallo, Julian. "Moblogs: The Map of Time." *Zone Zero.* 11 Feb. 2008. Web. 17 Sept. 2014.

Halle, David. "The Family Photograph." *Art Journal* 46.3 (1987): 217–25. *JSTOR.* Web. 15 Sept. 2014.

Blue = content issues   Red = format issues

Dong 9

Smith, Shawn Michelle. "Family Photographs and

    Kelly McKaig's Dreamworlds." *Frontiers: A*

    Journal of Women's Studies 19.3 (1998): 98–111.

    JSTOR. Web. 17 Sept. 2014.

Sontag, Susan. *On Photography*. New York: Farrar,

    1977. Print.

Presentation Matters

4a How to present your work

Follow these general guidelines for the final draft of an essay. The Model Papers in this book show you the specific formats for several recommended styles: MLA, APA, *Chicago*, and CSE (see chapters 9–11 for MLA, APA, and *Chicago*; see our Web site for CSE).

Paper and print White bond, unlined, 8½″ × 11″; not erasable paper. Clip or staple the pages. Use dark black printing ink.

Digital Word-processed document or portable document format (PDF). Save word-processed files as .rtf (Rich Text Format) to avoid compatibility issues between software programs. You can save word-processed documents as PDFs, too, in many software programs. PDFs can be read using the free download of Adobe Reader.

Margins One inch all around. Sometimes 1½ inches will be acceptable. Lines should *not* be justified (that is, not aligned on the right).

Space between lines Uniformly double-spaced, including any list of works cited. (However, notes in *Chicago* style and references in CSE may be single-spaced; consult your instructor, and see Model Paper 4 for *Chicago*; see our Web site for CSE.)

Spaces after a period, question mark, or exclamation point Most style manuals suggest one space. Your instructor may prefer two spaces in the text of your essay.

Type font and size Use a standard type font (such as Times New Roman or Arial or Cambria), and a regular type font size of 10 to 12 points.

Page numbers Place in the top right margin. In MLA and *Chicago* styles, put your last name before the page number. In APA and CSE styles, put a short version of the running head before the page number. Use Arabic numerals (that is, 1, 2, 3, 4) with no period.

Paragraphing Indent one-half inch (five spaces) from the left.

Title and identification Put on the first page for MLA style (see Model Paper 1, p. 14, and Model Paper 2, p. 98) or on a separate title page for APA, *Chicago*, and CSE styles (see p. 132 for APA and our Web site for CSE).

Parentheses around a source citation in the text In MLA style, place the author's name and page number(s) in parentheses after quoted or paraphrased material unless the author is already named in the text sentence. In APA style, put the year of publication in parentheses after the author's name in the text sentence. Add any page number(s) in parentheses after the quoted or paraphrased material. For electronic sources without page numbers in either MLA or APA style, indicate paragraph numbers or shortened section titles if they are available. At the end of your paper, add an alphabetical list with full publication details, including only the works you have cited in your paper.

KEY POINTS
Posting on the Web in HTML Format

If you are posting your work online in HTML format, also consider the following guidelines:

Internal hyperlinks: Insert internal hyperlinks to connect readers directly to relevant sections of your text, content notes, and visuals. Also provide links to the text from the table of contents and from a source cited in the text to the entry in your list of works cited.

External hyperlinks: Use external hyperlinks to connect to Web documents from references in the body of your paper and from your list of works cited. Useful for the works-cited list, word processors have a function that will automatically convert any string starting with <http://> into a hyperlink. Use the Help menu for instructions.

No paragraph indentation: Do not indent for a new paragraph. Instead, leave a line space between paragraphs.

Attribution of sources: For your instructor and your fellow students using the same licensed databases, provide a persistent link to a database article in the form of a DOI—Digital Object Identifier—or a stable URL assigned by the database, not a link that works only for a few hours or days; do not use the URL you see in the address box of a database article. The DOI will point to the most authoritative repository and is probably the best way to cite an electronic document.
(continued)

(continued)

For readers who will not necessarily have access to the database, give the link to the home page only. **NOTE:** A DOI is used in APA and *Chicago* styles only; see chapters 10 and 11.

List of works cited or list of references: Give a complete list, with visible hyperlinked URLs, even if you provide external links to the sources from the body of your paper. If a reader prints your paper, the exact references will then still be available.

4b Visual presentation of text (color, lists, and headings)

Color is not mentioned in academic style guides, but color can be distracting or make a document harder to read. When in doubt, avoid color for typefaces or highlighting in academic writing. However, in business, community, and online documents, color can be a useful tool to draw attention to important points. In those cases, use it sparingly so that it does not overwhelm your text.

Lists are useful in technical reports and oral presentations, making it easy for readers to scan and absorb information. Bulleted or numbered lists are also a common feature of presentation software slides, as in student Emily Luo's outline slide for a classroom presentation of her research, as shown in Figure 4.1. (For more on oral presentations, see 4e.)

FIGURE 4.1 Presentation Slide

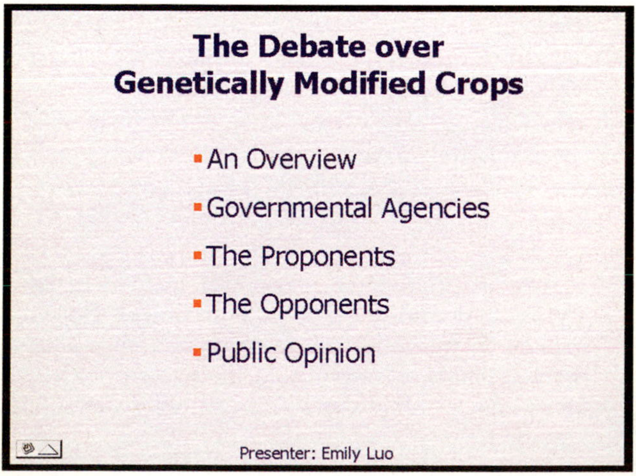

The Debate over Genetically Modified Crops

- An Overview
- Governmental Agencies
- The Proponents
- The Opponents
- Public Opinion

Presenter: Emily Luo

Ann Raimes

Headings such as *Abstract, Method, Results,* and *Discussion* are common in the social sciences and sciences (APA and CSE styles) and in business reports and online documents. Each level of heading and subheading should have a consistent typeface, grammatical structure, and position: centered or flush left. When writing a résumé, use bulleted lists and section headings, for example, *Education, Work Experience, Special Skills,* and *References.*

4c Photos and images

Include photographs and images to enhance your content and to illustrate a point you make in writing. For example, movie stills will add a great deal to a paper on film history; maps and aerial photographs can reinforce your points and tell a story in a geography paper.

KEY POINTS
Enhancing Your Argument with Visuals

1. Decide which type of material best fits your content, and determine where to place photographs and images; usually, it is best to place them within your text.

2. Introduce and discuss each visual before readers come across it. Indicate where the visual appears (such as "in the image on page 8"), and carefully interpret or analyze the visual for readers, using it as an aid that supports your points, not as something that can stand alone.

3. Give each visual a title, number each visual if you use more than one visual of the same type, and state the source for all images that you have not prepared yourself (see p. 99 for an example).

4. When you include a visual in an online document, check that the image file, especially of photographs, is not so large that it will take a long time to download. As a rule of thumb, do not use image files over 100 KB.

5. Make sure that every image you include makes a point and contributes to your argument. Do not include an image just to fill space in a page allotment or to jazz up your text. Including a silly or frivolous image could detract from an otherwise solid argument.

4d Visuals that present data: Tables, graphs, and charts

Preparing your own visuals You can create professional-looking tables, graphs, and charts in *Excel* or in *Word*. Go to the Help menu to find out how to construct a table or select a type of chart (such as a pie chart or a bar chart) and enter your own details, such as a title, labels for the vertical and horizontal axes of a bar graph, numbers, and data labels.

Honesty in visuals If you prepare your own visuals to make your point, remember to represent the data ethically. Never change a photograph, falsify data, or exaggerate or downplay changes over time in the way you plot the axes of a graph. Remember to include the percentage base, that is, the number on which any percentages are based. And whenever you prepare your own table, chart, or graph from source data that are not your own, be sure to cite the source of the figures you use.

Tables are good for presenting textual or numerical data in a more condensed way than can be done in running text. People may find it difficult to read tables with many numbers, however, so point out in your text discussion the significant features of any table that you are using. Figure 4.2 could be used in a paper discussing recent voting trends among the U.S. Hispanic population.

Line graphs show changes over time. Graphs using more than one line compare several pieces of information over time. The graph in Figure 4.3 could be useful in a paper on the need to eliminate hunger in America.

Pie charts (also called pie graphs) show how fractions and percentages relate to one another and make up a whole.

FIGURE 4.2 Party Affiliation among Hispanic Registered Voters in Florida, 2006 to 2012

	Republicans	Democrats	Other Party	No Party Affiliation	Total
2012*	452,619	564,513	25,657	431,131	1,473,920
2010	445,353	550,799	25,082	404,570	1,425,804
2008	445,526	513,252	23,500	372,992	1,355,270
2006	414,185	369,902	16,915	312,881	1,113,883

*NOTE: Data for 2012 as of January 3, 2012, the presidential preference primary book closing date. The Florida presidential preference primary election date is Tuesday January 31, 2012. For all other years, data reflect general election book closing dates.

SOURCE: Florida Division of Elections <http://election.dos.state.fl.us/voter-registration/statistics/elections.shtml>.

FIGURE 4.3 **Percentage of Children Ages 0–17 in Food-Insecure Households by Poverty Status, Selected Years 1995–2008.**

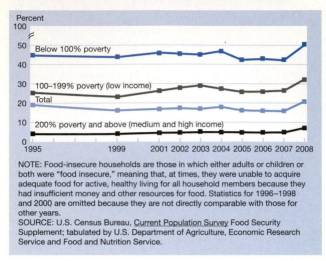

NOTE: Food-insecure households are those in which either adults or children or both were "food insecure," meaning that, at times, they were unable to acquire adequate food for active, healthy living for all household members because they had insufficient money and other resources for food. Statistics for 1996–1998 and 2000 are omitted because they are not directly comparable with those for other years.
SOURCE: U.S. Census Bureau, Current Population Survey Food Security Supplement; tabulated by U.S. Department of Agriculture, Economic Research Service and Food and Nutrition Service.

Bar charts show comparisons and correlations and can highlight differences among groups. A bar chart can also be presented horizontally, which makes it easier to attach labels to the bars.

Other visuals such as concept maps, scatter plots, statistical maps, and thematic maps can be useful for complex and large-scale projects.

4e   Oral and multimedia presentations, *PowerPoint,* and e-portfolios

Oral presentations You may be asked to give oral presentations in writing courses, in other college courses, and in the business world. Usually, you will do some writing as you prepare your oral presentation, and you might deliver your oral report—backed by other media—either from notes or from a manuscript text written especially for the oral presentation. If you are called on to do a multimedia presentation, use the Framework for Critical Thinking in chapter 2 to consider the background and expectations of your audience and other elements of your writing situation. Always ensure that any sound and images you use serve to illustrate and explain your content: Using media is no substitute for substance. If you use a tool such as *PowerPoint,* do not be tempted to let its gimmicks take over. Use the slides to structure your presentation and illustrate key concepts.

KEY POINTS
Tips for Preparing an Oral Presentation

1. Concentrate on a few main points that your audience will easily grasp. Do not go overboard with details.

2. Include signposts and signal phrases to help your audience follow your ideas (*first, next, finally, the most important point is . . .*).

3. Present the organizational framework of your talk in *PowerPoint* slides, posters, or other visuals, or make it available afterward on the Web or in handouts.

4. Use appropriate language, maintain eye contact with your audience, and avoid reading from a script.

5. Remind your audience periodically of the structure of your talk and the points you have already made.

6. Make sure you finish within the allotted time without rushing at the end. Bring your presentation to the planned conclusion.

7. Recap the main points of your presentation, and provide an easy-to-remember bottom line to your talk.

Multimedia presentations   The possibilities for supplementing a presentation with multiple media can seem almost limitless. You can use slide presentation software such as *PowerPoint, Prezi,* or *Google Docs* to embed graphics, photographs, charts, video, audio, or any combination of these to support and enhance your presentation.

Bear in mind, however, that simulations and virtual experiences can be complicated to prepare and present and will involve a great deal of technological know-how. And because electrical cords can be misplaced and computers can crash, always be prepared to give your presentation without visuals.

Using *PowerPoint, Prezi,* and *Google Docs*   Presentation software like *PowerPoint, Prezi,* and *Google Docs* allows you to integrate audio and visual components seamlessly to produce a dynamic multimedia presentation. As an organizing tool, these programs help you separate the main points from the supporting details, keeping you focused as you give your presentation. Slides of well-timed quotations, graphs, and visual images can also provide evidence, support, and even counterpoints in a presentation. But if you do include music, sound, and video clips to drive home your points, be careful not to overdo these effects. They should enhance your work, not dominate it.

E-portfolios E-portfolios provide a way for you to record achievements and samples of your visual, written, and audio work. Check whether your college has an e-portfolio site where you can establish and organize your material.

Colleges that offer an e-portfolio system typically also provide general advice on how to assemble an e-portfolio, along with examples (though some parts may apply to the specific software used only). The site at <www.eportfolio .lagcc.cuny.edu> provides good examples of students' work.

Alternatively, you could get an individual e-portfolio account from various developers or vendors. Usually, they charge a small annual fee, but some offer a free basic version (e.g., Epsilen developed at Indiana University-Purdue University Indianapolis).

4f   Multimodal composition

As new technologies emerge, new ways of writing have been designated as "multimodal." Multimodal practices encompass multiple modes of communication, including linguistic, visual, spatial, gestural, and aural ways of making meaning.

Multimodal compositions may be multimedia texts (born-digital compositions including image, animation, sound, as well as text), but they may also employ multiple modes in concrete form, such as the arrangement of physical objects, paintings, and analog sound recordings, and exhibit spaces. Multimodal compositions may also incorporate networking technologies, such as social networking sites (*Facebook*), social bookmarking sites (*Diigo*), SMS/texting applications (*Twitter*), content aggregators (using RSS feeds), and file sharing sites (*Instagram*).

Such complicated composition requires you, the writer/designer, to have a clear idea of how to convey meaning in each mode. While multimodal composition may be fun and creative, it requires more preparation and research than a print essay.

When designing a multimodal composition, remember to:

- address a specific audience with a specific purpose in mind
- organize your design around a primary controlling idea or metaphor
- provide transitions that guide the reader through the work
- make sure that you use all of your media (textual, architectural, visual, aural, or interactive) in accordance with the best practice for each type

PART TWO

Research: Finding and Evaluating Sources

EVALUATE	
PURPOSE	**AUDIENCE**
• What is the author's purpose in writing this piece? • Is it meant to be persuasive, informative, or something else? • What influence might that purpose have on the potential usefulness of the piece as a source in your own work?	• What audience is the author addressing? • How do you know? • Does the intended audience have any impact on what information is included in or excluded from the piece? If so, how?
VOICE	**MEDIUM**
• What are the credentials and reputation of the author? • What is the place of publication? • What or who does the author represent? • Is there a particular bias that the author demonstrated? If so, where do you see it, and what is the impact on credibility?	• In what medium was the piece published? • Why do you think it was published in that medium? • Was it peer reviewed or edited by someone else? • Is the publication venue subject to rapid change (like an article in *Wikipedia*), or is it fairly fixed, like a printed book or an online journal article?

© 2016 Cengage Learning®

Doing research involves looking for and collecting information on a topic in order to develop and refine your own views. When doing research for an academic paper, you gather information that you evaluate as valid, reliable, and relevant. Then you cite this source information in your paper.

No matter how many sources you find and use, your paper should still be *your* synthesis of the main issues that you come across in your research. In the sciences, structuring of information is more important than the personal opinion of the writer. In the humanities, the writer is often more present, offering a point of view as well as sources. A good research paper is not simply a mindless compilation of sources; it should instead establish your place in the ongoing conversation about the topic. Let it present you in interaction with your topic and engaged with the ways in which others have addressed that topic.

5 How to Search for Information

5a Considering primary and secondary sources

Primary sources　Primary sources are the firsthand, raw, or original materials that researchers study and analyze, such as historical documents, visuals, journals and letters, autobiographies, memoirs, government statistics, and speeches. You can examine works of art, literature, and architecture or watch or listen to performances and programs. You can also conduct case studies, experiments, observations, interviews or surveys, all of which are common in the sciences and social sciences. The use of such primary sources can bring an original note to your research and new information to your readers, but their use requires careful guidance and planning. You need to set up a system for collecting relevant data, taking notes, and allowing for follow-up. Surveys and questionnaires, for instance, involve complex sampling, design, and data analysis. Ask your instructor for guidance.

Secondary sources　Secondary sources are analytical works that comment on and interpret other works, such as primary sources. They are common in the humanities, and examples include reviews, discussions, biographies, critical studies, analyses of literary or artistic works or events, commentaries on current and historical events, class lectures, and electronic discussions.

5b Starting the search for sources

Turn to the following for materials:

1. **Your college library,** providing
   - Electronic holdings (licensed databases, e-books), which are typically available via the Internet from anywhere
   - Physical holdings (reference works, printed books, bound journals, current periodicals, reports, microforms)
   - Reference librarians (who often can be contacted via e-mail and/or through "Ask-a-Librarian," an Internet chat service providing 24/7 access)
   - Your college library Web site, the gateway to licensed resources on the Internet (not accessible via popular search engines like *Google*), also providing instruction on how best to use the various electronic services
   - Interlibrary loan (providing access to resources at other libraries by ordering them and having them sent to your school or local library)

2. **Your instructor** and any lists of references you find in your course readings

3. **The Internet:** Web directories, online library catalogs, online newspapers, books and journals, informational Web sites

A note on Internet resources The democratic nature of the Internet means that there is no editorial control over many Web pages, so although you will probably find a great deal of material, much of it could be inaccurate. On the plus side, you will find vast resources, current material, and frequent updates—all without leaving your computer. As you plan your research, consider which of the following Internet resources might be the most appropriate for your topic.

- Online magazines and online scholarly journals (you will find a useful directory at *Librarians' Internet Index*)
- Online literary texts
- Online news sites
- Nonprofit research sites

On using *Wikipedia* Be aware that while *Wikipedia* can be useful in getting you started with information on a topic, it is a work in progress and is constantly being revised. So check any information you find there, and do not include it as a source. If you consult *Wikipedia*, you might just scroll to the end of the article to see the list of references and use those as potential leads. In addition, your instructor may recommend not using *Wikipedia* at all.

KEY POINTS
What Every Librarian Wishes You Knew

- **Libraries do more than store books.** You might think of a library as a place that holds books, but libraries do that and more. These days they provide access to information that is available through multiple media. For this reason, many experienced researchers make the library their first stop for any new project.

- **Not everything is accessible online.** While you can probably access your library's databases online and perhaps even see what other books are on a shelf next to one you are interested in, some things are only available in person. Go to the physical library if you can, and spend some time learning about what is available.

- **Keywords should be chosen carefully.** Many students go to a library without having thought through the best way to phrase their search terms. Think of the specific words you should search for and any alternatives. Ask a librarian for help. Read through 5d for ideas about choosing keywords for searching.

- **Good researchers visit early and often.** You will need time to look through the resources that are available, assess whether they are credible, and determine which portions you want to use. Some resources may only be available through interlibrary loan, which can take several days.

- **Librarians are people, too.** Librarians are specialists in finding information of all types, and they want to help you. Go to the librarian with a specific question, and ask for help.

5c Good starting points

General reference sources, in print or online Ask librarians for their recommendations of useful reference sources, bibliographies, indexes, and Web sites. Encyclopedias (including *Wikipedia*), specialized dictionaries, bibliographies, and government documents will give you a sense of the field and the issues, but be sure to move beyond these starting points to more substantial sources.

Web directories Libraries, colleges, and other organizations provide valuable directories for researchers:

- *Research Quickstart* at the University of Minnesota, listing sources in many academic subjects
- *Michigan Electronic Library* (MeL), a University of Michigan site
- *Internet Public Library*, run by librarians, offering a guide to subject collections and an "Ask an IPL Librarian" feature
- *INFOMINE*, a University of California, Riverside, site, with scholarly resources in medical sciences, business, and visual arts, along with general references
- *Voice of the Shuttle*, a University of California, Santa Barbara, site, listing research sources in the humanities
- *Library of Congress*, important for the listing of its own collections
- *Intute*, an easy-to-use database published by seven universities, with sources in science and technology, arts and humanities, social sciences, and health and life sciences
- *The WWW Virtual Library*, providing a common access point to Web catalogs/directories maintained by different institutions around the world

Online library subscription databases Databases of published works are a good place to start serious online searching. Material is best accessed by keyword searching (5d). Databases with both abstracts and full texts of scholarly articles (most of which are also available in print) include EBSCO's *Academic Search Elite; Readers' Guide to Periodical Literature; Expanded Academic ASAP; InfoTrac; JSTOR;* OCLC *FirstSearch;* LexisNexis *Academic; ERIC* (for education); *PsycINFO* (for psychology); *PAIS International* (for public affairs); Sage *Sociology Collection; Art Index; Science Direct;* and *Web of Science.* In addition, some databases specialize in images (for example, *ARTstor*) or quantitative statistics (for example, *Social Explorer*).

Visit your college library's Web site to find out what is available at your school.

Online literary texts Complete works whose copyright has expired are available for downloading at, for example, *Project Bartleby, Project Gutenberg, Oxford Text Archive,* and *University of Virginia Electronic Text Center.*

NOTE: Once you have found a good source, make sure it will be readily available to you again for rereading, summarizing, discussing, and so on. See 7d for online sites that help with saving and organizing the sources you find.

5d   Efficient keyword searching

Search engines, directories, and licensed databases use keyword searching. Databases also offer options of searching for author, title, subject, and other features.

KEY POINTS
Tips on Using Search Engines

1. **Don't mistake popularity for quality.** Search engines do not assess the quality of a site's content, so make your search string as specific as possible in order to exercise greater control over your results.

2. **Be aware of "sponsored" Web sites and links.** "Sponsored" Web sites often appear at the very top of a result list and are in addition to the easily spotted sponsored links that appear in the sidebar on the right side of the screen. The owners of sponsored Web sites and links pay for their placement in your search results, so their inclusion is no indication of their quality, popularity, or even relevance.

3. **Try using search engines that are intended for academic work.** You probably use a search engine such as *Google* for your everyday Web searches. For your academic work, branch out and use *Google Scholar* and *Book Search*, the directories listed earlier in 5c, and your library's online licensed databases. To find material in journal and newspaper articles, use databases such as *Academic Search Premier, InfoTrac, LexisNexis*, and specialized subject-area databases; there you can find abstracts (when available) or full articles.

4. **Persist and be resourceful.** If a search yields only a few hits, try new keywords in new combinations. Also try variant spellings for names of people and places (such as *Chaikovsky, Tchaikovsky, Tschaikovsky*), and/or try a different search engine.

How to do efficient keyword searches for academic purposes

- **Know the system of the database or search engine.** Use Search Tips or locate a Help page to learn how to conduct a search. Some systems search for any or all of the words you type in, some need you to indicate whether the words make up a phrase, and others allow you to exclude search terms or search for alternatives.

- **Use Advanced Search Features.** Before you begin a search, read the instructions to learn how to perform both a simple search and an advanced search. Generally, begin a search by using keywords or subject terms, if you know them. A keyword search of an online database of full-text articles will produce articles with subject terms attached, as in Source Shot 3 in 9f, page 85. Use what the database provides to limit your search as to type of source, date, full-text articles or not, and scholarly, peer-reviewed articles.

- **Learn how to do Boolean searches.** Many database searches operate on the Boolean principle; that is, they use the "operators" *AND, OR,* and *NOT* in combination with keywords to define what you want the search to include and exclude. Imagine that you want to find out how music can affect intelligence. A search for "music AND intelligence" would find sources in the database that included both the word *music* and the word *intelligence.* A search for "music AND (intelligence OR learning)" would expand the search. You would find sources in the database that included both the word *music* and the word *intelligence* or the word *learning.* Some search engines let you use terms such as *NEAR* and *ADJ* (adjacent to) to find phrases close to each other in the searched text.

- **Know how to expand or narrow a search.** Many search engines, including *Google,* let you use signs such as + or – to include or prohibit a term, thereby expanding or narrowing your search. You do not need to insert the word *and.*

- **Use a wildcard character (*or?) to truncate a term and expand a search.** The truncated search term *podiatr** will produce references to *podiatry, podiatrist,* and *podiatric.* In *Google,* however, the wildcard character* is used to stand for a whole word only, as in "Foot doctor is a*," but *Google* automatically uses "stemming" and searches for "podiatrist" as well as "podiatry" if you have entered the latter term only.

- **Narrow a search by grouping words.** Enclose search terms in quotation marks (or, in some cases, parentheses) to group the words into a phrase; this is a useful technique for finding titles, names, and quotations.

- **Be flexible.** If you do not get good results, try using synonyms. *Google* will include synonyms in the search, for example, if you type a tilde (~) immediately before the search term, as in ~ *addiction*. Or try a different search engine or database.

Searching for and finding appropriate and interesting sources can take time and ingenuity. Start your research well in advance of a deadline.

5e Finding visual sources

Use visuals—tables, charts, photographs, and other artwork—to illustrate and enhance a point or to present information clearly and economically. Images may also help you strengthen an argument (3d).

Several of the major search engines, including *Google, Bing, AltaVista,* and *Yahoo!,* offer specific image searches, and by using the advanced search forms there, you will be able to narrow your search to certain types of images, including those that are licensed for noncommercial use, which means that you will not have to worry about copyright or whether to ask permission to use the image. Another useful source is *Flickr,* a repository providing access to a large number of amateur photographs.

Searching for images can often be difficult and frustrating because many "hits" may not interest you. So, rather than doing a general image search, it may be more productive to look for images on the Web sites where you found relevant textual information in the first place. Always be sure to record the URL of the images you use so that you are able to cite them appropriately. Remember, every image on the Web has some sort of copyright status: You do not need to seek permission to use images in a college paper, but you do for wider publication.

5f Getting the most out of *Google*

Google is by far the most popular search engine in the world. *Google* finds text, images, news, news archives, videos—and a great deal more. Students should use it with some caution, however. *Google* covers only a relatively limited number of the documents on the Web, and it will not display results that do not have a certain number of incoming links. Knowing how to use *Google* well, though, can make it more versatile, direct, and productive than when you just do a basic search.

KEY POINTS
What *Google* Can Do for You

- *Google Alerts* sends e-mail notifications to you about new information and content available for search terms or news stories that you are following.

- *Google Scholar,* an excellent resource for researchers, searches scholarly sources (such as research studies, dissertations, peer-reviewed papers) across many disciplines. You may also be able to customize the program to provide links to the full text of articles in your college library. Click on "Scholar preferences" and enter the name of the library. You can then import local links into bibliographical programs your college may own, such as *EndNote* or *RefWorks.*

- *Google Book Search* helps you find books and provides details of the contents, even allowing you to search the full text of many books for specific content.

- *Google Blog Search* helps you find blogs that might provide interesting, current information about topics of interest.

- *Google Earth* allows you to search for maps, detailed satellite images, and 3D images.

- *Google Advanced Search* provides many options for tailoring your search to your precise needs.

- *Google Reader* provides a way to subscribe to specific blogs, news sites, and other Web sites that are regularly updated by subscribing to RSS (Really Simple Syndication) feeds.

- *Google Docs* allows you to create or upload existing online materials, such as documents, presentations, and spreadsheets. Others can then access the material and make comments and changes, recording their contribution. This is a useful tool for collaborative projects.

5g Research in your pajamas: How to use online alerts to get information to come to you

Not only can you find a vast amount of source material online, but also you can arrange to be notified when materials on your specific topic become available. For example, *Google Alerts* will e-mail search results directly to you, and *Google Reader* allows you to keep up with Web sites' RSS feeds by notifying you of the latest news items, events, or discussion postings on a given topic at the time interval you specify. In addition, several journal databases, such as those sponsored by EBSCO, SAGE, and CSA, will run a search on a topic you specify as often as you request, even daily, and alert you via e-mail about articles that meet the criteria you establish. These RSS feeds mean that you get full-text research articles brought to you 24/7 without your having to remember to redo a search.

6 How to Evaluate Sources

6a Reading sources critically

To read sources critically, you follow the same process outlined in the framework for critical thinking in chapter 2. In other words, you should think about the source's purpose, audience, voice, and medium as you read—its *context*. Understanding the context of the sources you are reading while keeping in mind your own research context will help you find sources that will be a good match—sources that your readers will find credible, reliable, and relevant for your research goals.

6b Evaluating potential sources

Before you take detailed notes on a source that you might use for your research, be certain it will provide suitable information to help answer your research question. As you evaluate your sources, pay careful attention to how something was vetted before it was published, especially if it is published online. Pay attention to whether the piece was peer reviewed (a scholarly article) or just edited prior to publication (a magazine or newspaper article). You will find more help with evaluating Web sources in the Key Points box on page 43.

KEY POINTS
Questions to Evaluate a Source

1. **What does the work cover?** It should be long enough and detailed enough to provide adequate information.

2. **How objective is the information?** The author, publisher, or periodical should not be affiliated with an organization that has an ax to grind—unless, of course, your topic entails reading critically and making comparisons with other points of view.

3. **How current are the views?** Check the date of publication. The work should be up to date if you need a current perspective.

4. **How reputable is the publisher?** The work should be published by someone who is reputable and in a source that is academically reliable, not one devoted to gossip, advertising, propaganda, or sensationalism. Look online for information about the publisher of the print book/journal or host of the Web site.

5. **How reputable is the author?** The author should be an authority on the subject. Find out what else the author has written (in *Google*, in *Books in Print*, or at *Amazon*) and what his or her qualifications are as an authority.

6. **Is the piece well written?** A source filled with spelling and grammatical errors does not inspire confidence. If the language has not been checked, the ideas probably have not been given much scrutiny or thought either.

BOOKS

- Check who the publisher is, and do a quick Web search if you do not recognize the name.
- Check the date of publication, notes about the author, table of contents, and index.
- Skim the preface, introduction, chapter headings, and summaries to get an idea of the information found in the book and the book's theoretical basis and perspective.
- Do not waste time making detailed notes on a book that deals only tangentially with your topic or on an out-of-date book (unless your purpose is to discuss and critique its perspective or to examine a topic historically).

PERIODICAL ARTICLES

- Check the type of periodical, any organization with which it is affiliated, and the intended audience.
- Differentiate among the following types of articles (listed in descending order of reliability, with the most reliable first):
  - scholarly articles (see 6c)
  - articles in periodicals for nonspecialists but serious, well-educated readers, such as *New York Review of Books, Atlantic Monthly, The Economist, Scientific American,* and *Nation*
  - shorter articles, with sources not identified, in popular magazines for a general audience, such as *Ebony, Time, Newsweek, Parents, Psychology Today,* and *Vogue,* or in newspapers
  - articles with dubious sources, written for sensational tabloid magazines, such as *National Enquirer, Globe,* and *Star*

Newspaper articles and news articles The *New York Times, Washington Post,* and *Los Angeles Times,* for example, provide mostly reliable accounts of current events; daily editorial comments; and reviews of books, film, and art. Be aware that most newspapers (as well as televised news reports such as Fox News and MSNBC) have political leanings, so perspectives on the same event may differ.

Other sources found online What makes the Internet so fascinating is that it is wide open, free, and democratic. Anyone can publish anything, and anyone can read it. However, if you are looking for well-presented facts and informed opinion among the more than 800 million domain names registered as of January 2012 (ISC Internet Domain survey), the Internet can pose a challenge.

- **Postings found in e-mail discussion lists, blogs, and wikis** Discussion list postings, blogs (Web logs), and wiki entries (additions to or editing of a Web text appearing in a wiki) will often appear in a list of a search engine's findings. Many professionally moderated lists and other targeted discussion lists can be useful sources of information, although quality can vary considerably. If you look at such postings as possible sources, be sure to read and take into consideration the responses to the post in which you are interested.

• **Personal or Organizational Web sites** Evaluate Web sites with particular care. Individuals on a rant, as well as serious government or research agencies, can establish a site. Learn to separate good information from junk.

KEY POINTS
Locating Key Information on Web Sites

1. **Scrutinize the domain name of the URL.** Reliable information can usually be found on .gov and .edu addresses that are institutionally sponsored (but also see item 2). With .com ("dot com"), .net, .info, or .org sources, always assess whether the source provides factual information or advocates a specific point of view on an issue.

2. **Assess the originator of an .edu source.** Is the educational institution or a branch of it sponsoring the site? A tilde (~) followed by a name in the URL generally indicates a posting by an individual, with no approval from the institution. So follow up by finding out what else the individual has published.

3. **Locate missing information.** If you can't readily find information on the actual Web site, a good way to begin an evaluation is to look the site up on <http://www.betterwhois.com>. This site will provide information on the author, date, sponsor, and address and so will supply clues about the reliability of the site.

4. **Check the About page or the Home page.** If you find your way to a Web page, always go to Home or About (if available) to find out about the overall site. Look for the title of the site, its stated purpose, and sponsor. Check, too, for bias. For instance, does the site aim to persuade, convert, or sell?

5. **Follow the links.** See whether the links in a site take you to authoritative sources. If the links no longer work (you'll get a 404 message: "Site Not Found"), the home page with the links has not been updated in a while—not a good sign.

6. **Check for dates, updates, ways to respond, and ease of navigation.** A well-managed site will have recent updates, clear organization, up-to-date links, and easy-to-find contact information.

6c Recognizing a scholarly article

A scholarly article is not something you are likely to find in a magazine in a dentist's office. A scholarly article does the following—the first point being the most important:

1. It is reviewed by other scholars (peer reviewers) for their approval before publication.

2. It refers to the work of other scholars and includes notes, references, and/or a list of works cited, footnotes, or endnotes.

3. It names the author and may describe the author's affiliation and credentials.

4. It deals with a serious issue in depth. For example, a magazine might simply report on various findings and how they might apply to its targeted audience, but a scholarly journal would go further to discuss issues such as methodology, possible differing opinions, and potential future research directions.

5. It uses academic or technical language for informed readers.

   Scholarly articles in print generally do not appear in journals with colorful advertisements and eye-catching pictures. *Time, Newsweek,* and *The Economist* deal with some serious topics, but they are not scholarly. Note that a scholarly article may appear in a publication for the general population, such as *Psychology Today.* See Source Shot 2 on page 82 for an example of a table of contents from a scholarly journal.

Scholarly articles online Online articles in HTML or other digital formats, aside from PDFs, do not necessarily provide the immediate signals of color, illustrations, and varied advertisements that would identify nonscholarly work in print publications. If you find an online article and wish to check its credibility, try the following:

- Follow links from the author's name (if available) to find a résumé and more information.

- In *Google Scholar*, use the author's name as a search term to see publications and citations by others.

- Do a search for the title of the periodical in which the article appears to find out that periodical's purpose and its requirements for submitting and publishing articles. In some library databases (EBSCO's, for example), you can limit your search to articles that are peer-reviewed; that is, they are read by other scholars who are working on similar topics and are found to contribute new and important knowledge before they are accepted for publication.

FIGURE 6.1 Online scholarly journal

The table of contents shown in Figure 6.1 is a good example of what you will find searching for credible online journal articles.

PART THREE

Using and Citing Sources: Writing without Plagiarizing

CITE	
PURPOSE	**AUDIENCE**
• How can you use sources to support your purpose for writing? • When might quoting a source verbatim best support your purpose, and when would it be more effective to paraphrase or summarize?	• What kinds of sources will your audience expect you to use? • How can you integrate sources to make it easy for your audience to follow shifts between your own thinking and ideas from a source? • How might your audience use the citations you provide to find more information about your subject?
VOICE	**MEDIUM**
• How can you build credibility by citing sources accurately? • How can you incorporate sources into your writing and still stay true to your own authorial voice?	• What bibliographic software might help you manage and track your sources? • What types of sources are you using, and what information do you need to track about sources from different media?

© 2016 Cengage Learning®

Readers are impressed when you include in your writing references to what other writers have said on your topic. They know then that you are writing from an informed position, that you have thought long and hard, and that you have taken the time to find out the issues and views that experts see as important in their discussions. You have saved them work and earned their respect. Citing sources, quoting, and paraphrasing accurately are all essential in academic writing to avoid the serious charge of plagiarism (see 7b).

 7 **Citing Your Sources**

Acknowledge the research you have done by accurately citing your sources: who said it, where, and when.

7a　Why, how, and what to cite

Why you need to cite sources

- Citing sources shows your audience that you have done your homework. You will earn their respect for the depth and breadth of your research and for having worked hard to make your case.
- Citing responsible and recent sources lets your audience know that your arguments are both weighty and current.
- Citing sources draws your readers into the conversation about the issue and educates them. It also allows them to see you as engaged in the ongoing intellectual conversation. With full and accurate citations, they can follow up on your sources and learn more.
- Citing sources can be used to strengthen your argument, protect against counterclaims, or align your thinking with a particular scholar or institutional perspective.
- Citing all sources fully and accurately is essential if you are to avoid even the suspicion of plagiarizing.

How to cite sources
Citing a source means letting readers know whose words or ideas you are quoting, summarizing, or paraphrasing; where you found the information; when it was published; and, in the case of Web sites, when it was posted online. Styles of documentation vary in whether they ask initially for author and page number (MLA) or author and year of publication (APA), with a detailed list at the end of the paper of all the sources used. Other systems (*Chicago* and CSE) use numbering systems in the paper,

with a listing of source details at the end. Follow the models in part 4 for the MLA, APA, and *Chicago* systems. See our Web site for CSE style.

How to cite visuals Visual sources must be cited just as written sources are. Provide a number and a source note for all tables and figures that you include in your paper. In MLA style, put the visual close to the text it illustrates, with a credit line immediately beneath it. For APA papers, consult with your instructor. Some instructors recommend including visuals within the text of a college paper; others adhere to strict APA style, with tables and figures placed at the end of the paper. See chapters 9 and 10 for student papers with visuals.

What to cite Intentionally presenting another person's work as your own may be the most deceptive kind of plagiarism, but the effect is the same as if you neglect to acknowledge your sources because of sloppy research and writing practices. In both cases, readers will not be able to discern which ideas are yours and which are not. Always provide full documentation of sources, with a citation in your text and an entry in your list of sources. The following Key Points box shows you what you must always cite and also points out when citing is not necessary. If you are in doubt about whether you need to cite a source, it is always safer to cite it.

KEY POINTS
Sources to Cite or Not to Cite

WHAT TO CITE

- exact words, even facts, from a source, enclosed in quotation marks
- somebody else's ideas and opinions, even if you restate them in your own words in a summary or a paraphrase
- each sentence in a long paraphrase if it is not clear that all the sentences paraphrase the same source
- facts, theories, and statistics

WHAT NOT TO CITE

- common knowledge, such as nursery rhymes and folktales handed down through the ages
- information that is available from many sources, such as the dates of the Civil War and chronological events in the lives of public figures

7b   How to avoid plagiarism

The Council of Writing Program Administrators, a professional organization of writing teachers and program directors, says that plagiarism occurs "when a writer deliberately uses someone else's language, ideas, or other (not common-knowledge) material without acknowledging its source." It might be helpful to break down how such intentional use can occur into several different types of plagiarism.

KEY POINTS
The Seven Sins of Plagiarism

1. **Intentional grand larceny:** Presenting as your own work a whole essay bought from paper mills, "borrowed" or commissioned from a friend, intentionally copied and pasted from an online source, or otherwise obtained like a "takeout essay."

2. **Premeditated shoplifting:** Taking passages from a book, article, or Web site and intentionally inserting them into your paper without indicating who wrote them or where you found the passages. This type of plagiarism differs from item 1 only because passages, not the whole paper, are copied.

3. **Tinkering with the evidence:** Making a few word changes to source material and inserting the slightly altered version into your paper as if you wrote it, with no acknowledgment of the source. Minor changes are not enough to avoid charges of plagiarism.

4. **Idea kidnapping:** Using ideas written by others (even if you do use your own words) and neglecting to cite the author and source of the ideas.

5. **Unauthorized borrowing of private property:** Citing your source, but following its sentence structure and organization too closely or not indicating with quotation marks if and when you use any of your source's exact words.

6. **Trespassing over boundaries:** Failing to indicate in your paper where ideas from a source end and your ideas take over.

7. **Writing under the influence:** Being too tired, lazy, or disorganized, or facing an imminent deadline, and turning to any of the six previous sins in desperation or ignorance.

Consequences Obviously, these "sins" vary in their severity and in their intention to deceive. The types of plagiarism described in items 4 through 6 of the Key Points box sometimes occur unintentionally, but they may be perceived as plagiarism nevertheless. You have to work hard at avoiding them, especially since the consequences of plagiarism can be severe, ranging from an F on a paper or in a course to disciplinary measures or expulsion from college. In the world at large, plagiarism can lead to lawsuits and ruined careers. Those are reasons enough to do your own work and to learn to document your sources fully and correctly.

7c Keeping track of sources

The best method for avoiding plagiarism is to keep track of what your sources are and which ideas come from your sources and which come from you.

- **Keep a working bibliography.** Some options: Make a bibliography card (one for each source; use one side only); save screens or printouts from a library catalog, database listing, or Web site; or use as a research organizing tool any bibliographical software provided by your library, such as *EndNote* or *RefWorks,* or available freely online, such as *Zotero* or *Mendeley.* Record all the relevant information for each source that you read and plan to use, including reference works, and remember to record inclusive page numbers for all print sources as well as the date on which you access Web sites.

- **Make copies of print material.** While you are in the library, scan or photocopy complete journal or magazine articles and a periodical's table of contents (which will provide the date and volume number). Scan or copy book sections or chapters, too, along with the title page and copyright page of the book. You will need this information for your list of works cited.

- **Make a copy or take a screenshot of every Web source you may use.** Material you find online can change quickly, so always print a source, take a screenshot, e-mail it to yourself, add it to your bibliographical software file (7d), or save it on a flash drive, making sure you use highlighting or a special type font to distinguish your own comments and notes from the material you have copied and saved.

- **Use your browser's Bookmark or Favorites feature.** Save all the links to useful sites so that you can easily find them again. If you work on a networked computer and cannot save your work on the hard drive, export your bookmarks to your own computer or CD, or use an online bookmark manager such as *Diigo.*

- **Record complete online document information and URL.** If you do not take a screenshot of the whole site, record the name of the author, title, and date posted or updated, if available. Also note any sponsor/publisher/owner that is listed, if different from the site's title or author. Copy and paste to save the exact URL on your hard drive or flash drive, and note the date on which you accessed the online material.

- **Record the DOI (digital object identifier) of the article.** This permanent identifying number is usually found close to the copyright notice on the first page of an electronic journal article. You can also find it on the article's database landing page, which lists format and cataloging information. NOTE: DOIs are not used in MLA citations.

- **Highlight, copy, and paste.** As you read material on the Web, highlight a passage you find, copy it, and then paste it into your own file. Make sure that you indicate clearly in your new document that you have included a direct quotation. Use quotation marks and/or a larger or colored font or highlighting, along with an author/page citation, as in the following example:

Novelist John Lanchester has made a telling point about our image of self by having his narrator declare that we **"wouldn't care so much what people thought of us if we knew how seldom they did"** (62).

7d How bibliographical software and databases can help

Bibliographical software When you are asked to write research papers, you may find that your college library owns special software (such as *EndNote* or *RefWorks*) to help you search databases, store the results of your database searches, organize your research, insert citations while you write, and prepare a bibliography in one of many styles available. If your library does not provide access to this software, several free applications are available online, such as *Zotero, Mendeley,* and *CiteULike.*

KEY POINTS
Using Bibliographical Software

- Software can provide a way for you to record and easily save citations for sources you find in online databases.

- It will automatically create a bibliographical list or endnotes either in "cite while you write" (CWYW) mode or after completion of your text.

- It can prepare these lists in a variety of documentation styles, including those commonly required in college courses and covered in this handbook: MLA, APA, *Chicago*, and CSE. In fact, *EndNote* claims to offer 3,000 styles—more than enough for anyone.

- It does a lot but not everything. Using these programs requires a considerable initial investment of time and patience, but the investment will pay off eventually by making citations in research papers much easier to manage. Read the documentation and consult the Help menu whenever you need to.

- The software needs to be supplemented by your informed knowledge of the documentation system you are using. Do not let the program take over *all* the chores of recording the results of your research, inserting your citations, and preparing your list of works cited. You still need to be able to check citations for general accuracy and completeness, fix glitches, insert your anchors and hyperlinks in online papers, and handle the occasional obscure reference yourself.

Databases Several database screens, such as those sponsored by EBSCO, shown here, include useful features for writers of research papers.

From the Citation screen for an article, clicking on the "Cite" icon will take you to a screen that shows you how to cite the article in several documentation styles, including AMA, APA, *Chicago*, and MLA. The "Export" icon allows you to save citations in a file for export to *EndNote*, *RefWorks*, and other bibliographical software.

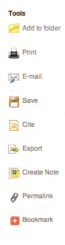

Tools »

- Add to folder
- Print
- E-mail
- Save
- Cite
- Export
- Create Note
- Permalink
- Bookmark

EBSCO Publishing

8 How to Use and Integrate Source Material

8a Driving the organization with ideas, not sources

As you consider how to incorporate your sources into your paper's organization, let your ideas, not your sources, drive your paper.

AVOID ORGANIZATION LIKE THIS

1. What points Smith makes
2. What points Jones makes
3. What points Fuentes makes
4. What points Jackson and Hayes make in opposition
5. What I think

This type of organization is driven by sources, with the bulk of the paper dealing with the views of Smith, Jones, and others. Instead, let your main point and then the supporting evidence for subpoints determine the organization.

IMPROVED ORGANIZATION

1. First point of support: what ideas I have to support my thesis and what evidence Fuentes and Jones provide
2. Second point of support: what ideas I have to support my thesis and what evidence Smith and Fuentes provide
3. Third point of support: what ideas I have to support my thesis and what evidence Jones provides
4. Opposing viewpoints of Jackson and Hayes
5. Common ground and refutation of those viewpoints
6. Synthesis

8b Summarizing and paraphrasing

Summaries are useful for giving readers basic information about the work you are discussing. A **summary** presents, briefly and in your own words and sentences, the main idea of a source.

ORIGINAL (PARAGRAPHS FROM A LONGER SOURCE)

Beauty might be particularly beastly for women going after highly masculine jobs. Whereas attractiveness benefited men seeking traditionally masculine and traditionally feminine jobs, a 2010 study found it hurt women applying for a masculine job, such as a prison guard. Once women have scored a position, their attractiveness provides a boost only when the job is nonmanagerial. Yet attractiveness seems to have no effect on performance evaluations of men.

"We have a conception of a beautiful woman, and 'leader' does not usually fit into that," says Lorri Sulpizio, Ph.D., coordinator of the Women's Leadership Academy at the University of San Diego.

Flora, Carlin. "The Beauty Paradox." *Psychology Today* 47.1 (2014): 36–37. *Academic Search Complete*. Web. 4 Apr. 2014.

SUMMARY (RECORDED IN A COMPUTER FILE)

Flora

Summary

"The Beauty Paradox"

Carlin Flora reports that women who are considered physically attractive might have more difficulty securing and keeping jobs that are usually considered more masculine, especially if those positions involve managing other employees (37).

A **paraphrase**, in contrast, is similar in length to the original material. Both paraphrases and summaries *avoid plagiarism by not using the author's exact words or sentence structure*. If you keep the source out of sight as you write a summary or a paraphrase, you will not be tempted to use any of the sentence patterns or phrases of the original. Even if you are careful to cite your source, your writing may still be regarded as plagiarized if your paraphrase or summary resembles the original too closely in wording or sentence structure. You can use common words and expressions without quotation marks, but if you use longer or more unusual expressions from the source, always enclose them in quotation marks.

PARAPHRASE TOO SIMILAR TO THE ORIGINAL (SIMILARITIES ARE HIGHLIGHTED)

Flora

Paraphrase

"The Beauty Paradox"

Once women have secured a position, being attractive is usually an asset. If a woman is in a management position, however, it might become a problem. By contrast, attractiveness usually has no effect on job evaluations of male coworkers (Flora 37).

REVISED PARAPHRASE

Flora explains the double standard that exists between men and women in management positions. For women, their attractiveness often becomes problematic in management, but a man's appearance does not seem to have any effect on his evaluations (37).

8c Quoting

Deciding what and when to quote Quote sparingly and only when the original words succinctly express the exact point you want to make. Ask yourself: Which point of mine does the quotation illustrate? Why am I considering quoting this particular passage rather than paraphrasing it? What do I need to tell my readers about the author of the quotation?

Quoting the exact words of the original Any words you use from a source must be included within quotation marks and quoted exactly as they appear in the original, with the same punctuation marks and capital letters. Include a page number for an article that is more than one page long.

NOT EXACT

Flora makes the point that "attractiveness has no effect on performance evaluations for men" (37).

EXACT

Flora makes the point that "attractiveness seems to have no effect on performance evaluations of men" (37).

Omitting words in the middle of a quotation If you omit as irrelevant to your purpose any words or passages from the middle of a quotation, signal this by using the ellipsis mark (three dots separated by spaces):

Flora reports, "Beauty might be particularly beastly for women going after highly masculine jobs … such as a prison guard" (37).

Use three dots after a period if you omit one or more complete sentences.

Adding or changing words If you add any comments or explanations in your own words or if you change a word or capitalization of the original to fit it grammatically into your sentence, enclose the added or changed material in square brackets. However, do not overuse this strategy.

> Flora's article shows that "[women's] attractiveness provides a boost only when the job is nonmanagerial" (37).

Quoting longer passages If you quote more than three lines of poetry or four typed lines of prose, do not use quotation marks. Begin the quotation on a new line.

- For MLA style, indent the quotation one inch from the left margin.
- For APA or *Chicago* style, indent the quotation one-half inch from the left margin.
- Double-space throughout.
- Do not indent from the right margin.
- If you quote from more than one paragraph, indent the first line of a new paragraph an additional one-quarter inch.
- Establish the context for a long quotation, and integrate it into your text by stating the point you want to make and naming the author of the quotation in your introductory statement.

> Flora describes research conducted on the effect of attractiveness for women seeking certain kinds of jobs:
>
> > Whereas attractiveness benefited men seeking traditionally masculine and traditionally feminine jobs, a 2010 study found it hurt women applying for a masculine job, such as a prison guard. Once women have scored a position, their attractiveness provides a boost only when the job is nonmanagerial. Yet attractiveness seems to have no effect on performance evaluations of men. (37)

NOTE: With a long indented quotation that has a parenthetical page citation, put the period before the parenthetical citation, not after it.

Avoiding a string of quotations Use quotations, especially long ones, sparingly and only when they help you make a good argument. Readers want to read your analysis of your sources and the conclusions you draw from your research, not a collection of passages from other writers. Quotations should not appear in a string, one after the other. If they do, your readers will wonder what purpose the quotations serve and will search for your voice in the paper.

8d Introducing and integrating source citations

Introduce information from your sources (summaries, paraphrases, and quotations) in a way that integrates them into the flow of your writing. They should not just pop up with no lead-in.

SOURCE NOT INTRODUCED AND INTEGRATED

> Women can have difficulty with securing jobs and keeping them if they are physically attractive. "Yet attractiveness seems to have no effect on performance evaluations of men" (Flora 37).

SOURCE INTRODUCED AND INTEGRATED

> In an article about how women can have difficulty securing and keeping their jobs if they are physically attractive, Carlin Flora describes that, by contrast, "attractiveness seems to have no effect on performance evaluations of men" (37).

Naming the author (Modern Language Association style) If you quote a complete sentence, or if you paraphrase or summarize a section of another work, introduce the source material by providing an introductory phrase with the author's full name (for the first reference to an author) and a brief mention of his or her expertise or credentials, as in the preceding example. For subsequent citations, the last name is sufficient.

Varying the introductory phrase The introductory verbs *say* and *write* are clear and direct. Occasionally, use one of the following verbs to express subtle shades of meaning: *acknowledge, agree, argue, ask, assert, believe, claim, comment, contend, declare, deny, emphasize, explain, insist, note, point out, propose, speculate,* or *suggest.*

8e How to indicate the boundaries of a source citation

Naming an author or title in your text tells readers that you are citing ideas from a source, and citing a page number at the end of a summary or paraphrase lets them know where your citation ends:

> At schools in the Patriot League, John Feinstein points out, athletes mix freely with other students and aren't segregated as they are at other Division I schools (112).

However, for one-page print articles and for Internet sources, a page citation is not necessary, so it is harder to indicate where your comments about a source begin and end. Convey the shift to readers by commenting on the source in a way that clearly announces a transition back to your own views. Use expressions such as *it follows that, X's explanation shows that, as a result, evidently, obviously,* or *clearly* to signal the shift.

UNCLEAR CITATION BOUNDARY

> According to promotional material on a Sony Web site more than ten years ago, the company decided to release a cassette and a CD based on a small research study indicating that listening to Mozart improved IQ. The products showed the ingenuity of commercial enterprise while taking the researchers' conclusions in new directions.

REVISED CITATION, WITH SOURCE BOUNDARY INDICATED

> According to promotional material on a Sony Web site more than ten years ago, the company decided to release a cassette and a CD based on research indicating that listening to Mozart improved IQ. Clearly, Sony's strategy demonstrated the ingenuity of commercial enterprise, but it cannot reflect what the researchers intended when they published their conclusions.

Another way to indicate the end of your citation is to include the name of the author or authors at the end of the citation:

> For people who hate shopping, Web shopping may be the perfect solution. An article exploring the "holiday hell" of shopping reminds us that we get more choice from online vendors than we do when we browse at our local mall because the online sellers, unlike mall owners, do not have to rent space to display their goods (Jerome and Taylor). In addition, one can buy almost anything

online, from music, cell phones, and books to cars and real estate.

Note that the citation has also been introduced ("An article exploring") and the writer has indicated the shift to his own thoughts ("In addition"). See part 4, "Documenting Sources," for complete instructions on documenting your sources.

PART FOUR

Documenting Sources

DOCUMENT

PURPOSE

Each citation style represents the values and concerns of specific academic communities.

- Which citation style is the most appropriate one for your project, given your purpose in writing? Why do you think so?

AUDIENCE

Academic writers document all of the sources they have used in their research to give credit to the original authors, providing a way for their audience to locate that source for themselves. All of this builds a writer's credibility.

- How do each of your citations help your audience know where to go to find additional information?
- Looking at your draft as a whole, where do you find opportunities to improve your credibility as a writer?

VOICE

Careful documentation guides an audience smoothly through an essay, allowing readers to trace easily how ideas have been developed, extended, and so on.

- Are there places where you need to revise your documentation to clearly distinguish your sources from your own voice?

MEDIUM

Some sources delivered via newer media may not be covered in the official stylebook for your discipline.

- What examples are similar to what you're looking for and how can you modify them to provide your audience with needed information?
- Some media, including those that allow for hyperlinked documents, may offer ways of documenting sources that traditional essays on paper do not. Does the medium in which you're working afford opportunities for documentation beyond the usual ones?

9 MLA Style

MLA AT A GLANCE: INDEX OF STYLE FEATURES

When you refer to, comment on, paraphrase, or quote another author's material, you must indicate that you have done so by inserting what is called a "citation." In MLA style, you give the name of the author(s) and the page number(s) to indicate where you found the material, if available. You can put the author's name in your own text to introduce the material, with the page number in parentheses at the end of the sentence; or, especially for a source you have cited previously, you can put both author and page number (not separated by a comma) in parentheses at the place in the sentence in which you cite the material. Then, all of the more detailed information about your sources goes into a list of works cited at the end of your paper so that readers can retrieve and read the same source.

Sections 9a-9h show you examples and variations on the basic principle of MLA citation—for instance, what to do when no author is named or how to cite an online source that has no page numbers.

9a Basic features of MLA style

MLA (Modern Language Association) style for the humanities for undergraduates is most recently explained and illustrated in the *MLA Handbook for Writers of Research Papers* (7th ed., New York: MLA, 2009) and on the MLA Web site at <http://www.mla.org>.

KEY POINTS
Handling Sources in MLA Style

1. *In your paper,* include the following information for each source:

   - the last name(s) of the author (or authors) either in your text or in parentheses—or the title (or a shortened form in the parentheses) if no author is known—after a quotation or a paraphrase

   - the page number(s) telling where the information is located (except when the source is online or only one page long), but do not include the word *page* or *pages* or the abbreviation *p.* or *pp.* Do not put a comma between the author's name or the title and the page numbers contained in parentheses.

(continued)

(continued)

2. *At the end of your paper,* include a list, alphabetized by authors' last names or by title (if the author is not known), of all of the sources you refer to in the paper. Begin the list on a new page and title it *Works Cited* (73–94).

Illustrations of the Basic Features

In-Text Citation	Entry in List of Works Cited
Print book	
Author named in your text and page(s) in parentheses The renowned scholar of language, David Crystal, has promoted the idea of "dialect democracy" (168).	Crystal, David. *The Stories of English*. Woodstock: Overlook, 2004. Print.
Author and page(s) in parentheses A renowned scholar of language has promoted the idea of "dialect democracy" (Crystal 168).	
Print article	
Author named in your text and page(s) in parentheses If indeed "anything goes" in art, Barry Gewen is right to question the role of an art critic (29).	Gewen, Barry. "State of the Art." *New York Times* 11 Dec. 2005, early ed., Book Review sec.: 28-32. Print.
Author and page(s) in parentheses If indeed "anything goes" in art, the role of an art critic can be questioned (Gewen 29).	
Web document	
Author named in text According to James Ledbetter of *Slate* magazine, the number of people who are texting while driving is increasing significantly every year.	Ledbetter, James. "Don't Write Off Texting-While-Driving Bans." Human Nature: Science, Technology, and Life. *Slate*. Washington Post. Newsweek Interactive, 29 Sept. 2010. Web. 1 Oct. 2014.

NOTE: Use endnotes (at the end of the paper) or footnotes (at the bottom of each page or at the end of each chapter) only for supplementary comments and additional information, not for regular source citations.[1] Number information notes consecutively in your text by placing a raised (superscript) numeral after the referenced material, as in the previous sentence. Indent the first line of each numbered note, and place the number and a period before the note content. The footnote example at the bottom of this page refers to the superscript number above.

9b How to cite sources in your paper (MLA)

You can get a great deal of help with the automatic "cite while you write" feature offered in bibliographic software programs such as *EndNote* and *RefWorks*. See 7d on the value of learning to use these programs, which are often offered by college libraries.

CITING A WORK WITH INDIVIDUAL AUTHOR OR AUTHORS (MLA)

A. One author quoted or mentioned in your text For the first mention of an author, use the full name and any relevant credentials. After that, use only the last name. Generally, use the present tense to cite an author.

author and credentials

National Book Award winner Paul Fussell points out that

even people in low-paying jobs show "all but universal pride

page number

in a uniform of any kind" (5).

When a quotation includes a question mark or an exclamation point, use an additional period only if you provide a parenthetical citation.

Fussell reminds us of our equating uniforms with seriousness of purpose when he begins a chapter by asking, "Would you get on an airplane with two pilots who are wearing cut-off jeans?" (85).

For a quotation longer than four lines, see 9b, item U.

B. Author cited in parentheses As an alternative to naming the author in your text, especially if you have referred

---

1. MLA allows you to make comments about your sources in endnotes and footnotes.

to the author previously or if you are citing statistics, simply include the author's last name before the page number within the final parentheses, with no comma between them.

The army retreated from Boston in disarray, making the

victors realize that they had defeated "the greatest military

author and page number

power on earth" (McCullough 76).

Note that, with a long indented quotation, when no quotation marks are necessary, the final period comes before the citation in parentheses. See 9b, item U, page 72.

C. Work written by two or more authors   For a work with two or three authors, include all of the names either in your text sentence or in parentheses.

Lakoff and Johnson have pointed out. . . . (42)

(Baumol, Litan, and Schramm 226-28).

For a work with four or more authors, either put the first author's last name, followed by *et al.* (the Latin words *et alii* mean *and others*), or list all of the authors. See 9d, item 2, for how to list a work with several authors in a works-cited list.

D. Work by author with more than one work cited Include the author and title of the work in your introductory text.

Alice Walker, in her book *In Search of Our Mothers' Gardens,*

describes learning about Flannery O'Connor (43-59).

If you do not mention the author in your text, include in your parenthetical reference the author's last name, followed by a comma, an abbreviated form of the title (not followed by a comma), and the page number.

O'Connor's house still stands and is looked after by a

caretaker (Walker, *In Search* 57).

To list more than one work by the same author in your works-cited list, see item 3 in the Key Points box in 9c on page 73.

E. Two authors with the same last name Include each author's first initial, or if the initials are the same, include the whole first name.

A writer can be seen as both "author" and "secretary," and

the two roles can be seen as competitive (F. Smith 19).

F. Author of work in an edited anthology Cite the author of the included or reprinted work and the page numbers of the work included in the anthology. Mention the editor of the anthology only in the entry in the works-cited list (as shown in 9d, items 14 and 15).

Des Pres asserts that "heroism is not necessarily a romantic notion" (20).

G. Indirect source (author quoted in another source) Use *qtd. in* (for *quoted in*) in your parenthetical citation, followed by the last name of the author of the source in which you find the quotation (the indirect source) and the page number, if it is a print source. List the indirect source in your list of works cited. In the following example, the indirect source, *Douthat,* not *Mansfield,* would be included in the list of works cited.

Harvey Mansfield of Harvard University has attributed grade inflation to "the prevalence in American education of the notion of self-esteem" (qtd. in Douthat 96).

H. More than one work in one citation Include all of the citations, separated by semicolons. Avoid making the list too long.

The links between a name and ancestry have occupied many writers and researchers (Waters 65; Antin 188).

If sources refer to different parts of your sentence, cite each one after the point it supports.

CITING A WORK WITH NO INDIVIDUAL AUTHOR NAMED (MLA)

I. Corporation, government agency, or organization as author See the Key Points box in 6b for help with finding the author of a Web site. When you use material authored not by an individual but by a corporation, government agency, or organization, cite the organization as the author, making sure it corresponds with the alphabetized entry in your works-cited list (shown in 9d, item 5, and 9g, item 47). Use the complete name in your text or a shortened form in parentheses. The following examples cite a Web site, so page numbers are not included.

——— full name ———
The United States Department of Education has projected an increase in college enrollment of 11 percent between 2003 and 2013.

An increase in college enrollment of 11 percent between 2003 ——— short name ———
and 2013 has been projected (US Dept. of Educ.)

J. No author or editor named If no author or editor is named for a source, refer to the book title (italicized), article or Web page title (within quotation marks), or name of the Web site (italicized). Within a parenthetical citation, shorten the title and begin with the first word alphabetized in the works-cited list (see 9d, item 6).

According to *The Chicago Manual of Style,* rules for writers are not meant "to foreclose breaking or bending rules" when necessary (xii).

Writers should not be afraid of "breaking or bending" usage rules when necessary (*Chicago* xii).

If you need help with reading a Web site to determine its author, see the Key Points box in 6b.

K. Unauthored entry in dictionary or encyclopedia For an unsigned entry, give the title of the entry. A page number is not necessary for an alphabetized work. Begin the entry in the works-cited list with the title of the alphabetized entry (see 9d, item 16).

Drypoint differs from etching in that it does not use acid ("Etching").

CITING A WORK WITH PAGE NUMBERS NOT AVAILABLE OR RELEVANT (MLA)

L. Reference to an entire work and not to one specific idea or page Use the author's name alone, with no page number.

Diaries tell about people's everyday lives and the worlds they create (Mallon).

M. Work only one page long If a print article is only one page long, you may mention the author's name alone in your text, but be sure to include the page number in your works-cited list (9e, item 24).

N. Web and electronic sources with no page numbers Electronic database material and Web sources, which appear on a screen, have no stable page numbers that apply across systems or when printed unless you access them in PDF (portable document format) files. If your source on the screen includes no visible numbered pages or numbered paragraphs, provide only the author's name or the title if no author is named. With no page number to indicate where your citation ends, be careful to define where the citation ends and your commentary takes over (see 8e).

Science writer Stephen Hart describes how researchers Edward Taub and Thomas Ebert conclude that for musicians, practicing "remaps the brain."

Provide page or paragraph numbers only if they appear on the screen as part of the document, and indicate the total number of paragraphs in your works-cited list (as in 9g, item 35).

Hatchuel discusses how film editing "can change points of view and turn objectivity into subjectivity" (par. 6).

You may also locate the information according to an internal heading of the document, such as *introduction, chapter,* or *section.* You may write out the name of a division or abbreviate it *(sec. 9).* If your source includes no visible numbered pages or paragraphs, include *n. pag.* in your works-cited list.

CITING MULTIMEDIA AND MISCELLANEOUS SOURCES (MLA)

O. Multimedia source For radio or television programs, interviews, live performances, films, computer software, recordings, works of art, or other multimedia sources, include only the author (or producer, actor, director, and so on) or title. Make sure that your text reference corresponds to the first element of the information you provide in your works-cited list; in the following example, *Shaw* is the actor Fiona Shaw. See 9h, item 62.

It takes an extraordinary actor to keep an audience enthralled even when buried up to the neck (Shaw).

P. Multivolume work Indicate the volume number, followed by a colon, a space, and the page number (Richardson 1: 25). Give the total number of volumes in your works-cited list (9d, item 10).

Q. Lecture, speech, personal communication, or interview Give the name of the person delivering the communication. In your works-cited list, state the type of communication after the author's name (9g, item 52, and 9h, items 64 and 65).

According to Roberta Bernstein, professor of art history at the University at Albany, the most challenging thing about contemporary art is understanding that it is meant to be challenging. This may mean that the artist wants to make us uncomfortable with our familiar ideas or present us with reconceived notions of beauty.

R. Frequently studied literary works: Fiction, poetry, and drama For a short story or a novel with no divisions or chapters, simply provide the author's name and page number. For other works, particularly classic works appearing in many editions, using the following guidelines will allow readers to find your reference in any edition. In your works-cited list, include details about the edition you use.

> **For a novel:** First give the page number in the edition you used, followed by a semicolon. Then give the chapter or section number: (Twain 104; ch. 5).

> **For a poem:** For the first reference, write *lines* and give line numbers, not page numbers: (lines 62–68). Omit the word *lines* in subsequent line references. See 29d and 29e for help with punctuation in quoting poetry.

> **For classic poems such as *The Iliad* with divisions into books or parts:** Give the book, canto, or part, followed by a period (with no space) and line numbers, not page numbers, separated by a hyphen: (8.21-25).

> **Classic verse plays:** Rather than page numbers, give act, scene, and line numbers in Arabic numerals, separated by periods. For classic works by Chaucer, Homer, Wordsworth, Shakespeare, and others, titles such as *A Midsummer Night's Dream* can be abbreviated in parentheses: (*MND* 1.1.133-36).

S. The Bible and other sacred texts Give book, chapter, and verse(s) in your text (Genesis 27.29) or abbreviate the book in a parenthetical citation (*New Jerusalem Bible*, Gen. 27.29). Give the edition of the Bible or other sacred text in your works-cited list, as in 9d, item 19.

T. Historical or legal document Cite any article and section number of a familiar historical document such as the Constitution (usually abbreviated and not in italics or quotation marks) in parentheses in your text (US Const., art. 2, sec. 4), with no entry in the works-cited list. Italicize the name of a court case (*Roe v. Wade*) in your text but not in your works-cited list. Do not italicize laws and acts in either place. List cases and acts in your works-cited list, as in 9h, item 66.

U. A long (block) quotation Indent a quotation of four or more lines one inch (or ten spaces), without using quotation marks. See an example in 8c, page 57.

V. A footnote To cite a footnote in a source, give the page number (or, in the case of a sacred text, the chapter and verse), followed by *n* or *nn* (*New Oxford Annotated Bible*, Gen. 35.1-4n).

9c How to set up an MLA list of works cited

The references that you make in your text to sources should be brief—usually only the author's last name and a page number—so they allow readers to continue reading without interruption. For complete information about the source, readers use the in-text citation as a guide to the full reference in your list of works cited.

KEY POINTS
Guidelines for MLA List of Works Cited

1. *What to list*: List only works you actually cited in the text of your paper, not works you read but did not mention, unless your instructor requires you to include all of the works you consulted as well as those mentioned in your text.

2. *Format of the list*: Begin the list on a new numbered page after the last of the paper or any endnotes. Center the heading (*Works Cited*) without quotation marks, underlining, or a period. Double-space throughout the list. Do not number the entries.

3. *What to put first in an entry* (*author or title*): List works alphabetically by the author's last name. For multiple authors, reverse the names of the first author only (9d, item 2). If the author is a corporation or an organization, use that name (9d, item 5). List works with no stated author by the first main word of the title (9d, item 6, and 9e, item 27). For several works by one author, after the first entry, use three hyphens and a period in place of the author's name, listing the author's works alphabetically by title (see an example in Model Paper 2 on page 104).

4. *Indentation:* To help readers find a source and to differentiate one entry from another, indent all lines of each entry—except the first—one-half inch (or five spaces). A word processor can provide these "hanging indents" (go to your Help menu).

NOTE: If you intend to publish on the Internet, it is often preferable to use no indentation at all; HTML does not support hanging indents well. Instead, follow each bibliographical entry with a
(continued)

(continued)

line space. Consult your instructor about using this format.

5. *Periods:* Separate the main parts of each entry—author, title, publishing information—with a period, followed by one space.

6. *Capitals in titles:* Capitalize the first letter of the first and last words in titles and subtitles of books and articles and all other words except *a, an, the,* coordinating conjunctions, *to* in an infinitive, and prepositions (such as *in, to, for, with, without, against*).

7. *Italics in titles:* Italicize the titles of books; the names of journals, newspapers, and magazines; and the titles of Web sites, online databases, films, and other media, as shown in the examples in this section.

8. *Page numbers:*
   • Give inclusive page numbers for print articles and sections of books, with a hyphen rather than a dash between numbers: 146-54.
   • Do not use *p.* (or *pp.*) or the word *page* (or *pages*) before page numbers in any reference.
   • For citations of page numbers greater than 100 and sharing the same first number(s), use only the last two digits for the second number (for instance, 683-89,, but 798-805).
   • For an unpaginated work, write *n. pag.*
   • Do not include page numbers for online works unless they are in PDF or are provided on the screen for an original print source. See 9b, item N for more on page numbers in online sources.

9. *Abbreviations:* Use abbreviations for publishers' names; well-known religious and literary works; some common words in references, such as *fig.*, *assn.*, and *introd.*; countries (as in *Can.* or *UK*); and common terms such as *e.g.* and *i.e.* Use *n.d.* when no date of publication is given and *n.p.* when no publisher or no place of publication is given.

10. *Publication medium:* Always include the medium of publication, e.g., *Print, Web, Film, CD, Performance, MP3 file, Television.*

NOTE: Provide a URL only when a source may otherwise be difficult to locate or when your instructor asks for it. See examples in 9g, items 49-51.

9d Listing print books, parts of books, and pamphlets

Find the necessary information for an entry on the title page of a book and on the copyright page. Use the most recent copyright date, and list only the first city on the title page. Use a shortened form of the publisher's name; usually one word is sufficient: *Cengage,* not *Cengage Learning; Basic,* not *Basic Books.* For university presses, use the abbreviations *U* and *P* with no periods. End each entry with the word *Print.*

1. Book with one author Give the name of the author, last name first. Then give the title and any subtitle, italicized. Follow this with the city of publication, a colon, the name of the publisher in short form (using *UP* for university presses), a comma, the year of publication (often found only on the copyright page), and a period. Then give the medium of publication: *Print.* See Source Shot 1 on page 76.

2. Book with two or more authors Separate the names of authors with commas. Reverse the order of the first author's name only.

Baumol, William J., Robert E. Litan, and Carl J. Schramm.

Good Capitalism, Bad Capitalism, and the Economics

of Growth and Prosperity. New Haven: Yale UP, 2007.

Print.

With four or more authors, either list all of the names or use only the first author's name, followed by *et al.* (Latin for *and others*).

3. Book with editor or editors Include the abbreviation *ed.* or *eds.* after the name(s).

Sebold, Alice, ed. *The Best American Short Stories 2009*.

Boston: Houghton, 2009. Print.

Treat a book with more than one editor as you would a book with more than one author.

4. Book with author and editor When an editor has prepared an author's work for publication, list the book under the author's name if you cite the author's work. Then, in your listing, include the name(s) of the editor or editors after the title, introduced by *Ed.* (*edited by*) for one or more editors.

Bishop, Elizabeth. *One Art: Letters*. Ed. Robert Giroux.

New York: Farrar, 1994. Print.

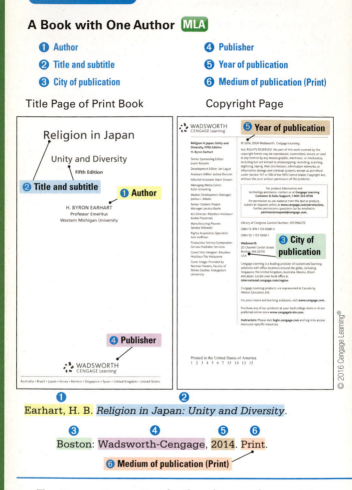

SOURCE SHOT 1

A Book with One Author   MLA

① Author
② Title and subtitle
③ City of publication
④ Publisher
⑤ Year of publication
⑥ Medium of publication (Print)

Title Page of Print Book

Religion in Japan

Unity and Diversity

Fifth Edition

② **Title and subtitle**

① **Author**

H. BYRON EARHART
Professor Emeritus
Western Michigan University

④ **Publisher**

WADSWORTH
CENGAGE Learning·

Australia · Brazil · Japan · Korea · Mexico · Singapore · Spain · United Kingdom · United States

Copyright Page

WADSWORTH
CENGAGE Learning

⑤ **Year of publication**

Religion in Japan: Unity and Diversity, Fifth Edition
H. Byron Earhart

Senior Sponsoring Editor: Joann Kozyrev
Development Editor: Ian Lague
Assistant Editor: Joshua Duncan
Editorial Assistant: Marri Straton
Managing Media Editor: Katie Schooling
Market Development Manager: Joshua I. Adams
Senior Content Project Manager: Jessica Rasile
Art Director: Faceless Holdbaur/ Andrei Pasternak
Manufacturing Planner: Sandee Milewski
Rights Acquisition Specialist: Ann Hoffman
Production Service/Compositor: Cenveo Publisher Services
Cover/Text Designer: Rosebox Holdbaur/Tac Hatayama
Cover Image: Provided by Norman Havens, Faculty of Shinto Studies, Kokugakuin University

© 2014, 2004 Wadsworth, Cengage Learning

ALL RIGHTS RESERVED. No part of this work covered by the copyright herein may be reproduced, transmitted, stored, or used in any form or by any means graphic, electronic, or mechanical, including but not limited to photocopying, recording, scanning, digitizing, taping, Web distribution, information networks, or information storage and retrieval systems, except as permitted under Section 107 or 108 of the 1976 United States Copyright Act, without the prior written permission of the publisher.

For product information and technology assistance, contact us at **Cengage Learning Customer & Sales Support, 1-800-354-9706**
For permission to use material from this text or product, submit all requests online at **www.cengage.com/permissions.**
Further permissions questions can be emailed to **permissionrequest@cengage.com.**

Library of Congress Control Number: 2012946272
ISBN-13: 978-1-133-93481-3
ISBN-10: 1-133-93481-1

③ **City of publication**

Wadsworth
20 Channel Center Street
Boston, MA 02210
USA

Cengage Learning is a leading provider of customized learning solutions with office locations around the globe, including Singapore, the United Kingdom, Australia, Mexico, Brazil and Japan. Locate your local office at **international.cengage.com/region**

Cengage Learning products are represented in Canada by Nelson Education, Ltd.

For your course and learning solutions, visit **www.cengage.com.**

Purchase any of our products at your local college store or at our preferred online store **www.cengagebrain.com.**

Instructors: Please visit **login.cengage.com** and log in to access instructor-specific resources.

Printed in the United States of America
1 2 3 4 5 6 7 15 14 13 12

①   ②
Earhart, H. B. *Religion in Japan: Unity and Diversity*.

③   ④   ⑤   ⑥
Boston: Wadsworth-Cengage, 2014. Print.

⑥ **Medium of publication (Print)**

To cite a section written by the editor, such as an introduction or a note, begin with the name of the editor, followed by a label such as *Introduction*. Continue with the title and the word *By,* followed by the author's name, and give the section's page numbers.

Giroux, Robert, ed. Introduction. *One Art: Letters.* By

Elizabeth Bishop. New York: Farrar, 1994. vii-xxii. Print.

See 9d, item 14, to cite a section written by neither the author nor the editor.

5. Book written by a corporation, organization, or government agency   Alphabetize by the name of the corporate author or the branch of government. If the publisher is the same as the author, include the name again as publisher.

Hoover's. *Hoover's Handbook of World Business.* Austin:

Hoover's, 2010. Print.

If no author is named for a government publication, begin the entry with the name of the federal, state, or local government, followed by the name of the agency.

United States. Natl. Commission on Terrorist Attacks upon

the United States. *The 9/11 Commission Report.* New

York: Norton, 2004. Print.

6. Book or pamphlet with no author named Put the title first. Do not consider the words *A, An,* and *The* when alphabetizing the entries. The following entry would be alphabetized under *C.*

The Chicago Manual of Style. 16th ed. Chicago: U of Chicago

P, 2010. Print.

7. Translated book After the title, include *Trans.*, followed by the name of the translator, not in inverted order.

Saviano, Roberto. *Gomorrah: A Personal Journey into the*

Violent International Empire of Naples' Organized

Crime System. Trans. Virginia Jewiss. New York: Farrar,

2008. Print.

8. Book not in first edition Give the edition number (*ed.*) after the title or the name of the editor (if there is one).

Raimes, Ann, and Susan Miller-Cochran. *Keys for Writers.*

7th ed. Boston: Wadsworth-Cengage, 2014. Print.

9. Republished book Give the original date of publication after the title. The reprint publication information and the date should be followed by the medium of publication.

King, Stephen. *On Writing.* 2000. New York: Scribner,

2010. Print.

10. Multivolume work If you refer to more than one volume of a multivolume work, give the total number of volumes (*vols.*) after the title, editor's name, or edition and before the publication information.

Einstein, Albert. *Collected Papers of Albert Einstein.* 10 vols.

Princeton: Princeton UP, 1987-2006. Print.

If you refer to only one volume, limit the information in the entry to that one volume (for example, *Vol. 3*).

11. Book in a series End the entry with the title of the series (using the abbreviation *ser.*) after the medium (*Print*).

Connor, Ulla. *Contrastive Rhetoric: Cross-Cultural Aspects of*

    Second Language Writing. New York: Cambridge UP,

    1996. Print. Cambridge Applied Linguistics Ser.

Add any series number after the series name.

12. Book published under a publisher's imprint First state the name of the imprint (the publisher within a larger publishing house), and then follow with the name of the larger publishing house, separated by a hyphen.

Atwood, Margaret. *Negotiation with the Dead: A Writer on*

    Writing. New York: Anchor-Doubleday, 2003. Print.

13. Foreword, preface, introduction, or afterword List the name of the author of the book element cited, followed by the name of the element, with no quotation marks. Give the title of the work; then use *By* to introduce the name of the author(s) of the book (first name first). After the publication information, give inclusive page numbers for the book element cited, and conclude with the medium of publication.

Remnick, David. Introduction. *Politics.* By Hendrik Hertzberg.

    New York: Penguin, 2004. xvii-xxiv. Print.

If the element has a title, put it in quotation marks before the description of the element.

14. One work in an anthology (original or reprinted) For a work included in an anthology, first list the author and the title of the work. Follow this information with the title of the anthology, the name of the editor(s), the edition, publication information (place, publisher, date) for the anthology, the inclusive page numbers in the anthology where the work can be found, and the medium of publication.

Alvarez, Julia. "Grounds for Fiction." *The Riverside Reader.* Ed.

    Joseph Trimmer and Maxine Hairston. 9th ed. Boston:

    Houghton, 2008. 121-34. Print.

If the work in the anthology is a reprint of a previously published scholarly article, supply the complete information for both the original publication (placed first in the entry) and the reprint in the anthology (preceded by *Rpt. in).*

Gates, Henry Louis, Jr. "The Fire Last Time." *New Republic*

1 June 1992: 37-43. Rpt. in *Contemporary Literary*

Criticism. Ed. Jeffrey W. Hunter. Vol. 127. Detroit: Gale,

2000. 113-19. Print.

15. More than one work in an anthology, cross-referenced If you refer to more than one work from the same anthology, list the anthology separately in a complete entry. Then cross-reference each work from the anthology in a separate entry containing the author's full name, the title of the work, the last name of the editor(s) of the anthology, and the work's inclusive page numbers. Include the medium of publication only with the anthology entry.

Des Pres, Terrence. "Poetry and Politics." Gibbons 17-29.

Gibbons, Reginald, ed. *The Writer in Our World*. Boston:

Atlantic Monthly P, 1986. Print.

Walcott, Derek. "A Colonial's Eye View of America." Gibbons

73-77.

16. Entry in a reference book For a well-known reference book, give only the edition number and the year of publication. When entries are arranged alphabetically, omit any volume and page numbers.

"Etching." *Columbia Encyclopedia*. 6th ed. 2000. Print.

17. Book title including a title Do not italicize a book title included in the italicized title of the work you list. (However, if the title of a short work, such as a poem or a short story, is included, enclose it in quotation marks.)

Hays, Kevin J., ed. *The Critical Response to Herman Melville's*

Moby Dick. Westport: Greenwood, 1994. Print.

18. Illustrated book or graphic narrative If illustrations are part of a literary work, give *Illus.* and the illustrator's name after the title.

For collaborative graphic narratives, such as a graphic novel, use labels to indicate the roles of individuals (*writer*, *illus.*, *adapt.*, *trans.*, and so on). Begin your entry with the name of the person whose work you are emphasizing.

Pekar, Harvey, and Joyce Brabner, writers. *Our Cancer*

Year. Illus. Frank Stack. New York: Four Walls Eight

Windows, 1994. Print.

19. The Bible and other sacred texts Give the usual bibliographical details for a book, including the name of an editor or a translator. If the work is based on a specific version of the text, put that information at the end of the entry.

Enuma Elish. Ed. Leonard W. King. Escondido: Book Tree,

   1998. Print.

The Holy Bible. Peabody: Hendrickson, 2003. Print. King

   James Vers.

The Koran. Trans. George Sale. London: Warne, n.d. Print.

(Use *n.d.* when no date is given.)

20. Dissertation Cite a published dissertation as you would a book, with the place of publication, publisher, and date, but also include dissertation information after the title (for example, Diss. U of California, 2014.).

   If the dissertation is published by University Microfilms International (UMI), italicize the title, and, after the dissertation information, add *Ann Arbor: UMI* and the UMI publication date before the medium of publication.

Jerskey, Maria. *Writing Handbooks, English Language*

   Learners, and the Selective Tradition. Diss. New York U,

   2006. Ann Arbor: UMI, 2006. Print.

For an unpublished dissertation, follow the title (in quotation marks) with *Diss.,* the degree-granting university and date, and the medium of publication.

Hidalgo, Stephen Paul. "Vietnam War Poetry: A Genre of

   Witness." Diss. U of Notre Dame, 1995. Print.

If you cite an abstract published in *Dissertation Abstracts International,* give the relevant volume number, issue number, year (in parentheses), item or page number, and medium of publication.

Hidalgo, Stephen Paul. "Vietnam War Poetry: A Genre of

   Witness." Diss. U of Notre Dame, 1995. *DAI* 56.8 (1995):

   item 0931A. Print.

9e Listing print articles in periodicals (MLA)

The conventions for listing articles differ according to the type of publication in which they appear: newspapers, popular magazines, or scholarly journals. For information about distinguishing scholarly journals from other periodicals, see 6c. Note: If the article is accessed through an online database, see 9f for information about how to list the database in the citation.

21. Article in a scholarly journal   After the italicized journal title (not followed by a comma), give the volume number and the issue number (if there is one), separated by a period; the year in parentheses, followed by a colon; the inclusive page numbers, separated by a hyphen; and the medium, *Print*. Repeat only the last two digits of the second page number. See Source Shot 2 on page 82.

22. Article in a scholarly journal with no volume number Include the issue number alone if no volume number is given.

23. Article in a magazine   Do not include *The* in the name of a magazine: *Atlantic,* not *The Atlantic.* For a weekly or a biweekly magazine, give the complete date (day, month, and year, in that order, with no commas between them), as in the second example below. For a monthly or a bimonthly magazine, give only the month and year, as in the example by Pritchard below. In MLA style, do not include volume and issue numbers for magazines. If the article is on only one page, give that page number. If the article covers two or more consecutive pages, list inclusive page numbers. See 9e, item 25, for an article that skips pages.

Pritchard, Jonathan K. "How We Are Evolving." *Scientific*

　　American Oct. 2010: 40-47. Print.

Remnick, David. "Putin and the Exile." *New Yorker* 28 Apr.

　　2014: 19. Print.

24. Article in a newspaper   After the newspaper title (omit the word *The*), give the date, followed by any edition (such as *late ed., natl. ed.*) and a colon. For a newspaper that uses letters to designate sections, give the letter before the page number: A23. For numbered or named sections, as in Sunday editions, write, for example, sec. 2: 23. See an example on page 66. (Also see 9g, item 36, for the entry for the online version of the following article.)

Shear, Michael D., and Jonathan Weisman. "Veteran Scandal

　　Aggravates Woes of White House." *New York Times*

　　21 May 2014, natl. ed.: A1+. Print.

SOURCE SHOT 2*

Listing an Article in a Scholarly Journal MLA

❶ Author
❷ Title of article
❸ Title of journal
❹ Volume and issue number

❺ Date of publication
❻ Page span
❼ Medium of publication (Print)

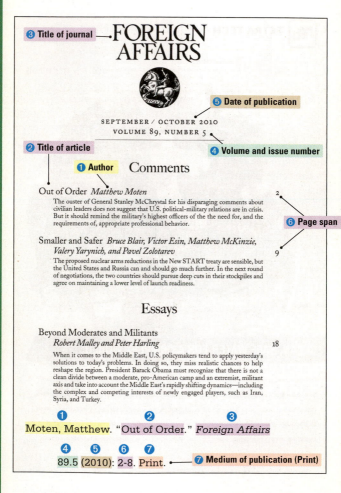

❸ Title of journal   FOREIGN AFFAIRS

❺ Date of publication

SEPTEMBER / OCTOBER 2010
VOLUME 89, NUMBER 5

❹ Volume and issue number

❷ Title of article

❶ Author   Comments

Out of Order *Matthew Moten*   2

The ouster of General Stanley McChrystal for his disparaging comments about
civilian leaders does not suggest that U.S. political-military relations are in crisis.
But it should remind the military's highest officers of the the need for, and the
requirements of, appropriate professional behavior.

❻ Page span

Smaller and Safer *Bruce Blair, Victor Esin, Matthew McKinzie,
Valery Yarynich, and Pavel Zolotarev*   9

The proposed nuclear arms reductions in the New START treaty are sensible, but
the United States and Russia can and should go much further. In the next round
of negotiations, the two countries should pursue deep cuts in their stockpiles and
agree on maintaining a lower level of launch readiness.

Essays

Beyond Moderates and Militants
Robert Malley and Peter Harling   18

When it comes to the Middle East, U.S. policymakers tend to apply yesterday's
solutions to today's problems. In doing so, they miss realistic chances to help
reshape the region. President Barack Obama must recognize that there is not a
clean divide between a moderate, pro-American camp and an extremist, militant
axis and take into account the Middle East's rapidly shifting dynamics—including
the complex and competing interests of newly engaged players, such as Iran,
Syria, and Turkey.

❶   ❷   ❸
Moten, Matthew. "Out of Order." *Foreign Affairs*

❹   ❺   ❻   ❼
89.5 (2010): 2-8. Print.   ❼ Medium of publication (Print)

25. Article that skips pages When a magazine or a news-paper article does not appear on consecutive pages, give only the first page number, followed by a plus sign. The following article by Thompson is on pages 18–19 and 68.

Thompson, Clive. "Take This Job and Unplug It." *Mother*

   Jones May-June 2014: 18+. Print.

26. Review Begin with the name of the reviewer and the title of the review article, if these are available. After *Rev. of,* provide the title, a comma, the word *By,* and the author of the work reviewed, followed by the publication information for the review. Conclude with the medium of publication.

McCarter, Jeremy. "Drama Queen." Rev. of *Sarah*, by Robert

   Gottlieb. *Newsweek* 27 Sept. 2010: 58-59. Print.

27. Unsigned editorial or article Begin with the title. For an editorial, include the label *Editorial* after the title. In alphabetizing, ignore an initial *A, An,* or *The.*

"Put Out to Pasture: Controversy Surrounds the

   Government's Management of Wild Horses."

   Economist 24 Sept. 2011: 40. Print.

 "The Repeal Pledge." Editorial. *Wall Street Journal* 30 Sept.

   2010: A24. Print.

28. Letter to the editor Write *Letter* or *Reply to letter of* . . . after the name of the author or the title of the letter (if there is one).

Gonzalez, Wayne. "Survival of the Fittest." Letter.

   Smithsonian Oct. 2010: 6. Print.

Lisle, Laurie. Letter. *Authors Guild Bulletin* Spring 2010: 2+. Print.

(Lisle's letter begins on page 2 and continues on page 54.)

29. Abstract in an abstracts journal Provide exact information for the original work, and then add information about your source for the abstract: the title of the abstract journal, volume number, issue number, year (in parentheses), item number and/or page number, and medium of publication. (For dissertation abstracts, see 9d, item 20.)

Powers, R. S., and R. A. Wojtkiewicz. "Occupational

   Aspirations, Gender, and Educational Attainment."

Sociological Spectrum 24.5 (2004): 601-22. *Studies on*

Women and Gender Abstracts 23.8 (Dec. 2005): 435,

item 05W/710. Print.

9f Listing works accessed in online databases (MLA)

Libraries subscribe to large online databases such as *Academic Search Premier, Academic Search Complete*, and *LexisNexis*, as well as to specialized databases such as *ERIC, Contemporary Literary Criticism,* and *PsycINFO.* You can use these databases to locate abstracts and full texts of thousands of articles previously published in print form.

Include whatever is available of the following information for an article in an online database:

1. Author(s): individual, company or government agency.
2. Title and subtitle of work, in quotation marks.
3. Print publication information for the source: name of journal (italicized), volume and issue number for a scholarly journal, date of publication, and the range of page numbers if given, or *n. pag.* if no exact page span is given. Use a PDF rather than an HTML version to see original page numbers of a source previously in print.
4. Title of the database (italicized), such as *Academic Search Premier* or *PsycArticles.*
5. The medium: *Web.*
6. Date of access: day, month (abbreviated), year.

30. Scholarly article in an online library database

Miller-Cochran, Susan, and Dana Gierdowski. "Making

Peace with the Rising Cost of Writing Technologies:

Flexible Classroom Design as a Sustainable Solution."

title of journal   volume number. issue number   year   page span
Computers and Composition 30.1 (2013): 50–60.

title of database   medium of publication   date of access
Academic Search Premier. Web. 21 May 2014.

31. Magazine article in an online library database See Source Shot 3 on page 85.

32. Newspaper article in an online database

Mehta, Seema. "Meaner Bullying Is Stirring New Tactics." *Los*

Angeles Times 7 Mar. 2008: B1. *LexisNexis*. Web. 9 Mar. 2011.

SOURCE SHOT 3

Listing a Magazine Article in an Online Database MLA

❶ Author   **❷ Title of article**

Lindsey, Brink. "Culture of Success." *New Republic*

❸ Print publication:
– magazine, date: pages   **❹ Database title**

12 Mar. 2008: 30-31. *Academic Search Complete*.

❺ Medium of publication ❻ Date of access

Web. 14 Mar. 2011.

9g Listing Web sources (MLA)

NOTE: No URL is necessary, unless the source is difficult to locate without it. If you include a URL, place it in angle brackets, and only split the URL across a line after a slash. Do not split the protocol *http://* across lines.

33. Entry in an online reference work

"Vicarious." *Cambridge Advanced Learner's Dictionary*.

    Cambridge UP, 2004. Web. 6 Feb. 2014.

34. Article in an online scholarly journal Give the author, title of the article, title of the journal, volume and issue numbers, and date of online publication. Include the page number or the number of paragraphs only if pages or paragraphs are numbered in the actual source, as they are in the example below. End with the medium of publication and your date of access.

author   title of article
Hatchuel, Sarah. "Leading the Gaze: From Showing to

Telling in Kenneth Branagh's *Henry V* and *Hamlet*."

                                        issue   year of publication
    title of online journal   volume   number of paragraphs
    Early Modern Literary Studies 6.1 (2000): 22 pars.
    medium of publication   date of access
    Web. 1 Feb. 2008.

35. Article in an online magazine

Kinsley, Michael. "The Least We Can Do." *Atlantic*. Atlantic

Monthly Group, Oct. 2010. Web. 29 Nov. 2013.

36. Article in an online newspaper

Shear, Michael D., and Jonathan Weisman. "Veteran Scandal

Aggravates Woes of White House." *New York Times*.

New York Times, 21 May 2014. Web. 25 May 2014.

37. Online book with a print source Give whatever is available of the following: author, title, editor or translator, and print publication information. Then give the electronic publication information: name of the Web site or database, medium of publication (*Web*), and your date of access.

author   title
Darwin, Charles. *The Voyage of the Beagle*. New York:
    print publication
    —information—   title of database   medium
    Collier, 1909. *Oxford Text Archive*. Web.

    date of access
    19 Jan. 2014.

38. Book published only online Cite a book that is only published electronically as you would a print book by listing the author, title, and other publication information. Next, give the title of the Web site (if different from the work's title) or database, the sponsor of the site, the date of publication, the medium of publication, and the date of access.

Goldberg, David Theo, Stretka Hristova, and Erik Loyer. *Blue

Velvet: Re-dressing New Orleans in Katrina's Wake.*

Vectors Journal. Vectors Journal, 2008. Web. 25 Mar. 2012.

39. Online poem with a print source   Give the print publication information first, listing *n. pag.* if no page numbers are visible on-screen. Then give the Web site or database, the medium of publication, and the date of access.

Levine, Philip. "What Work Is." *What Work Is.* New York:

Knopf, 1991. N. pag. *Internet Poetry Archive.* Web.

20 Jan. 2014.

(labels: title of poem; print publication information; no page numbers in Web source; title of database; date of access)

40. Poem published only online   For a poem that is only published on a Web site, give the author, title, name of the Web site, name of the sponsor, date of the posting, medium of publication, and the date of access.

Aechtner, Chris D. "Goddess of the Night." *PoetrySoup.*

PoetrySoup, 2011. Web. 2 Feb. 2014.

41. Online review, editorial, or letter with a print source   Give the author, title, identification of the type of text: *Letter, Editorial*, or *Rev. of . . . by . . .* (see 9e, items 26–28), and other print publication information. Give the page numbers, if they are visible on-screen. Then add the name of the Web site or database, medium of publication, and date of access.

McGuinan, Cathleen. "A Fiennes Romance This Is." Rev. of

The End of the Affair. Dir. Neil Jordan. *Newsweek* 12 June

1999: 82. *Academic Search Elite.* Web. 4 Feb. 2014.

42. Review, editorial, or letter published only online   Give the author, title, and identification of the type of text. Then continue with the name of the Web site, the sponsor of the site, the date of online posting, the medium of publication, and the date of access.

Raimes, Ann. Rev. of *Dog World: And the Humans Who Live*

There, by Alfred Gingold. *Amazon.com.* Amazon.com,

11 Feb. 2005. Web. 1 Feb. 2014.

43. Authored document on a Web site

Cohen, Elizabeth. "A Lesson from Mom: Don't Be a 'Good'

Patient." *CNN.com/health.* Cable News Network,

30 Sept. 2010. Web. 8 Oct. 2013.

(labels: sponsor; date of posting; medium; date of access)

44. Web site document, no author named Begin with the title, and then include other information as you would for an authored website. See item 43 for an example.

"Execution Deadline: Missouri Inmate with Birth Defect

Appeals." *NBC News*. NBCNews.com, 20 May 2014.

Web. 20 May 2014.

45. Entire Web site, no author named

name of site   sponsor   online update
MLA. Mod. Lang. Assn. of Amer., 18 June 2013.

medium   date of access
Web. 15 May 2014.

46. Government publication online Begin with the government, agency, and title of the work. Include the date if the work was published in print. Follow this information with the date of posting (if the work is only available online), the Web site, the medium of publication, and the date of access.

United States. Dept. of Educ. Inst. of Educ. Sciences. Natl.

Center for Educ. Statistics. *Digest of Education*

Statistics: 2009. April 2010. *National Center for*

Education Statistics. Web. 14 Oct. 2013.

47. Scholarly project online If the site shows the name of the editor, give it after the title. If no date is given for site creation, write *n.d.*

editors
Victorian Women Writers Project. Ed. Angela Courtney and

sponsor   date of posting
Michelle Dalmau. Trustees of Indiana U, 2010.

medium of publication   date of access
Web. 2 Mar. 2014.

48. Personal Web site or home page If a personal Web site has a title, supply it, italicized. For a home page within a Web site, use the designation *Home page* and the name of the Web site. Use *N.p.* for "no publisher" and *n.d.* for "no date."

Gilpatrick, Eleanor. Online Fine Art Gallery. N.p., n.d. Web.

date of access
22 Feb. 2014.

Politzer, Sally. Home page. Architectural Glass. N.p., 2006.

Web. 20 Jan. 2014.

49. Course home page For a course home page, give the name of the instructor, the course title, the words *Course home page,* the dates of the course, the department, the name of the Web site, the sponsor, the date of posting or update, the medium of publication, and the access date. Only include a URL (as is done here) if the site otherwise may be difficult to access.

Casana, Jesse. "ANTH 3023: Approaches to Archaeology."

> Course home page. Spring 2012. Dept. of Anthropology.
>
> *University of Arkansas.* Fulbright College of Arts and
>
> Sciences, U of Arkansas, 2012. Web. 22 Apr. 2012.
>
> <http://blackboard.tufts.edu/webapps/portal/>.

50. Blogs, discussion boards, wikis, electronic mailing lists Give the author's name and the document title. If there is no title or if an explanation is needed, use a descriptive label such as *Online posting.* Follow this with the name of the list or forum or the title of the blog or wiki (if available), the date of posting, the medium of publication (*Web*), the date of access, and the URL of the list or blog if it would help readers find the source.

Althouse, Ann. "Patti Smith Nominated for a National Book

> Award." *Althouse.* 14 Oct. 2010. Web. 15 Oct. 2014.
>
> <http://althouse.blogspot.com>.

Krugman, Paul. "Healthcare Politics in One Sentence." The

> Conscience of a Liberal. *New York Times.* 28 Apr. 2014.
>
> Web. 30 Apr. 2014. <http://krugman.blogs.nytimes.com>.

To make it easy for readers to find a posting in an electronic discussion list, whenever possible, refer to one stored in Web archives.

Kuechler, Manfred. "Google Docs: A New Tool for

> Collaborative Writing." Online posting. Hunter-L
>
> Archives, 5 Dec. 2007. Web. 21 Jan. 2014.
>
> <http://hunter.listserv.cuny.edu>.

51. Forwarded document To cite a forwarded document in an online posting, include the author, title, and date, followed by *Fwd. by* and the name of the person forwarding the document. End with the name of the discussion group, the date of the forwarding, the medium, the date of access, and the URL of the discussion list.

Beaky, Lenore A. "Chronicle Article." 18 Mar. 2011. Fwd. by

Jack Hammond. Hunter-L. 18 Mar. 2011. Web. 20 Mar.

2014. <http://hunter.listserv.cuny.edu>.

52. Personal e-mail message   Treat an e-mail like a letter, adding in quotation marks any title from the subject line. End with the medium of delivery: *E-mail.*

McBride, Tom. "Multimedia Composition." Message to the

author. 29 Sept. 2013. E-mail.

53. Synchronous communication   When citing a source from a chat room, give the name of the person speaking or posting information, title of the message, name of the forum, date of posting, medium (*Web*), date of access, and URL. Refer to archived material whenever possible.

9h   Listing visual, performance, multimedia, and miscellaneous sources: Live, print, and online (MLA)

Identify online interviews, maps, charts, films and film clips, videos, television programs, radio programs, sound recordings, works of art, cartoons, and advertisements as you would sources that are not online, with the addition of electronic publication information (such as the site name and date of publication or posting), the medium of publication, and the date of access. Items 54, 57, 58, 59, 62, and 66 show examples of sources accessed online.

54. Work of art   List the name of the artist; the title of the work (italicized); the date of composition; the medium of composition; the name of the museum, gallery, site, or owner; and the location. Omit the medium of composition for a work of art accessed online (see the second example below) or in print (see the fourth example below).

Christo and Jeanne-Claude. *The Gates*. Feb. 2005. Steel and

fabric. Central Park, New York.

Warren, Rebecca. *The Main Feeling*. 2009. Art Inst. of

Chicago. Web. 29 Sept. 2013.

Johns, Jasper. *Racing Thoughts*. 1983. Encaustic and

    collage on canvas. Whitney Museum of Amer. Art,

    New York.

For a photograph in a book, give complete publication information, including the number of the page on which the photograph appears.

Johns, Jasper. *Racing Thoughts*. 1983. Whitney Museum of

    Amer. Art, New York. *The American Century: Art and*

    Culture 1950–2000. By Lisa Phillips. New York: Norton,

    1999. 311. Print.

For a slide in a collection, include the slide number (*Slide 17).

55. Cartoon or comic strip Give the artist's name, the title (if any) in quotation marks, and the label (*Cartoon*). Follow these with the usual information about the source, and give the page number for a print source. Conclude with the medium of publication.

Chast, Roz. "New Chess Pieces." Cartoon. *New Yorker*

    27 Sept. 2010: 65. Print.

56. Advertisement or museum wall placard Give the name of the product or company, followed by the label *Advertisement* and the publication information. If a page is not numbered, write *n. pag.*

Bose headphones. Advertisement. *Scientific American*

    Sept. 2010: 5. Print.

For a placard such as a museum wall label, include the word *Placard* after the name of the work. Also give the name of the museum and the dates of the show, if relevant, and the medium of publication.

Matisse, Henri. *Bathers by a River*. Placard. New York:

    Museum of Modern Art, 18 July-11 Oct. 2010. Print.

57. Map or chart Cite a map or a chart like an article or a book; include the designation after the title. Give the appropriate information for material on the Web.

"Attack Map." *Remembering Pearl Harbor*. Multimedia map.

    National Geographic. Natl. Geographic Soc., 2001.

    Web. 28 Jan. 2014.

58. Film or video List the title (italicized), director, and any other pertinent information, such as performers. End with the name of the distributor, the year of release, and the medium.

Atonement. Dir. Joe Wright. Perf. Keira Knightley. Working

    Title Films, 2007. Film.

Cite a videocassette, laser disc, slide program, filmstrip, or DVD as you would a film, ending with the appropriate medium. When relevant, include the date of the original film.

The Girl with the Dragon Tattoo. Dir. Niels Arden Oplev. Perf.

    Michael Nyqvist and Noomi Rapace. 2009. Music Box

    Films Home Entertainment, 2010. DVD.

For an online video, include the Web site, the medium, and the date of access.

Phillips, Barnaby, narr. *South Africa's Threatened Rhinos*.

    AlJazeeraEnglish, 2010. *YouTube*. Web. 27 Sept. 2010.

59. Television or radio program Give the title of the program episode (in quotation marks); the title of the program or series (in italics); any pertinent information such as performers, narrator, adapter, or director after the episode or the series, wherever applicable; the network; the local station and city (if any); the date of broadcast; and the medium of reception. (Note the punctuation in the examples below.)

"Stuck in the Middle." *This American Life*. Narr. Ira Glass.

    Public Radio Intl. WBEZ, Chicago, 17 Jan. 2014. Radio.

NOTE: When a radio or television program such as the above is accessed on the Web, give *Web* as the medium of reception and the date of access. If you downloaded it as a podcast, give *MP3 file* as the medium. See also item 62.

To emphasize the work of an individual, begin with the person's name.

Shergold, Adrian, dir. "*Persuasion*." By Jane Austen. Adapt.

    Simon Burke. *Masterpiece Theatre*. PBS. WTTW,

    Chicago, 21 Feb. 2010. Television.

60. Sound recording List the composer or author, the title of the work (in italics), the names of the artists, the manufacturer, and the date of issue. Conclude with the medium: *CD, LP, Audiotape*, or *Audiocassette*. Put the title of a specific song in quotation marks.

Bustin, Dillon. *Willow of the Wilderness: Emersonian Songs*.

Emerson Umbrella Center for the Arts, 2003. CD.

Lorde. "Royals." *Pure Heroine*. Universal, 2013. CD.

Walker, Alice. Interview by Kay Bonetti. Columbia: American

Audio Prose Library, 1981. Audiocassette.

61. Live performance   Give the title of the play, opera, concert, or dance; the author; any pertinent information about the director and performers; the name of the theater or other venue; its location (city); the date of the performance; and the word *Performance*. If you are citing an individual's role in the work, begin your citation with the person's name.

In Paris. By Ivan Bunin. Dir. and Adapt. Dmitry Krymov. Perf.

Mikhail Baryshnikov. Broad Stage, Santa Monica.

15 Apr. 2012. Performance.

Mikhail Baryshnikov, perf. *In Paris*. By Ivan Bunin. Dir. Dmitry

Krymov. Broad Stage, Santa Monica. 15 Apr. 2012.

Performance.

62. Podcast   Cite a podcast that you download and access on an audio player as you would cite the work in its original medium (book, online newspaper, sound recording, and so on), but use *MP3 file* as the medium. You do not need to give the date of access.

Lehrer, Jonah. "How Creativity Works." Interview by June

Thomas. *Slate*. Washington Post, 30 Mar. 2012. MP3 file.

63. Interview: Personal, published, broadcast, or online
If you conduct the interview, list the name of the person interviewed, the type of interview (telephone, personal, and so on), and the date.

Gingold, Toby. Telephone interview. 3 Aug. 2013.

For a published interview, give the name of the person interviewed, the title (if any), the word *Interview* or phrase *Interview by . . .* , and the print publication information.

Parker, Dorothy. Interview by Marion Capron. *Writers at Work*:

The Paris Review *Interviews*. London: Secker, 1958.

66-75. Print.

For a broadcast or online interview, give the source, date, and medium.

Erdrich, Louise. Interview by Bill Moyers. *Bill Moyers Journal*.

PBS. WNET, New York, 9 Apr. 2010. Radio.

For a sound recording of an interview, see item 60.

64. Lecture, reading, speech, or address Give the speaker and title (if known), the meeting, the name of the sponsoring organization (if pertinent), the location (city), the date, and the medium of delivery.

Simon, James. "What's Happening to Newspapers in the

Digital Age?" Beloit College, Beloit, WI. 21 Oct. 2010.

Lecture.

65. Letter or personal communication Cite a published letter as you would cite a work in an anthology. Include the page numbers, any identifying number, and the date when the letter was written. Conclude with the medium of publication.

Bishop, Elizabeth. "To Robert Lowell." 26 Nov. 1951. *One*

Art: Letters. Ed. Robert Giroux. New York: Farrar, 1994.

224-26. Print.

Describe the type of personal communication you received, and conclude with the medium of delivery: *TS (typescript,* as in this example), *MS (manuscript), Telephone call,* or other form. (See also 9g, item 52.)

Rodrigo, Shelley. Letter to the author. 18 Sept. 2014. TS.

66. Legal or historical document For a legal case, give the name of the case (short form with the plaintiff first and then the defendant) with no italics or quotation marks, the volume and page or reference number of the case, the name of the court deciding the case, the date of the decision, and the medium of publication. Also give the Web site and the date of access for an online source. Use familiar abbreviations.

Roe v. Wade. No. 70-18. Supreme Ct. of the US. 22 Jan. 1973.

Print.

However, if you mention the case in your text, italicize the name.

Chief Justice Burger, in *Roe v. Wade,* noted that. . . .

For an act, in your list of works cited, give its name, its Public Law number, its Statutes at Large volume number and inclusive pages, the date it was passed, the source, and the medium of publication.

USA Patriot Act. Pub. L. 107-56. 115 Stat. 272-402. 26 Oct.

    2001. Web. 10 Feb. 2013.

Do not include well-known historical documents such as the Constitution in your works-cited list. See 9b, item T.

67. CD-ROM or DVD-ROM Cite material from a CD-ROM or DVD published as a single edition (that is, with no regular updating or revising) in the same way you cite a book, but include any version or release number and the medium of publication.

Keats, John. "To Autumn." *Columbia Granger's World of*

    Poetry. Rel. 3. New York: Columbia UP, 1999. CD-ROM.

Model Paper 2: A student's research paper, MLA style **

Here is Patti Suchan's research paper written for her first-year composition course at High Point University in North Carolina. For this essay, students were asked to develop an argument that presented a radical perspective, or "re-seeing," on the topic of globalization. The citations and the list of works cited are in the style recommended in the 2009 *MLA Handbook for Writers of Research Papers,* 7th edition.

NOTE: Annotations have been added here to point out features of her paper that you may find useful when you write your own research paper in MLA style. Blue annotations point out issues of content and organization; red annotations point out MLA format issues.

Suchan 1

Patti Suchan

Dr. Kozma

ENG-1103-10

6 December 2013

Originality Died and Made Profit King

There was a time when the theater was known for dramatics and creativity, but also for being an unstable and unprofitable way to make a living. Only a few truly gifted people could survive in such an industry, where freedom of expression did not always achieve public resonance and equate to a regular payday, or even an occasional paycheck. The renowned American playwright Arthur Miller remarked, "The theater is so endlessly fascinating because it's so accidental" ("Arthur Miller"), and many believe that this is undoubtedly true. But those days of spontaneity and insecurity have been on the wane, unbeknownst to the world's hoi polloi. Although they are often not included in discussions about how globalization is changing the world, the arts are actually an area that is leading the charge. Back in the Elizabethan age, William Shakespeare created a worldwide theater phenomenon that has resulted in both positive and negative repercussions in modern times. Thomas Friedman, a journalist for the *New York Times*, notes in his book *The Lexus and the Olive Tree* that the present era of globalization began in 1989, with the end of the Cold War (xvii). Jonathan Burston, a professor in the Department of Information and Media Studies at the University of Western Ontario who specializes in

Blue = content issues   Red = format issues

Used by permission of Patti Suchan.

Suchan 2

music, media, and globalization, also connects history and theater to argue that globally driven changes to theater, and "cultural industries in general," began in the early 1980s ("Recombinant" 161). With the advent of globalization, the destruction of the art form that is theater has been almost completely actualized for the benefit of increased profitability and the ruination of originality.

Author with more than one work cited—shortened title used

Thesis

Globalization is a difficult subject to define. There are many different elements that together create the concept of globalization. The coming together of cultures, ideas, religions, and industries are some of the more essential pieces of globalization. The most important aspect of globalization is the maximizing of profits in a market that has a broader reach than ever before, regardless of what that particular market may be. Michael Moore wrote an article about American business owners who would frequently "tell [him] that 'a company must do whatever is necessary to create the biggest profit possible'" (410). This ideology is not limited to major businesses in the United States, though. It is a mindset that has spread around the world and into atypical market sectors, such as theater, as globalization has become prevalent.

Defin-ing term so that audience can follow argument

Quotation in source quoted by student writer; word changed in brack-ets within quotation

In the history of theater, going as far back as its origins and as recently as about a half century ago, productions of shows were vastly different from others done previously. The script of the show would be the same, but since the actors would be different, the whole show would have a different essence. The sets, costumes, and props could all be different as well, but what would really make the critical difference would be the new life that each actor's interpretation breathed into a character. Since this was how the theater worked for such a long period of time, theater became irrevocably known as a creative art form. One of the most important and formative time periods for theater was the Elizabethan age of William Shakespeare. His legacy has been a blessing and a curse to theater worldwide. (See fig. 1.)

Shakespeare greatly contributed to the prominence of theater in not just English-speaking countries but around the globe, which has been very beneficial to the theater community. The popularity becomes a problem when many new shows are just repetitions of common themes. Shakespeare's works have been adapted into many modern works, such as *West Side Story* and *Kiss Me, Kate,* but even his "original" works are not thought to be original ideas. *The Taming of the Shrew*, known as a tale of "achieving rapid dominance" (Fhloinn 188), is based on a common story of the time. Jan Harald Brunvand believes that "Shakespeare's source for the taming plot was most likely an oral text of the folklore" (qtd. in Fhloinn 190), but it has also been suggested that the "story originated in the east" (Fhloinn 191). The possible origin comes from the famous fifth century BC Chinese strategist and philosopher, Sun Tzu, by way of Chinese historian Sima Qian. Sun Tzu, author of *The Art of War*, is said to have performed acts of violence to "achieve rapid dominance," which, in turn, inspired such a tale (Fhloinn 192). Shakespeare's works themselves

Indirect source: cites work in which another author is quoted

Suchan 4

English School/The Bridgeman Art Library/Getty Images

Fig. 1. The First Globe Theatre, where many of Shakespeare's plays were performed, from Visscher's View of London (1616); rpt. in Joseph Quincy Adams, *Shakespearean Playhouses: A History of English Theatres from the Beginnings to the Restoration* (Gloucester, MA: Peter Smith, 1960; print; 254). *Project Gutenberg eBook*. 21 Nov. 2013.

can therefore be said to represent globalization long before globalization was even acknowledged, which helped with their popularity, but which has also created world-renowned clichés. With the continued success of all things Shakespearean, though, the clichés have been oft-repeated, which is unsurprising. When profit

Clear transition; writer is forming an evidence chain. is king, a popular storyline is the surest route to success.

There are new shows created every year that are re-creations of already well-liked stories. International blockbusters are frequently being brought to the stage, especially since the Disney Company achieved such wide success with the productions of *Beauty and the Beast* and *The Lion King*. Broadway producers are **Quotation and para- phrase both used in sentence** "choosing bankable titles more and more regularly in order to reduce risk" because, even if the show does poorly, it will attract enough attention to run for an adequate period of time and, more importantly, boost global sales of related products (Burston, "Recombinant" 166). *Shrek the Musical* is a fairly recent adaptation that joined the lineup on the Great White Way (fig. 2). Many negative critiques of the show, by both experts and audience members, revolved around the fact that the storyline of the show was exactly the same as that of the movie. While this is true, it is also true for the Disney musicals, in which no fault is generally found.

The difference, I believe, comes from the musical nature of the movie on which the show is based, which Disney has and Dreamworks does not. Regardless, *Shrek the Musical* characters are portrayed in a manner similar to their counterparts in the movie. This is especially surprising since Daniel Breaker, the actor playing Donkey, and possibly the character that was **Substi- tuted words in brackets** most similar between the two mediums, said in an interview that he had "never seen the movies . . . and didn't want to [because he] didn't want to be lost in

Blue = content issues   Red = format issues

Suchan 6

ZUMA Press, Inc./Alamy

Fig. 2. Publicity photograph from *Shrek the Musical*. By David Lindsay-Abaire. Dir. Jason Moore and Rob Ashford. 2012 Touring Performance.

trying to re-create Eddie Murphy's role." Is his portrayal **Web source, no page number for quotation** so similar to that of Eddie Murphy because the part is written in such a way as to lend itself to such an interpretation, or is it that the director of the show was guiding the actor into making the character the same as is found in the movie? Either way, the actor was not organically creating the character. Someone else, either the writer or the director, was pushing him to act in such a way, and it wasn't of his own volition. This repetition of characters from silver screen to stage

Suchan 7

has become a popular trend, possibly in part because foreign audiences who have seen the movie can enjoy the show despite the language barrier, since they already know the storyline.

Another type of show, those that do not have storylines that are popular from films, is becoming widely famous for another reason: they are being designed for worldwide success. Starting in the early 1980s, when the theater industry was struggling, Andrew Lloyd Webber and Cameron Mackintosh discovered a way to take the theater industry from a risky endeavor and make it into a largely profitable business. Their new musical *Cats* had become a smashing success on Broadway in London's West End and on tours of both North America and Europe, but they realized that the demand to see the show was greater than what they were meeting. They decided to create permanent productions in "emerging major markets like Hamburg, Tokyo, and Toronto" (Burston, "Recombinant" 161) for as long as they were attracting a sufficient audience. The decisive factor about these productions that changed theater forever is that "Lloyd Webber and Mackintosh also concluded that each show should look, feel, and sound *exactly* like the originating production . . . if the producers were to maximize the new levels of profitability" (Burston, "Recombinant" 161). Thus, the megamusical, designed for megaprofits by stifling originality, was born.

Today, productions of shows that are running in different parts of the world are exactly the same,

Quotation integrated into writer's sentence

Ellipsis points signal part of quoted material omitted

Suchan 8

"based upon a *template* of an original production whose cast and creative team have already completed all the exciting collaborative work of turning written page into breathing performance" (Burston, "Recombinant" 166). The actors and musicians now have greater job security, but they complain about having to work "McTheater jobs," where they are more "acting machines" and less artists (Burston, "Recombinant" 162; also Burston, "Spectacle"; Russell). Have the global audiences' expectations become such that actors can compare their profession to that of a fast-food worker? Sadly, this has become a trending phenomenon in the theater worldwide.

The magic of theater still exists, but the magic is often not the invention of the actors performing. The story they are acting out is clichéd and the characters are hackneyed. Shakespeare helped the theater become a globally recognized art form and kept it prevalent for many years, but he also damaged theater by starting the trend of reusing ideas to create new shows. The business of Broadway, and its counterparts worldwide, is booming for both the producers and the actors, with profits that were unimaginable several decades ago. Nevertheless, many actors resist the death of creativity and try to keep the originality of the theater alive in our new, globalized world.

Suchan 9

1" **New page**

Works Cited

Title first: no author named: "Arthur Miller Quotes." *BrainyQuote*. BookRags

Media Network, 2011. Web. 2 Dec. 2013.

Breaker, Daniel. "Daniel Breaker on Fatherhood,

Donkey-hood (in *Shrek*), and His Strange New

Movie." Interview by Melissa Rose Bernardo.

Broadway.com. Key Brand Entertainment, 27

July 2009. Web. 13 Nov. 2013.

Two works by same author; entries listed by author and then alphabetically by title. Burston, Jonathan. "Recombinant Broadway."

Continuum: Journal of Media and Cultural

Studies 23.2 (2009): 159-69. *Academic Search*

Premier. Web. 14 Nov. 2013.

Three hyphens used instead of author's name for second work by same author. ----. "Spectacle, Synergy, and Megamusicals: The

Global-Industrialisation of Live-Theatrical

Production." *Media Organisations in Society*.

Ed. James Curran. London: Arnold, 2000.

69-81. Print.

Sponsor of Web site, date site last updated, medium of publication (Web), date site accessed "Faculty Member Profile: Jonathan Burston."

Faculty of Information and Media Studies at

the University of Western Ontario. U of

Western Ontario, 2010. Web. 30 Nov. 2013.

Fhloinn, Bairbre Ní. "From Medieval Literature to

Missiles: Aspects of ATU 901 in the Twenty-

First Century." *Fabula* 51.3/4 (2010): 187-200.

Academic Search Premier. Web. 14 Nov. 2013.

Friedman, Thomas L. *The Lexus and the Olive Tree*.

New York: Anchor-Doubleday, 1999. Print.

Blue = content issues   Red = format issues

Suchan 10

Moore, Michael. "Why Doesn't GM Sell Crack?"

> The Composition of Everyday Life: A Guide to
> Writing. Ed. John Mauk and John Metz. 3rd ed.
> Boston: Cengage, 2010. 410-11. Print.

Russell, Susan. "The Performance of Discipline on

> Broadway." Studies in Musical Theatre 1.1
> (2007): 97-108. Print.

Page range for essay in anthology

Print scholarly journal article accessed in online database

10 APA Style

APA AT A GLANCE: INDEX OF STYLE FEATURES

This section gives details about the documentation style recommended for the social sciences by the *Publication Manual of the American Psychological Association* (6th ed., Washington, DC: Amer. Psychological Assn., 2010), and the Web site for the *APA Publication Manual* at <http://www.apastyle.org>.

10a Basic features of APA style

KEY POINTS
How to Document Sources in APA Style

1. *In the text of your paper,* include at least two pieces of information each time you cite a source:
   - the last name(s) of the author or authors, or the first words of the title if no author's name is available
   - the year of publication or posting online

   Also give the page number for a quotation, summary, or paraphrase.

2. *At the end of the paper,* on a new numbered page, include a list entitled *References,* double-spaced and arranged alphabetically by authors' last names, followed by initials of first and other names, the date in parentheses, and other bibliographical information. See 116–131 for forty sample entries.

Illustrations of the Basic Features

In-Text Citation	Entry in List of References
Print book	
Author and year	
The speed at which we live can be cause for concern as well as derision (Gleick, 1999).	Gleick, J. (1999). Faster: The acceleration of just about everything. New York, NY: Pantheon.
Print article	
Author and year in your text	
According to Bruck (2010), the multibillionaire Eli Broad "is the Lorenzo de' Medici of Los Angeles" (p. 50).	Bruck, C. (2010, December 6). The art of the billionaire. *The New Yorker*, 50–61.
[Page number included for quotation]	

In-Text Citation	Entry in List of References
Print article	
Author and year within parentheses	
The multibillionaire Eli Broad "is the Lorenzo de' Medici of Los Angeles" (Bruck, 2010, p. 50).	Bruck, C. (2010, December 6). The art of the billionaire. *The New Yorker*, 50–61.
Author and year for article with digital online identifier (DOI) in an online database	
Research has shown that cross-cultural identification does not begin before eight years of age (Sousa, Neto, & Mullet, 2005). (See 10f and item 20 for more on DOIs.)	Sousa, R. M., Neto, F., & Mullet, E. (2005). Can music change ethnic attitudes among children? *Psychology of Music, 33*(3), 304–316. doi:10.1177/0305735605053735
Author and year for a document on a Web site	
Quittner (2010) has reported on the future of reading.	Quittner, J. (2010, March 1). The future of reading. *Fortune*. Retrieved from http://money .cnn.com/ magazines/fortune/ fortune_archive/ 2010/03/01/toc.html

NOTE: In APA style, you can use content notes to amplify information in your text. Number notes consecutively with superscript numerals. After the list of references, attach a separate page containing your numbered notes and headed *Footnotes*. As an alternative, you may place footnotes at the bottom of pages with cited material. Use notes sparingly; include all important information in your text, not in footnotes.

10b How to cite sources (author/year) in your paper (APA)

CITING AN AUTHOR OR AUTHORS (APA)

A. Author named in your text If you mention the author's name in your own text, include the year in parentheses directly after the author's name.

author　year

Wilson (1994) has described in detail his fascination with insects.

B. Author cited in parentheses If you do not name the author in your text sentence (perhaps because you have referred to the author previously), include both the name and the year, separated by a comma, in parentheses. Put a period after the closing parenthesis.

The army retreated from Boston in disarray, making the rebels realize that they had achieved a great victory (McCullough, 2001).

author　comma　year

C. Author quoted or paraphrased If you use a direct quotation or a paraphrase, include in the parentheses the abbreviation *p.* or *pp.,* followed by a space and the page number(s). Use commas to separate items within parentheses.

Memories are "built around a small collection of dominating images" (Wilson, 1994, p. 5).

See 10b, item R for how to present a long quotation (more than forty words).

D. A work with more than one author

Two authors For a work by two authors, in all your references cite both authors in the order in which their names appear on the work. Within parenthetical citations, use an ampersand (*&*) between the names in place of the word *and*. However, use the word *and* if you name the authors in your text.

The word *and* in your text

Kanazawa and Still (2000), in their analysis of a large set of data, showed that the statistical likelihood of being divorced increased if one was male and a secondary school teacher or college professor.

Analysis of a large set of data showed that the statistical likelihood of being divorced increased if one was male and a secondary school teacher or college professor (Kanazawa & Still, 2000).

ampersand in parentheses

Three to five authors Identify all of the authors the first time you mention the work in your text and in the first parenthetical citation.

Baumol, Litan, and Schramm (2007) posit the existence of
several types of capitalist economies around the world.

In later references in your text and in parenthetical
citations, give the name of only the first author, followed
by *et al.* (the Latin abbreviation for *et alii*—"and others") in
place of the other names, along with the year of publication
and any necessary page reference.

In the United States, the dominant type of capitalism called
"entrepreneurial capitalism" shows significant differences
from the capitalism in Japan and Europe, which tends to
avoid "radical entrepreneurship" (Baumol et al., 2007, p. viii).

Six or more authors Give the name of only the first
author, followed by *et al.* for both a citation in your text and
one in parentheses.

See also 10d, item 2, for how to enter works by multiple
authors in your list of references.

E. Author of work in an edited anthology In your text,
refer to the author of the work itself, not to the editor of the
anthology (although you will include information about the
anthology in your list of references). The essay referred to
below is in an anthology of writing about race (see 10d, item 4).

The voice of W. E. B. Dubois (2007) resonates today as
soldiers return from a different war, hoping to find change in
their country.

**F. Author's work cited in another source (secondary
source)** After quoting the author's work in your text, in
parentheses give the author or title of the work in which you
found the reference, preceded by the words *as cited in* to
indicate that you are referring to a citation in that work. List
that secondary source in your list of references. In the following example, *Smith* will appear in the list, but *Britton* will not.

The words we use simply appear, as Britton says, "at the
point of utterance" (as cited in Smith, 1982, p. 108).

G. Entire work or an idea in a work Use only an author
and a year to refer to a complete work. For a paraphrase or a
comment on a specific idea, a page number is not required
but is recommended.

H. More than one work in one citation List the sources
in alphabetical order, separated by semicolons.

"Voice" in writing means many things to many people
(Bowden, 2003; Coles, 1998; Elbow, 2007; Kesler, 2012).

I. Author with more than one work published in one year Identify each work with a lowercase letter after the year to correspond to the work's order in the reference list: (Schell, 2012a, 2012b). Separate the dates with commas. In the reference list, repeat the author's name in each work's entry, and alphabetize the works by title.

J. Two authors with the same last name In your text, also give the authors' initials, even if the dates of publication differ.

F. Smith (1982) described a writer as playing the competitive roles of author and secretary.

CITING A WORK WITH NO INDIVIDUAL AUTHOR NAMED (APA)

K. Corporation, government agency, or organization as author In the initial citation, use the organization's full name; in subsequent references, use an abbreviation, if one exists.

first text mention: full name and abbreviation in parentheses

In its annual survey of college costs, the College Board (CB) (2013) gives examples of rapid increases. These increases can cause hardships to students and their families. In four-year colleges, in-state tuition and fees increased 2.9% during the 2013-2014 school year (College Board [CB], 2013).

first parenthetical citation: full name with abbreviation in brackets

See 10d, item 6, for this work in a list of references.

L. No author named If a print or Web source has no named individual or organization as author, use the first few words of the title in your text or parenthetical citation (capitalizing major words). Put book titles in italics and article or Web page titles in quotation marks.

Many Hurricane Katrina survivors were relocated to trailers whose materials caused health problems from breathing disorders to cancer (*World Almanac*, 2009, p. 55).

An estimated 27 million Americans are said to be afflicted by osteoarthritis ("What Is Osteoarthritis?" 2011).

See 10d, item 5, and 10f, item 27, for how to list these source items.

CITING INTERNET, MULTIMEDIA, AND MISCELLANEOUS SOURCES (APA)

M. Internet source Give the author's name, if it is available, or a short form of the title, followed by the year of electronic publication or update. In your text, put titles of

Web pages in quotation marks as you would an article title. Use *n.d.* if no date is given. To locate a section of text that you quote, paraphrase, or comment on in a source with no page or paragraph numbers visible on the screen, give any available section heading, and indicate the paragraph within the section: (Conclusion section, para. 2).

When citing an entire Web site rather than a specific document or a page on the site in your text, you need only name the site (not in italics) and give the Web address (URL) in parentheses after the cited material. Do not list the Web site in your reference list.

The Arthritis Foundation website contains much valuable information about treatments for the disease (http://www.arthritis.org).

Be wary of citing e-mail messages (personal, bulletin board, discussion list, or Usenet group), because they are not peer-reviewed or easily retrievable. If you need to refer to an e-mail message, cite from an archived list whenever possible (see the example in 10f, item 32); otherwise, cite the message in your text as a personal communication (see 10b, item O), but do not include it in your list of references.

N. Visual, multimedia, or nonprint source For a film, television or radio broadcast, podcast, MP3 file, video recording, Web presentation, live performance, artwork, or other nonprint source, include in your citation the name of the originator or main contributor (such as the writer, interviewer, narrator, director, performer, or producer), along with the year of production.

An Al Jazeera video highlights the plight of the South African rhino (Phillips, 2010).

O. Personal communication (such as a letter, telephone conversation, interview, e-mail, or unarchived electronic discussion group message) Cite only sources that have scholarly content. Mention these only in your paper, followed by the words *personal communication*, a comma, and the complete date in parentheses. Do not include these sources in your list of references. Give the last name and initial(s) of the author of the communication.

According to V. Sand, executive director of the Atwater Kent Museum of Philadelphia, "Museums engage our spirit, help us understand the natural world, and frame our identities" (personal communication, February 7, 2014).

For including archived postings in the list of references, see 10f, item 32.

P. A multivolume work In your citation, give the author and the publication date of the volume you are citing: (Einstein, 2006). If you refer to more than one volume, give inclusive dates for all volumes you cite: (Einstein, 1987–2006). See 10d, item 8, for this work in a list of references.

Q. A classical or religious work If the date of publication of a classical work is not known, cite the year of the translation (preceded by *trans.*) or the year of the version you used (followed by *version*). You do not need a reference list entry for the Bible or other religious or ancient classical works. Just give information about book, chapter, verse, and line numbers in your text, and identify the version you used in your first citation: Gen. 35:1–4 (Revised Standard Version).

R. A long quotation If you quote more than forty words of prose, do not enclose the quotation in quotation marks. Start the quotation on a new line, and indent the whole quotation half an inch from the left margin. Double-space the quotation. Any necessary parenthetical citation should come after the final period of the quotation.

10c How to set up an APA list of references

NOTE: This handbook has been written in MLA style, which prefers *Web site*. APA style prefers *website* (only capitalized if it begins a sentence or follows a period in a citation).

KEY POINTS
Setting Up the APA List of References

- *What to list:* List only the works you cited (quoted, summarized, paraphrased, or commented on) in the text of your paper, not every source you examined.
- *Format:* Start the list on a new numbered page after the last page of the text of your paper. Center the heading *References* in uppercase and lowercase letters; without quotation marks; not bold, underlined, or italicized; and with no period following it. Double-space throughout the list, with no additional spaces between entries. Place any footnotes, tables, or charts after the reference list, or consult your instructor.
- *Indentation:* Use hanging indents. Begin the first line of each entry at the left margin; indent subsequent lines five spaces (or one-half inch).

(continued)

(continued)

- *How to list works and authors:* List the works alphabetically by the last name of the first author of each work or by the name of a corporation or organization that acts as the author. Do not number the entries. Begin each entry with the first author's name, last name first, followed by a comma and an initial or initials. For a work with up to six authors, give any additional authors' names in the same inverted form, separated by commas (see 10d, item 2, for works with seven or more authors). Use an ampersand (&) rather than the word *and* to connect two or more authors' names. List works with no author by title, alphabetized by the first main word.

  For two or more works by the same author(s), list the entries by year of publication, with the earliest first. List works by the same author(s) published in the same year by alphabetizing the titles and adding a corresponding *a, b, c,* and so on after the year.

- *Date:* Put the year of publication in parentheses after the authors' names. For journal, magazine, or newspaper articles, also add a comma and include the month and day, but do not abbreviate the names of the months.

- *Periods:* Use a period and one space to separate the main parts of each entry.

- *Titles and capitals:* In titles of books, reports, articles, and Web pages, capitalize *only* the first word of the title, any subtitle, and any proper nouns or adjectives. For magazines, newspapers, and journals, give the name in full, using uppercase and lowercase letters.

- *Titles and italics* Italicize the titles of books, but do not italicize or use quotation marks around the titles of articles, chapters, or Web pages. Italicize the titles of newspapers (including the word *The*), reports, brochures, and newsletters. For magazines and journals, italicize the title of the periodical, the comma following it, and the volume number—but not the issue number contained in parentheses (see an example in **, item 16) or the comma that follows it. Identify a specific format in square brackets immediately after the title, followed by a period: [Brochure], [Review], [Press release], [Audio file], [Abstract], [PowerPoint slide].

(continued)

(continued)

- *Sources found online:* Give as much information as you would for a print source, with the addition of enough retrieval information to enable your readers to find the same source. Use a DOI (Digital Object Identifier)—a permanent identification number that enables easy retrieval—rather than a URL if one is available. See 10f, items 20–32, for examples of how to list online sources.

- *Page numbers:* Give inclusive page numbers for print articles, online PDF articles (portable document format, which is used for photographed print works), and sections of books, using complete page spans and repeating all digits (251–259). Use the abbreviation *p.* or *pp.* only for newspaper articles and sections of books (such as chapters or anthologized articles). List document sections in place of page numbers for articles written for online use (in HTML).

10d Listing print books and parts of books (APA)

You will find all of the necessary information on the title page and the copyright page of a book. Use the most recent copyright date. Include the city and state or country of publication, omitting the state when its name appears in the name of the publisher. Use post office abbreviations for states, and spell out names of countries. Give the publisher's name in a shortened but intelligible form, including *Press* and *Books* but omitting *Co.* or *Inc.*

1. Book with one author   Give the author's last name first, followed by initials. See Source Shot 1 on page 76, where the following source is illustrated for MLA style.

last name   initial   year in parentheses   book title italicized
Earhart, H. B. (2014). *Religion in Japan: Unity and diversity*.

place of publication   publisher
Boston, MA: Wadsworth-Cengage.

2. Book with two or more authors   For up to and including **seven authors**, give all of the authors' names (last name first, followed by initials). Separate all names by commas, and use an ampersand (*&*) before the last name.

Baumol, W. J., Litan, R. E., & Schramm, C. J. (2007). *Good capitalism, bad capitalism, and the economics of growth and prosperity*. New Haven, CT: Yale University Press.

For **eight or more authors**, give the reversed names of the first **six authors**, followed by a comma, three ellipsis dots, and then the reversed name of the last author listed (, . . . Kleinschmidt, A.).

See also 10d, item 9, for how to list a book from which you cite only one element, such as a preface or an introduction.

3. Edited book   Begin with the editor's name in the author position. Then put *Ed.* or *Eds.* in parentheses, followed by a period after the name(s) of one or more editors.

Gates, L., Jr., & Jarrett, G. A. (Eds.). (2007). *The new Negro:*

  Readings on race, representation, and African American

  culture, 1892–1938. Princeton, NJ: Princeton University

  Press.

4. Work in an edited collection or reference book   List the author, the date of publication of the book, and the title of the work. Follow these with *In* and the name(s) of the editor(s) (not inverted and followed by *Ed.* or *Eds.* in parentheses), the title of the book, and (in parentheses) the inclusive page numbers (preceded by *pp.*) of the chapter or work. End with the place of publication and the publisher. If you cite more than one article in an edited work in your reference list, include full bibliographical details in each entry.

DuBois, W. E. B. (2007). Returning soldiers. In L. Gates, Jr.,

  & G. A. Jarrett (Eds.), *The new Negro: Readings on*

  race, representation, and African American culture,

  1892–1938 (pp. 85–91). Princeton, NJ: Princeton

  University Press.

For a well-known reference book with unsigned alphabetical entries, begin with the title of the entry, and include the page number(s).

Antarctica. (2000). In *The Columbia Encyclopedia* (6th ed.,

  pp. 116–118). New York, NY: Columbia University Press.

5. Book, pamphlet, or brochure with no author named   Put the title first. Ignore *A, An,* and *The* when alphabetizing. Alphabetize the following entry under *W.*

The world almanac and book of facts 2009. (2009).

  Pleasantville, NY: World Almanac Books.

6. Book, pamphlet, or brochure by a corporation, government agency, or other organization   Give the name of the corporate author first. If the publisher is the same as the author, write *Author* for the name of the publisher.

College Board. (2013). *Trends in college pricing 2013.*

   Washington, DC: Author.

For a brochure, include after the title the word *Brochure* in square brackets, followed by a period: [Brochure].
   If no author is named for a government publication, begin with the name of the federal, state, or local government, followed by the name of the agency.

U.S. Department of Homeland Security, Federal Emergency

   Management Agency. (2004). *Preparing for disaster*

   for people with disabilities and other special needs.

   Washington, DC: Author.

7. Translation   If there is a translator as well as an author, give the initials and last name of the translator in parentheses after the title of the work, followed by a comma and *Trans.*

Jung, C. G. (1960). *On the nature of the psyche* (R. F. C. Hull,

   Trans.). Princeton, NJ: Princeton University Press.

8. Multivolume work   Give the number of volumes in parentheses after the title. When appropriate, the date should include the range of years of publication.

Einstein, A. (1987–2006). *Collected papers of Albert Einstein*

   (Vols. 1–10). Princeton, NJ: Princeton University Press.

9. Foreword, preface, introduction, or afterword   List the name of the author of the book element cited. Follow the date with the name of the element, the title of the book, and in parentheses the page number(s) for the element, preceded by *p.* or *pp.*

Baumol, W. J., Litan, R. E., & Schramm, C. J. (2007). Preface.

   Good capitalism, bad capitalism, and the economics of

   growth and prosperity (pp. vii–x). New Haven, CT: Yale

   University Press.

10. New edition of book or revised, republished, or reprinted work   For a new edition of a book, give the edition number in parentheses after the title and follow with a period.

Raimes, A., & Miller-Cochran, S. K. (2014). *Keys for writers*

    (7th ed.). Boston, MA: Cengage.

For a revised edition, put *Rev. ed.* in parentheses instead of an edition number. For a republished work, after the author's name, give the most recent date of publication in parentheses and continue with the rest of the current publication information. At the end of the entry, add *Original work published* and the date in parentheses. Do not add a final period. In your parenthetical citation in the text of your paper, give both dates: (Smith, 1793/1976).

Smith, A. (1976). *An inquiry into the nature and causes of*

    the wealth of nations. New York, NY: Bantam Classics.

    (Original work published 1793)

For a reprint of a work originally published in another book, give the author, current date of publication, and current publication details, including page numbers. Then in parentheses write *Reprinted from* and give the title, page numbers of the work, *by* and the author or editor, date, place, and publisher of the book in which the work was first published.

11. Technical report Give the report number in parentheses (*Report No.*) after the title, followed by a period.

National Endowment for the Arts. (2007, November). *To read*

    or not to read: A question of national consequence

    (Report No. 47). Washington, DC: Author.

12. Dissertation or abstract Italicize the dissertation or master's thesis title, and identify the work as such in parentheses. If you retrieved it from a database, add *Available from* and the database name, with the order or accession number in parentheses at the end of the entry (not followed by a period).

Jerskey, M. (2006). *Writing handbooks, English language*

    learners, and the selective tradition (Doctoral

    dissertation). Available from Proquest Dissertations

    and Theses database. (UMI No. 3235697)

If you retrieve the work from an institutional database or Web site, add the words *Retrieved from* and the URL.

For a Web source, add the granting institution's name after the identifying phrase in parentheses.

For an abstract published in *DAI,* give the author, date, and dissertation title (not in italics), followed by *Dissertation Abstracts International* and the name of the section (*Section B. Sciences and Engineering*). After a comma, add the volume, (issue), and page numbers.

10e Listing print articles in periodicals (APA)

Do not use quotation marks for article titles. Only capitalize the first word of the title and subtitle and proper nouns or adjectives. After the title, include the italicized periodical name in uppercase and lowercase; then follow with a comma and the volume number (both italicized), a comma, and the inclusive page numbers, using all digits—not 125–26, but 125–126. For a periodical with each issue paged separately, immediately after the volume number (with no space) give the issue number, contained in parentheses and not italicized (as shown in Source Shot 4 on page 122).

13. Article in a scholarly journal Give the year of publication and the volume number. Include an issue number if each issue is paged separately and begins with page 1. As in the following example, include a DOI (digital object identifier) (with no following period) if one has been assigned to the article so that readers can easily access the source online. (See the Key Points box on p. 124 for more information on DOIs.) (See 6c on recognizing scholarly articles.) Do not use *p.* or *pp.* with page numbers. (See 10d, item 2 on listing multiple authors.)

authors' names reversed connected by ampersand (&)

Shi, Y. P., Cheng, Y. M., Van Slyke, A. C., & Claydon,

no quotation marks around or capitals within title

T. W. (2014). External protons destabilize the activated

journal title, comma, and volume number italicized

voltage sensor in hERG channels. *European Biophysics*

no p. or pp. before page numbers   DOI

Journal, 43, 59-69. doi:10.1007/s00249-013-0940-y

14. Article in a magazine Include the year, a comma, the month, and any exact date of publication in parentheses. Do not abbreviate months. Italicize the magazine title, the comma following it, and the volume number if there is one. Give the issue number (if there is one) in parentheses, a comma, and the page number(s) of the article. See Source Shot 4, page 122.

15. Article in a newspaper In parentheses, give the month and date of publication after the year. Include any necessary *The* in the title of a newspaper. Use *p.* and *pp.* with page numbers. Give the section letter or number as part of the page number, where applicable. For articles with no author, begin with the title.

Tanner, L. (2012, April 10). Study links autism to obesity

during pregnancy. *The Washington Post,* p. A3.

16. Article that skips pages Give all of the page numbers, separated by commas.

Strom, S. (2012, April 6). A case long ripening: For two

food giants, defining fresh fruit is not cut and dried.

The New York Times, pp. B1, B3.

17. Review or interview After the title of a review, add in brackets a description of the work reviewed and identify the medium: book, film, or video, for example.

Ayala, F. J. (2012, Spring). All for one and one for all? An

eminent scientist reconsiders natural selection [Review

of the book *The social conquest of Earth,* by E. O.

Wilson]. *The American Scholar, 81*(2), 112–113.

For a print interview, give the title of the interview (if there is one) and the name of the person interviewed. Add the word *Interview* and any other necessary information in brackets after the interview title and follow with a period.

Jeffrey, C. (2009, January/February). The Maddow knows

[Interview with Rachel Maddow]. *Mother Jones, 34*(1),

72–73.

18. Unsigned article or editorial For a work with no author named, begin the listing with the title of the article; for an editorial, add the word *Editorial* in brackets after the title.

Ready for day one. (2009, January 17–February 23).

The Economist, 390(8614), 31–32.

Healthcare Reality Check [Editorial]. (2011, February 7).

The Nation, 292(6), 3.

19. Letter to the editor Write *Letter to the editor* in brackets after the date or the title of the letter, if it has one. Give the page number.

Bogorad, H. C. (2012, April 10). The price of not voting [Letter

to the editor]. *The Washington Post,* p. A12.

SOURCE SHOT 4

Listing a Print Magazine Article APA

When listing a print magazine article, include the following:

❶ Author(s) Last name, initials (see 10c on how to list authors)

❷ (Date of publication) In parentheses: year, comma, month (not abbreviated) and day (if given), followed by a period.

❸ Title of article: Any subtitle Not in quotation marks or italics; capitalize only the first word of the title and subtitle and proper nouns or adjectives; end with a period.

❹ *Periodical Title, volume* (issue number) All italicized, except for the issue number. For periodicals with each issue paged separately, put the issue number in parentheses immediately following the volume number, with no space between. Use a comma (italicized) to separate a periodical title from the volume number, and use another before the page numbers.

❺ Inclusive range of page numbers All digits included and separated by an en dash (as in 67–68). Do not use *p.* or *pp.* End with a period.

    ❶   ❷   ❸

Del Frate, J. (2005, Winter). Old journey, new heights.

        ❹   ❺

ASK Magazine, 6(21), 6–9.

10f Listing online sources (APA)

Include in your citation whatever information is available of the following to enable your readers to locate your sources:

1. **name of author(s)**, if available

2. **year and date** of print publication or of online posting (use *n.d.* if no date is available)

3. **title of work and subtitle**, along with an identification in square brackets of any special type of source, such as [Review], [Abstract], or [Multimedia presentation]

4. **source details:** any available **print publication information for online books and journal articles,** as in items 1–19 above, such as the name of the journal, volume and issue number if each issue is paginated separately, and page numbers if they are shown (use a PDF version of an article when you can, because it provides on-screen page numbers and figures for reference)

Title page and Table of Contents of a Magazine APA

5. **retrieval statement:**

- If a work has a **DOI** (digital object identifier), give it as the retrieval information. The DOI, a permanent identification number for a source as published in any medium, will never change, even if the URL does. Many articles in restricted subscription databases have a DOI that is listed with citation information. Copy and paste the DOI, and use it as a retrieval statement (as in item 20).

- If there is no DOI, cite the URL. Write *Retrieved from* and the URL (for a database, use the home or menu page URL). Write *Available from* in place of *Retrieved from* when a URL does not provide the actual source but instead tells how to retrieve it. If the content may be changed or updated, such as content on a Web site or in a wiki, also add the retrieval date (month, day, and year).

KEY POINTS
Working with DOIs and URLs

- Copy and paste a DOI or URL from its site to be sure it is accurate. Many DOIs and URLs can be long and complex.

- In subscription databases, such as the ones sponsored by EBSCO (Source Shot 5, p. 126), the DOI is easy to find on the citation page. On some sites, however, the DOI may lurk behind a button such as *Article, CrossRef,* or the name of a supplier of full-text articles. Remember to search the site fully for a DOI.

- If you give a DOI, a reader can then easily turn the DOI string into a URL by going to <http://www.crossref .org> or by appending the DOI string after <http://dx .doi.org> to access the work or the database in which it is located.

- In your reference list entry, add the DOI after the period, following the inclusive page numbers. Write *doi* and add a colon (with no space after the colon) and the DOI numbers.

- Split a URL or DOI across lines only before a slash, a period, or other punctuation mark (exception: split after the double slashes in http://).

- Do not italicize or underline a DOI or URL, which will be the last item in your reference, and do not follow it with a period.

20. Online scholarly journal article with a DOI Universities and libraries subscribe to large searchable databases of print publications, such as Gale *InfoTrac,* EBSCO *Academic Search Premier, ERIC, LexisNexis,* EBSCO *PsycARTICLES,* and WilsonWeb *Education Full Text,* providing access to abstracts and full-text articles. In addition to print information, give the DOI for electronic retrieval information in a reference list entry. Source Shot 5, page 126, shows the relevant part of the EBSCO *PsycARTICLES* database citation page that provides the information needed for the reference. You do not need to give the name of the database if the DOI is available.

A reader attaching the DOI string to <http://dx.doi.org> as <http://dx.doi.org/10.1037/0022-3514.94.1.168> would then be taken directly to a *PsycARTICLES* Web site containing the abstract and could then either purchase the full text or access it free by logging on to a database offered by the reader's library.

NOTE: The DOI leads to a URL. For college papers, it may be quicker and more convenient to give a persistent URL to a database that the school has licensed. Consult with your instructor about such a divergence from APA style recommendations.

21. Online scholarly journal article with no DOI Give the URL of the home page of the journal (not followed by a period). The following journal is paginated by issue, so the issue number is given. No retrieval date is necessary.

Boudiny, K., & Mortelmans, D. (2011). A critical perspective:

Towards a broader understanding of "active ageing."

E-Journal of Applied Psychology, 7(1), 8–14. Retrieved

from http://ojs.lib.swin.edu.au/index.php/ejap

Some articles, such as those in discontinued journals, can only be found in electronic databases, such as *JSTOR or ERIC.* If such an article has no DOI, cite the home or entry page of the online archive.

22. Online article with a PDF print source Cite an article originally published in print and retrieved in PDF format as you would cite a print article, adding a DOI, if one exists, after the page numbers.

Kemp, C. B. (2012). Public health in the age of health

care reform. *Preventing Chronic Disease, 9,* 1–4.

doi:10.5888/pcd9.120151

If there is no DOI, give the URL of the journal's home page.

23. Article in an online journal or magazine with no print source available If only an HTML version is available, with information such as page numbers or figures missing, just give the journal or magazine publication information and the DOI or URL.

Marshall, M. (2012, June 14). Oldest cave art is a single red dot.

New Scientist. Retrieved from http://newscientist.com

If you have a choice, always access the PDF version.

24. Newspaper article retrieved from a Web site or a database Newspaper articles as well as journal articles are often available from several sources, in several databases, and in a variety of formats, such as in the newspaper's database and a library's online subscription database. No page numbers are listed in the entry. Give the URL of the newspaper's home page when the article is available by search to avoid citing URLs that may change.

SOURCE SHOT 5

Listing an Article in an Online Scholarly Journal with a DOI APA

Include the following in your reference list entry:

❶ Author(s) Last name, initials

❷ (Publication date) Year in parentheses followed by a period

❸ Title of work: Any subtitle No quotation marks or italics; only capitalize the first word of the title and of any subtitle and proper nouns and adjectives; end with a period.

❹ *Periodical Title, volume* (issue number) Capitalize all major words in the title. Italicize the title, comma, and volume number, but not the issue number (contained in parentheses). If each issue of the periodical is paged separately (beginning with page 1, not the case here), put the issue number immediately after the volume number, with no space between them. Follow with a comma.

❺ Inclusive range of page numbers Repeat all digits, and separate numbers with an en dash. Do not use the abbreviation *p.* or *pp*. End with a period.

❻ Digital object identifier (DOI) End with the article's DOI (see Key Points box on p. 124). Only break a DOI before a punctuation mark, and do not add a hyphen to break a DOI at the end of a line. Do not add a period after the DOI.

Do not list the name of the database or your date of retrieval of the article.

       ❶   ❷

Burstein, M., Ameli-Grillon, L., & Merikangas, K. (2011). Shyness

             ❸   ❹

versus social phobia in U.S. youth. *Pediatrics, 128,*

  ❺   ❻

917–925. doi:10.1542/peds.2011-1434

Belluck, P. (2010, December 6). Math puzzles' oldest ancestors

    took form on Egyptian papyrus. *The New York Times.*

              No period at end when a URL ends the entry

    Retrieved from http://www.nytimes.com /

25. Online abstract, review, editorial, or letter For an abstract retrieved from a Web site, begin the retrieval statement with the words *Abstract retrieved from,* followed by

Online Database Citation Page (from ProQuest PsycINFO database)

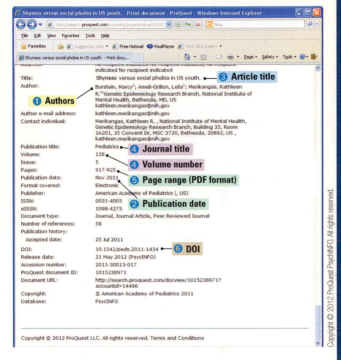

the URL of the home page of the journal's Web site, with no period at the end.

Frith, H., & Gleeson, K. (2004). Clothing and embodiment:

Men managing body image and appearance.

Psychology of Men & Masculinity, 5, 40–48. Abstract

retrieved from http://content.apa.org

For an abstract in a database, give the print publication information and then write *Abstract retrieved from* and the name of the database, followed by any identifying number in parentheses. Do not end with a period.

For a review, editorial, or letter to the editor in an online periodical, cite as you would for a print version and provide the appropriate content identifier in brackets after the title, such as *Review of . . .*, followed by the date of retrieval. If there is no author or title, begin with the bracketed material. End with the DOI or URL. See 10e, items 17–19.

26. Web page, author identified Do not put the title in quotation marks or italics. Capitalize only the first word of the title or subtitle and proper nouns and adjectives. Give the URL and the date of retrieval for content that may be changed or updated.

Landau, E. (2010, October 22). Parents: How to raise a

   creative genius. Retrieved October 23, 2010, from

   http://www.cnn.com

27. Web page, no author identified Begin with the page title. See 10f, item 26, for the rest of the entry details. In your list of references, alphabetize by the first major word of the title.

What is osteoarthritis? (2011). Retrieved June 30, 2011, from

   http://www.arthritis.org

28. Entire Web site Give the complete URL in parentheses in the text of your paper, after material referenced from the site; do not include the Web site in your list of references (see 10b, item M).

29. Technical or research report on a university or government agency site Italicize the title of a technical or research report and follow with any identifying number *(Report No. 351)* in parentheses. Then write *Retrieved from,* and give the name of the university or government agency (and the department or division if it is named) Web site. Follow this with a colon and the URL.

McClintock, R. (2000, September 20). *Cities, youth, and*

   technology: Toward a pedagogy of autonomy. Retrieved

   from Columbia University, Institute for Learning

   Technologies website: http://www.ilt.columbia.edu

30. Online book Give a DOI if one is available; otherwise, give the URL.

Freud, S. (1923). *A young girl's diary*. New York, NY: Thomas

    Seltzer. Retrieved from http://books.google.com

31. Online reference work Give the retrieval date for a work that is likely to be updated, especially from a source such as *Wikipedia* that anyone can update and change.

Hilgevoord, J., & Uffink, J. (2006). The uncertainty principle.

    In E. N. Zalta (Ed.), *The Stanford encyclopedia of*

    philosophy. Retrieved October 16, 2013, from

    http://plato.stanford.edu

32. Blogs, discussion boards, wikis, newsgroups, and archived electronic mailing lists Include in your list of sources only academic material posted on archived lists or blogs. (If no archives exist, cite an entry on a discussion board or message board in your text as a personal communication; see 10g, item 38). In your entry, include a description of the message in brackets after the title; include the name of the discussion list if it is not part of the URL. Write *Retrieved from* and the URL.

Baron, D. (2010, October 14). Killer app: Seven dirty words

    you can't say on your iPhone. [Web log post to The

    Web of Language]. Retrieved from http://illinois.edu/

    db/view/ 25/36000?count=1&ACTION=DIALOG

Always give the retrieval date for wiki pages, which may change constantly.

McCreary, D. (Ed.). (2013, November 9). XForms/Background.

    Retrieved May 21, 2014, from http://en.wikibooks.org/

    wiki/XForms/Background

10g Listing visual, multimedia, and miscellaneous sources (APA)

33. Film, recording, DVD, CD-ROM, or other video Identify the medium in brackets after the title. For a film, give the producer and director and the country where the film was released. Give the city and state or country and the publisher or recording label for other formats.

Lee, S. (Director). (2010). *The warrior's way* [Motion picture].

    United States: Relativity Media.

Jacquet, L. (Director). (2005). *The march of the penguins*

[DVD]. Burbank, CA: Warner Home Video.

For an online video, add the label in brackets [Video], the date of retrieval, and the URL.

34. Television or radio program

Gazit, C. (Writer). (2004). The seeds of destruction [Television

series episode]. In D. J. James (Producer), *Slavery and*

the making of America. New York, NY: WNET.

35. Podcast or MP3 download For a podcast, give the producer or editor, complete date, italicized title, identification of format and any other supplementary information in brackets, and *Retrieved from,* followed by the URL.

Tanenhaus, S. (Editor). (2010, October 22). *Book update*

[Interview with Jonathan Alter and Christopher

Caldwell on political books] [Audio podcast]. Retrieved

from http://www.nytimes.com/services/xml/rss/nyt/

podcasts/bookupdate.xml

For an MP3 download, begin with the author or performer. Also give the place of production and the recording label.

Davis, A. (2007, October 2). *Angela Davis speaks: Panel*

discussion with Burnham, Mitchell, and Noble

[MP3 download]. Washington, DC: Folkways Records.

Retrieved from http://www.amazon.com

36. Video blog posting Use a screen name if it is the only one available.

nnnicck. (2007, February 7). The march of the librarians

[Video file]. Retrieved from http://www.youtube.com/

watch?v=Td922l0NoDQ

37. Presentation slides

Norvig, P. (2000). *The Gettysburg PowerPoint presentation*

[PowerPoint slides]. Retrieved from http://norvig

.com/Gettysburg/index.htm

38. Personal communication or interview Cite a letter, telephone conversation, interview, personal e-mail, or message on a discussion board only in your text (10b, item O). Do not include it in your list of references.

39. Conference paper or poster session Cite published proceedings of meetings and symposia as you would cite a book or a chapter of a book. If the proceedings are published regularly, cite them in a periodical format. If they are published online, also give the DOI.

If contributions to symposia or conference papers or poster presentations have not been formally published, cite them as follows:

Szenher, M. (2005, September). *Visual homing in natural*

environments. Poster session presented at the annual

meeting of Towards Autonomous Robotic Systems,

London, England.

If the material is posted online, also give the retrieval information.

Szenher, M. (2005, September). *Visual homing with learned*

goal distance information. Paper presented at the Third

International Symposium on Autonomous Minirobots

for Research and Edutainment, Fukui, Japan. Retrieved

from http://books.google.com

40. Computer software Do not use italics for the name of the software.

SnagIt (Version 9.0) [Computer software]. (2008). Okemos,

MI: TechSmith.

Model Paper 3: A student's research paper, APA style

The following paper was written by Maria Saparauskaite in a required first-year course at Hunter College. The assignment was to explore a current issue. Using the APA style of documentation, she provides a title page, an abstract, and section headings. Her citations and the list of references at the end of the paper follow APA guidelines and serve to answer any questions that readers may have about the authors, dates, and publication details of her source material. Note the position of the running head and the page number on each page.

NOTE: Blue annotations point out issues of content and organization; red annotations point out APA format issues.

Title Page (APA)

Running head and page number on every page

SECRET OF SAVANT   1
In capitals

Midway on page,
centered in capital and
lowercase letters

The Secret of the Savant

Maria Saparauskaite

Hunter College of the City University of New York

Abstract Page (APA)

SECRET OF SAVANT   2

Abstract

Heading centered, capital and lowercase letters

This paper investigates the phenomenon of

savants, people with unusual mental talents, and

describes some of their extraordinary feats. Theories

of the development of the rare savant syndrome

are explored, especially the connection between a

savant's abilities and whether the effects of brain

damage on the hemispheres of the brain cause savant

talents to emerge spontaneously. A study by Snyder,

Bahramali, Hawker, and Mitchell (2006) is explored

in detail. The researchers wanted to examine how

stimulation of the brain affected mental functions,

with participants experiencing either brain stimulation

or a sham session and then being asked to make

judgments about what they saw. The study suggests

that the savant condition could be stimulated, thus

raising questions about not only whether rewiring

of the brain is advisable but also to what ends any

newfound intelligence may be applied.

Length:
137 words
(aim for
100–200)

Passive
voice
common
in APA

Summary
of findings

Double-
spaced
text

Blue = content issues   Red = format issues

The Paper (APA)

SECRET OF SAVANT   3

The Secret of the Savant

Many of us struggle with learning and memorization. We may long to be able to do math problems quickly in our heads, play a favorite song on the piano after hearing it only once, or recapture details from an event we have observed. We may wish we could learn a second language as easily as we did our first. For a few individuals among us, these talents are as natural as breathing. These individuals are *savants*, and they are capable of unusual mental feats. Some recent studies have shown that there may be a savant within all of us, which means that our brains may be capable of the same abilities as savants. Through artificial means these talents can in some cases be accessed temporarily.

Background Review of the Literature

Savants and Their Accomplishments

Savants exhibit extraordinary talents. Researchers Treffert and Wallace (2004) have reported that at the age of 14, Leslie Lemke was able to play Tchaikovsky's Piano Concerto No. 1 without a single mistake after hearing it only once. He had never had a piano lesson in his life, but today he tours all over the world playing in concerts even though he is blind and developmentally disabled. Lemke even composes his own music. Another savant, Kim Peek, the inspiration for the Oscar-winning film *Rain Man,* has memorized more than 7,600 books. It would take him less than 3 seconds to tell you which day of the week your birthday fell on and which day of the week you will

Blue = content issues   Red = format issues

SECRET OF SAVANT   4

be collecting your first pension. Like Lemke, Peek is
also developmentally disabled. The artwork of another
savant, Richard Wawro, is known all over the world.
His childhood oil paintings left people speechless
(Treffert & Wallace, 2004). He is an autistic savant,
as is David Tammet, who can calculate 37 to the 4th
power in his head (Heffernan, 2005).

The Savant Syndrome

The savant syndrome is an extremely rare
condition most often found in people with IQs
ranging from 40 to 70, though sometimes it can
occur in people with IQs up to 114 or higher (Treffert
& Wallace, 2004). Most savants are physically
disabled or suffer from autism, which is a "pervasive
development disorder [that] is characterized by a
severe disturbance of communication, social, and
cognitive skills, and is often associated with mental
retardation" (Sternberg, 2004, p. 352). Despite that,
savants exhibit amazing mental superiority in specific
areas, such as arithmetic, drawing, music, or memory.
However, their way of thinking is very literal, and
they have problems understanding abstract concepts.
Their abilities emerge spontaneously and cannot be
improved over time. Also, savants cannot explain how
they do what they do (Snyder, Bahramali, Hawker, &
Mitchell, 2006).

Theories of Development of the Syndrome

Scientists have only a vague idea of how the
savant syndrome develops. Recent studies have
illustrated that developmental problems in the left
brain hemisphere are most commonly seen in savants.

Marginal annotations (format issues):

Ampersand (&) within parentheses

Inserted word enclosed in brackets

Page number for a quotation

Blue = content issues   Red = format issues

SECRET OF SAVANT   5

Bernard Rimland of the Autism Research Institute has
observed that most abilities in autistic savants are
associated with the right hemisphere, whereas the
abilities they are deficient in are associated with the
left hemisphere (Treffert & Wallace, 2004). The left
hemisphere is thought to be responsible for forming
hypotheses and concepts. This observation helps to
explain why savants tend to be so literal. Another set
of evidence for this theory is the occasional emergence
of savant-like talents in people suffering from dementia.
Bruce Miller of the University of California observed
five elderly patients who spontaneously developed
exceptional artistic skills in music and painting. All
of these patients had what is called *frontotemporal
dementia* (FTD). Miller discovered that most brain
damage caused by FTD was localized in the left
hemisphere (Treffert & Wallace, 2004). Another case
of brain damage examined by psychologist T. L. Brink
reported that a 9-year-old boy developed "unusual
savant mechanical skills" (Treffert & Wallace, 2004)
after a bullet damaged his left hemisphere. According
to Treffert and Wallace, these reports of spontaneous
emergence of the savant syndrome in people with brain
damage could point to a possibility that savant talents
may be innate to everyone. So, as reporter Lawrence
Osborne (2003) provocatively asked, "Could brain
damage, in short, actually make you brilliant?"

Snyder's Experiment

Allan Snyder of the University of Sidney, "one
of the world's most remarkable scientists of human
cognition" (Osborne, 2003), became interested in the
prospect of hidden genius when observing patients

Annotations (margin notes):
- Mentions authority of source
- Present perfect tense used to introduce source
- Past tense for a research study
- Question for research
- New section of paper: heading bold, centered
- Credentials of researcher

Blue = content issues   Red = format issues

who underwent a procedure called *transcranial
magnetic stimulation* (TMS). The TMS was "originally
developed as a tool for brain surgery: By stimulating
or slowing down specific regions of the brain, it
allowed doctors to monitor the effects of surgery in
real time" (Osborne, 2003). Interestingly enough,
this procedure had very noticeable side effects on
the patients' mental functioning. A patient would
either temporarily lose his ability to speak or make
odd mistakes while speaking. But one side effect
intrigued Snyder the most: Some patients undergoing
TMS would gain savant-like intelligence for a limited
amount of time. With his colleague D. J. Mitchell,
he came up with the theory that savants have a
privileged access to lower levels of cognition whereas
normal persons do not (Snyder & Mitchell, 1999).

Participants and Method

    To test this theory, Snyder, along with Bahramali,
Hawker, and Mitchell, led an experiment (2006) that
was based on the finding that some savants are able
to guess the exact number of items, such as matches,
just by glancing at them. He tells of autistic twins
who were able to estimate correctly the number of
matches (111) fallen on the floor. By using TMS on the
brains of 12 volunteers, Snyder wanted to find out if a
normal person could accomplish the same thing. The
goal was to create virtual lesions in the left anterior
temporal lobes of the volunteers, thus suppressing
mental activity in that region of the brain.

    The participants underwent two sessions. During
one of them, they received TMS stimulation, while

Claim of researchers

Year in parenthesis

Description of experiment

Blue = content issues   **Red = format issues**

during the other "sham" session, they did not.
The participants were not able to tell the difference.
During each session, the participants were shown
a random number of dots on a computer screen
(as shown in Figure 1) and then told to estimate
the number of dots they saw. They were asked
to do this before the TMS stimulation, then
15 minutes afterward, and finally, an hour later.
The same procedure was used in both real and
sham sessions.

Results of the Experiment

Purpose of figure explained

The results, summarized in Figure 2, are surprising.
Eight of the 12 participants improved their ability to
estimate the number of dots within an accuracy range
of five after the TMS stimulation. The probability for
this to happen merely by chance alone is less than
1 in 1,000. Clearly there is a significant increase in
the number of correct estimations after the TMS
stimulation. The sham session shows relatively little
variation.

Confirmation of hypothesis

Snyder and the other researchers concluded
that the experiment "demonstrated an enhanced
ability of healthy normal individuals to guess the
absolute number of discrete elements by attempting
to artificially stimulate the savant condition"
(2006, p. 842). They described savants as being able
to see the parts of the holistic picture, thus having
access to raw information, unlike normal healthy
individuals.

Blue = content issues   Red = format issues

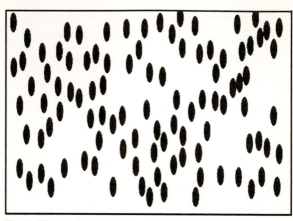

Fig. 1. The task—to estimate the number of dots, A. H. Snyder et al., 2006, p. 838.

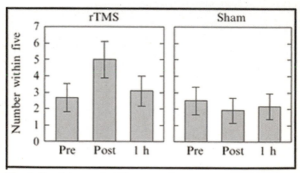

Fig. 2. Participants' ability to make guesses within an accuracy range of 5, both with repetitive transcranial magnetic stimulation and without (the sham session), Snyder et al., 2006, p. 841.

Blue = content issues   Red = format issues

From A. Snyder, H. Bahramali, T. Hawker, and D. J. Mitchell, "Savant-Like Numerosity Skills Revealed in Normal People by Magnetic Impulses," *Perception* 35(6), 837–845, doi:10.1068/p5539.

SECRET OF SAVANT   9

Conclusion

The line separating a normal person from a savant may thus be less "hard wired" than previously assumed. If a person could become brilliant by having his or her brain rewired, how would this newfound intelligence be used? For personal gain or for selfless good? Whatever directions and possibilities such research may reveal, understanding the savant syndrome brings us closer to understanding the human brain. Perhaps, in the future, research on savants will not only teach us more about what intelligence is and where it lies but will also help people who are born mentally retarded or brain damaged. The research that is just beginning opens up many possibilities.

Questions for further research

Thesis

Organized alphabetically   References   **New page, double-spaced**

Heffernan, V. (2005, February 23). A savant

   aided by the sparks that he sees inside his

   head. *The New York Times*. Retrieved from

   http://www.nytimes.com

Osborne, L. (2003, June 22). Savant for a day. *The*

   New York Times Magazine. Retrieved from

   http://www.nytimes.com

Snyder, A., Bahramali, H., Hawker, T., & Mitchell, D. J.

   (2006). Savant-like numerosity skills revealed

   in normal people by magnetic impulses.

   Perception, 35, 837–845. doi:10.1068/p5539

Snyder, A. W., & Mitchell, D. J. (1999). Is integer

   arithmetic fundamental to mental processing?

   The mind's secret arithmetic. *Proceedings of*

   the Royal Society B: Biological Sciences, 266,

   287–292. doi:10.1098/rspb.1999.0676.

Sternberg, R. J. (2004). *Psychology* (4th ed.). Toronto,

   Canada: Wadsworth.

Treffert, D. A., & Wallace, G. L. (2004, January).

   Islands of genius. *Scientific American Mind*.

   Retrieved from http://scientificamerican.com

Retrieval information: URL

No period after URL

Scholarly article

Volume number italicized

The DOI of the article

URL of the periodical home page

11 *Chicago* Style

In addition to its author-year parenthetical reference system that is similar to the APA system, *The Chicago Manual of Style,* 16th edition (Chicago: U of Chicago P, 2010), has a system that documents sources in footnotes or endnotes and a bibliography. This system is used widely in the humanities, especially in history, art history, literature, and the arts. For a *Chicago*-style humanities paper, include an unnumbered title page, and number the first page of your paper *2*.

11a **Basic features of the *Chicago* note style**

KEY POINTS
Documenting Sources in *Chicago* Style

1. *In your text,* place a superscript numeral at the end of the quotation or the sentence in which you mention your source material; place the number after all punctuation marks except a dash.

2. *On a separate numbered page at the end of the paper,* list all endnotes (single-spaced but double-spaced between notes), and number the notes sequentially, as they appear in your paper. If you use footnotes, a word processing program can automatically place them at the bottom of a page.

Example of an Endnote or Footnote for a Book

In-Text Citation with Numeral	Numbered Endnote or Footnote (single-spaced)
For footnote (source at bottom of page): Mondrian planned his compositions with colored tape.[3]	3. H. Harvard Arnason and Marla F. Prather, *History of Modern Art* (New York: Abrams, 1998), 393.
For endnote (mentioning source): According to Arnason and Prather, Mondrian planned his compositions with colored tape.[3]	

11b How to cite sources in your paper (*Chicago*)

Use the following format. Number your notes sequentially.

George Eliot thought that *Eliot* was a "good, mouthfilling, easy to pronounce word."[1]

See 11c, page 144, for the endnote for this citation.

11c How to prepare *Chicago* endnotes and footnotes

KEY POINTS
Chicago Endnotes and Footnotes

1. In the list of endnotes, place each number on the line (not as a superscript), followed by a period and one space. Follow the same format for footnotes. Word processing software will often automatically make a footnote number superscript; just be consistent with the format you use.

2. Indent the first line of each entry three or five spaces. Single-space within a note, and double-space between notes, unless your instructor prefers double-spacing throughout.

3. Use the author's full name, not inverted, followed by a comma and the title of the work. Put quotation marks around article titles, and italicize titles of books and periodicals.

(continued)

(continued)

4. Capitalize all words in the titles of books, periodicals, and articles except *a, an, the,* coordinating conjunctions, *to* in an infinitive, and prepositions. Capitalize any word that begins or ends a title or a subtitle.

5. Follow a book title with publishing information in parentheses (city—and state if necessary—name of publisher, and year), followed by a comma and the page number(s), with no *p.* or *pp.* Follow an article title with the name of the periodical and pertinent publication information (volume, issue, date, and page numbers where appropriate). Do not abbreviate months.

6. Separate major parts of the citation with commas, not periods.

7. For online sources, provide the date of publication or revision and a DOI or URL. For time-sensitive or undated material, give an access date.

First note for a source

author's name in normal order

book title italicized,
all important words capitalized

1. Margaret Crompton, *George Eliot: The Woman*

comma

place, publisher, and date in parentheses

(London: Cox and Wyman, 1960), 123.

comma   page number

First note for a source if a bibliography is provided If your paper includes a bibliography that lists all of the sources cited in your notes, the note citation can be concise.

1. Crompton, *George Eliot,* 123.

A bibliography supplies full publication details. All lines after the first line should be indented, and the parts of each entry should be separated with periods, not commas, with no mention of page numbers in books, as in the following bibliography entry:

last name first, not indented

Crompton, Margaret. *George Eliot: The Woman.* London: Cox

and Wyman, 1960.

See also the sample bibliography in 11h.

Note referring to the immediately preceding source Use *Ibid.* (Latin for *ibidem*—"in the same place") if the author, work, and page number(s) are the same as those in the preceding entry. If the page number is different, add it after *Ibid.* and a comma:

2. Ibid., 127.

However, avoid a series of *ibid.* notes. These are likely to irritate your reader. Instead, place page references within your text: *As Crompton points out (127), . . .*

Any subsequent reference to a previously cited source For a reference to a source cited in a previous note but not in the immediately preceding note, give only the author and page number. However, if you cite more than one work by the same author, include a short title to identify the source.

6. Crompton, 124.

11d Notes for print books and parts of books (*Chicago*)

Indent the first line, give the full name of the author, use commas to separate major sections of the note, and cite the publication details in parentheses (city: publisher, year of publication). For an edited or translated book, use *ed.* or *trans.* after the name. If you quote or refer to a specific page of the source, provide the page number after the publication details and a comma, as in item 1. For a general reference or one to the work as a whole, end the note after the closing parenthesis, as in item 2.

1. Book with one author

1. Robert A. Caro, *Master of the Senate: The Years of Lyndon Johnson* (New York: Knopf, 2002), 8.

2. Book with two or more authors

2. George Lakoff and Mark Johnson, *Metaphors We Live By* (Chicago: University of Chicago Press, 1980).

For a book with four or more authors, use the name of only the first author, followed by *et al. ("and others").*

3. Book with no author identified

3. *Chicago Manual of Style*, 16th ed. (Chicago: University of Chicago Press, 2010).

4. Government document

4. US Department of Education, National Center for Education Statistics, *The Condition of Education, 2013* (Washington, DC: Government Printing Office, 2013).

Note that in *Chicago* style, *US* and *USA* don't have periods.

5. Book with editor or translator

5. John Updike, ed., *The Best American Short Stories of the Century* (Boston: Houghton Mifflin, 1999).

For a translated work, begin with the translator's name, a comma, and *trans.*

6. Contribution to an edited volume or anthology (essay, chapter, poem, short story)

6. Terrence Des Pres, "Poetry and Politics," in *The Writer in Our World*, ed. Reginald Gibbons (Boston: Atlantic Monthly Press, 1986), 20.

7. Author's work quoted in another work

7. E. M. Forster, *Two Cheers for Democracy* (New York: Harcourt, Brace, and World, 1942), 242, quoted in Phyllis Rose, *Woman of Letters, A Life of Virginia Woolf* (New York: Oxford University Press, 1978), 219.

8. Scriptures and classics Provide the reference in the text or in a note. For the Bible, include the book (in abbreviated form, chapter, and verse, not a page number) and the version used. Do not include the Bible in a bibliography.

8. Gen. 27:29 (New Revised Standard Version).

For Greek and Roman works and for classic plays in English, locate by the number of book, section, and line or by act, scene, and line. Cite a classic poem by book, canto, stanza, and line, whichever is appropriate. Specify the edition used only in the first reference in a note.

11e Notes for print articles (*Chicago*)

9. Article in a scholarly journal Give the author(s), title of the article, title of the journal, volume and issue numbers, and date. End with the page number(s) that you refer to. (In a bibliography, give the page span of the article.)

9. Warren Wilner, "The Lone Ranger as a Metaphor for the Psychoanalytic Movement from Conscious to Unconscious Experience," *Psychoanalytic Review* 92, no. 5 (2005): 764.

To cite an abstract, include the word *abstract* before the title of the journal.

10. Article in a magazine Include the month for monthly magazines and the complete date for weekly magazines (month, day, year). Cite only a specific page number in a note. In a bibliography, however, provide the range of pages of the whole article.

10. Peter Ludlow, "WikiLeaks and Hacktivist Culture," *Nation*, October 4, 2010, 25.

11. Article or editorial in a newspaper Do not include an initial *The* in the name of a newspaper. Give the edition and any section number, but not the page number, last.

11. John Noble Wilford, "Extinct Penguins Wore Earth Tones, Fossil Shows," *New York Times*, September 29, 2010, late edition, sec. A.

If no author is given, begin the note with the title.

12. Letter to the editor

12. Allyssa McCabe, letter to the editor, *New Yorker*, October 4, 2010, 8.

13. Review (of a book, play, film, performance)

13. Evelyn Toynton, "Waugh vs. Waugh: The Family Ties That Bind," review of *Fathers and Sons: The Autobiography of a Family,* by Alexander Waugh, *Harper's,* August 2007, 92.

11f Notes for online sources (*Chicago*)

- To cite an online article, poem, government publication, or book, provide the same available information that you would for a nonelectronic source, but add a DOI or URL at the end.

- Give the DOI (digital object identifier), a permanent identifying number for locating a work in all media in which it is published, rather than a URL (uniform resource locator), if one is available.

- To split a DOI or URL across lines, do not insert a hyphen. Make the split *after* a colon or a double slash;

before a single slash, period, comma, hyphen, and most other punctuation; and either *before* or *after* an ampersand or equals sign.

- Provide a date of access, separated by commas, before the DOI or URL only if the material is undated or time sensitive, as shown in item 17.
- End the entry with a period after the DOI or URL.

14. Online reference work   Cite an online dictionary or an encyclopedia in a note, but do not include it in a bibliography. Because reference works are frequently updated, give the date when you accessed the material. Precede the title of an alphabetized article with the initials *s.v.* (Latin for *sub verbo*—"under the word").

   14. *Encyclopedia Brittanica*, Academic ed., s.v. "Religious dress," accessed May 22, 2014, http://www.britannica.com/EBchecked/topic/497306/religious-dress.

15. Online book   For books that are available both in print and online, cite the source that you consult. Include the DOI (if available) or the URL as the last part of the citation. Include the date of access only for a book that may be revised in new editions.

   15. Mary Wollstonecraft Shelley, *Frankenstein, or, the Modern Prometheus* (London: Dent, 1912), http://ota.ahds.ac.uk.

16. Article retrieved from an online database   List a stable URL if the database includes one with the archived article. If it does not, give the name of the database and (in parentheses) any identifying number provided.

   16. Geoffrey Bent, "Vermeer's Hapless Peer," *North American Review* 282, no. 5 (1997), http://www.jstor.org/stable/2516155.

See 11h for a bibliography entry.

17. Web page or document from a Web site   Give the author (if known), title of the document, title of the Web site, owner or sponsor of the site (if needed), date of posting, and URL.

   17. Tammy Worth, "Why Your Job Is Making You Depressed," Cable News Network, October 1, 2010, http://www.cnn.com/2010/HEALTH/10/01/health.job.making.depressed/index.html.

18. Article in an online journal, magazine, or newspaper
Cite as you would for a print publication, with the DOI or URL added at the end after a comma.

18. Caroline Ford, "Museums After Empire in Metropolitan and Overseas France," *Journal of Modern History* 82 (September 2010): 625–61, doi:10.1086/654828.

19. Government publication online

19. US Department of Education, National Center for Education Statistics, *The Condition of Education, 2007*, http://nces.ed.gov/pubs2007/2007064.pdf.

20. E-mail communication

20. Toby Gingold, e-mail message to the author, August 23, 2010.

21. Material posted on an electronic discussion list, wiki, or mailing list
Whenever possible, cite the name of the list, the date of the individual posting, and the URL for the archived material.

21. David Schwalm to WPA-L mailing list, August 30, 2010, https://lists.asu.edu/cgi-bin/wa?A0=WPA-L.

11g Notes for audiovisual, multimedia, and miscellaneous sources (*Chicago*)

22. Interview, lecture, or speech
Treat a published interview like an article or a book chapter, and include the phrase *interview with*. For unpublished interviews, include the type of interview and the date. Include a DOI or URL for interviews conducted online.

22. Douglass Mignone, telephone interview with the author, October 19, 2010.

For a lecture or speech, also provide the location and date in parentheses: *(lecture, Hunter College, New York, April 7, 2010)*.

23. Audiovisual sources
Include the date of copyright, production, or performance. Give the type of medium (such as *CD-ROM, compact disc, DVD, film,* or *audiocassette*) at the end of the entry, followed by any optional supplementary information (number of discs, length of film). Recordings consulted online should include a URL or DOI.

23. *Citizen Kane*, produced, written, and directed by Orson Welles, RKO, 1941, film, 119 min.

24. Other multimedia Give the author, title, and date, and include the type of medium (such as *podcast, MP3,* or *MPEG audio file*), indicating where you accessed the source.

24. Sam Tanenhaus, *Book Update*, November 23, 2010, *New York Times* podcast, http://www.apple.com/itunes.

25. E-books Cite books that you downloaded from libraries or booksellers as you would cite printed books, but indicate the format at the end of the citation.

25. Stephen Hawking. *The Grand Design* (New York: Bantam Books, 2010), Kindle edition, chap. 1.

Since e-books often do not have stable page numbers, cite the chapter, section, or other division instead.

11h A student's *Chicago* bibliography

Find out whether your instructor wants you to include a bibliography of works cited (or of works consulted) in addition to notes. If he or she does want you to include this information, you can use the short form for notes (11c, p. 145). Include complete page spans for articles.

Note form (with commas separating the three major parts of the note)

note number, indented

7. Peter C. Sutton, *Pieter de Hooch, 1629–1684*

publication details in parentheses   page number of exact citation

(New Haven: Yale University Press, 1988), 57.

Bibliography form (with periods separating the three major parts of the entry)

no note number, indented only after first line of entry

Sutton, Peter C. *Pieter de Hooch, 1629–1684*. New Haven:

Yale University Press, 1988.

The following bibliography is from a student's paper on the seventeenth-century Dutch painter Pieter de Hooch.

Bibliography

Bent, Geoffrey. "Vermeer's Hapless Peer." *North American Review* 282, no. 5 (1997): 10–13. http://www.jstor.org /stable/2516155.

Botton, Alain de. "Domestic Bliss: Pieter de Hooch Exhibition." *New Statesman*, October 9, 1998, 34–35.

Hollander, Martha. "Public and Private Life in the Art of Pieter de Hooch." *Nederlands Kunsthistorisch Jaarboek* 51 (2000), 272–93.

Sutton, Peter. *Pieter de Hooch: Complete Edition, with a Catalogue Raisonné*. Ithaca, NY: Cornell University Press, 1980.

Model Paper 4: Sample pages from a student's *Chicago* research paper

Here is the third paragraph (along with its corresponding endnotes) of an essay by Lynn McCarthy, written for Professor Roberta Bernstein's course in modern art at the State University of New York at Albany. Page 1 of her paper was a numbered title page. The assignment was to analyze a work of art by Piet Mondrian. In her paper, she included a visual image of *Trafalgar Square*.

NOTE: Blue annotations point out issues of content and organization; red annotations point out *Chicago* format issues.

Paragraph on Third Page of Essay (*Chicago* Style)

McCarthy 3

Trafalgar Square, an oil on canvas measuring 145.2 by 120 cm, today is housed in the Museum of Modern Art in New York City. It is interesting to discover that Mondrian planned out his compositions with colored tape before he applied any paint.[3] Some tape actually still remains on his *Victory Boogie Woogie* (1942–44), which is an unfinished work he was involved in at the time of his death. But what is even more interesting is that although Mondrian preplanned the compositions, we know from x-rays that he reworked the paint on his canvases over and over again.[4] So as methodical and mathematical as we may think Mondrian was, he still felt constant inspiration and intuitive urges to make changes along the way. It is interesting, too, to note that he worked on a flat, horizontal table rather than at an easel.[5] Maybe he did this for practical or comfort reasons, but it also can be seen as a break from the conventional way artists created their works just as their subject matter broke from tradition. I think of how an artist like Jackson Pollock takes this even further by laying his canvas on the floor and walking on and around it, dropping and splattering the paint.

Super-script number refers to list at end

Brings in own knowledge

Blue = content issues   Red = format issues

Endnotes (*Chicago* Style), Beginning on a New Page

Notes

1. Harry Cooper and Ron Spronk, *Mondrian: The Transatlantic Paintings* (New Haven, CT: Yale University Press, 2001), 24.

2. Ibid., 24–25.

Refers to source 1, directly above

3. H. Harvard Arnason and Marla F. Prather, *History of Modern Art* (New York: Abrams, 1998), 393.

4. Cooper and Spronk, 237.

5. Arnason and Prather, 383.

Same source as in note 1, with a different page number

6. Cooper and Spronk, 34.

7. Arnason and Prather, 233.

Five C's for Clear Style

SHAPE	
PURPOSE	**AUDIENCE**
• Where is your language wordy, obscuring your purpose? Where can you cut unnecessary words? • Are there places where more direct and active language would make your purpose clearer?	• How can you revise your text to connect ideas for your audience? • Have you chosen vivid, specific words, avoiding terms that might be confusing or offensive to your audience?
VOICE	**MEDIUM**
• Does your writing demonstrate a committed, confident stance? • Do you directly refer to your intentions in your text, and if so, is it potentially distracting to your readers?	• What language choices are most effective for the medium in which you are writing? • How could the design of your text help connect ideas in your writing?

Readers sometimes suffer from what has been called the MEGO—"My Eyes Glaze Over"—reaction to a piece of writing, even when ideas are well organized and there are no grammatical errors. This reaction happens when readers are turned off by a style that obscures meaning and is characterized by wordiness, flatness, inappropriate word choice, clichés, and sentences constructed without interesting variations. Consider your audience as you are revising: When you read your own draft prior to revision, use the convenient mnemonic of the five C's to remind you what to look for and consider for revision. Keep clarity and directness in mind as the basics of academic writing. Of course, graceful and elegant writing may ultimately be your aim, but grace and elegance always need an underlay of clarity.

Try this quick test: Read your draft aloud. If *you* have to pause anywhere to make sense of what you have written (watch out for a stumble, a pause, discomfort, or the occasions when "Huh?" flashes through your mind), use the five C's to revise for style and to get rid of the glitch.

12 The First C: Cut

When you write, do not underdevelop your ideas because you fear taxing your audience's patience. Work on developing ideas and presenting material that has substance, persuasive detail, explanation, and original expression. But once you are happy with the ideas and content in your draft, scrutinize it for obvious redundancies, fumbling phrases, weak expressions, and obscurities that can easily creep into a first draft.

12a Cut wordiness.

Say something only once and in the best possible place.

▶ The Lilly Library ~~contains many rare books. The books in the library are~~ carefully preserved~~s~~. ~~The library also houses a manuscript collection.~~ many rare books and manuscripts

▶ Steven Spielberg, ~~who has directed~~ the movie ~~that has been~~ described as the best war movie ever made, ~~is someone who~~ knows many politicians. director of

▶ California residents have voted to abolish bilingual education, ~~The main reason for their voting to abolish~~
  because
  ~~bilingual education was that~~ many children were being placed indiscriminately into programs and kept there too long.

In addition, trim words that simply repeat an idea expressed in another word in the same phrase: *basic* essentials, *true* facts, circle *around*, consensus *of opinion*, *completely* unanimous, my *personal* opinion. Edit redundant pairs: *various and sundry, each and every.*

▶ The task took ~~diligence and~~ perseverance.

  has
▶ His surgeon ~~is a doctor with~~ a great deal of clinical experience. ˄

12b Cut formulaic phrases.

Replace wordy phrases with shorter or more direct expressions.

Formulaic	Concise
at the present time	now
at this point in time	
in this day and age	
in today's society	
because of the fact that	because
due to the fact that	
are of the opinion that	believe
have the ability to	can
in spite of the fact that	although, despite
last but not least	finally
prior to	before
concerning the matter of	about

12c Cut references to your intentions.

Eliminate references to the organization of your text and your own planning, such as *In this essay, I intend to prove that . . .*; or *In the next few paragraphs, I hope to show that . . .*; or *In conclusion, I have demonstrated. . . .* In a short essay, there is no need to announce a plan. However, in the sciences and social sciences, where information is often provided in a set order, such signals are more appropriate and more frequent: *This paper describes three approaches to treating depression.*

13 The Second C: Check for Action

Vigorous sentences show clearly who or what is doing the action. Use vivid, expressive verbs when you can. Do not overuse the verb *be* (*be, am, is, are, was, were, being, been*), and save the passive voice for times when it is necessary.

13a Show "Who's doing what?" as subject and verb.

The subject shows the doer of the action, and the verb tells what the subject is or does. They carry the weight of the meaning of the sentence. Make sure not to waste the directness they can lend to your meaning. Read your draft and mark subjects and verbs with *S* and *V*.

Wordy
$\overbrace{\text{The mayor's approval of the new law}}^{S}$ $\overset{V}{\text{was}}$ due to the voters' suspicion of the concealment of campaign funds by his deputy.

The subject and verb here tell us "the mayor's approval . . . was"—not a very powerful statement! Ask "Who's doing what?" and you come up with a tougher, leaner sentence:

Subject	Verb
the mayor	approved
the voters	suspected
his deputy	had concealed

Revised
The mayor approved the new law because the voters suspected that his deputy had concealed campaign funds.

The revision is not only shorter but more direct; it gets rid of three nouns formed from verbs (*approval, suspicion,* and *concealment*) as well as five phrases using prepositions (words used before nouns and pronouns): *of, to, of, of, by.*

13b Scrutinize sentences beginning with *there* or *it*.

Use the Find feature of your word processing program to find all instances of *there* and *it* in your document. Rewriting a sentence that begins with *there* or *it* often makes the sentence more direct. Try revising by asking "Who's doing what?" and then using an action verb and a subject that does the action.

Wordy	There was a discussion of the new health care system by the politicians. [Who's doing what here?]
Revised	The politicians discussed the new health care system.
Wordy	It is clear that Baker admires Updike.
Revised	Clearly, Baker admires Updike.

13c Avoid unnecessary passive voice constructions.

The passive voice tells what is done to something or someone: "The turkey was cooked too long." Extensive use of the passive voice can make your style seem pedantic and wordy.

Passive	The problem will be discussed thoroughly by the committee.
Revised	The committee will discuss the problem thoroughly.

The passive voice occurs frequently in scientific writing because readers are primarily interested in data, procedures, and results, not in who developed or produced them. In a scientific report, you are likely to read, for example, *The rats were fed,* not *The researchers fed the rats.* See 21g for more on when it is stylistically appropriate to use the passive voice.

14 The Third C: Connect

When you read your draft, pay attention to a smooth flow, with clear connections between sentences and paragraphs. Avoid a series of grasshopper-like jumps.

14a Apply the principle of consistent subjects.

Readers need a way to connect the ideas beginning a sentence with what has gone before. So when you move from one sentence to the next, avoid jarring shifts of subjects.

Shift of subject	*Memoirs* are becoming increasingly popular.
	Readers all over the continent are finding them appealing.
Revised	*Memoirs* are becoming increasingly popular.
	They appeal to readers all over the continent.

14b Make logical connections with transitional words and expressions.

Transitional expressions connect independent clauses and paragraphs. They are usually followed by a comma.

Transitional words and expressions
Adding an aside: incidentally, by the way, besides
Adding an idea: also, in addition, further, furthermore, moreover
Affirming: of course, in fact, certainly, obviously, to be sure, undoubtedly, indeed
Contrasting: however, nevertheless, nonetheless, on the other hand, in contrast, still, on the contrary, rather, conversely
Explaining: in other words, that is
Giving examples: for example, for instance
Showing order of time or order of ideas: first, second, third (and so on), then, next, later, subsequently, meanwhile, previously, finally
Showing result: as a result, consequently, therefore, thus, hence, accordingly, for this reason
Showing similarity: similarly, likewise
Summarizing: in short, generally, overall, all in all, in conclusion, above all

For punctuation with these transitional words and expressions, see 26a and 29b.

14c Vary the ways to connect and combine ideas.

To avoid a series of short, choppy sentences, consider the logical connection between ideas. Frequently, you will have several alternatives: a transition, a coordinator (*and, but, or, nor, so, for, or yet*), or a subordinator (a word such as *because, if, although, while, who,* or *which* used to introduce a dependent clause), as in the following examples. Note the punctuation in each example.

▶ The flight was long and cramped. The varied entertainment program made it bearable.

Transition The flight was long and cramped; *however,* the varied entertainment program made it bearable.

The flight was long and cramped; the varied entertainment program, *however,* made it bearable.

Coordination The flight was long and cramped, *but* the varied entertainment program made it bearable.

Subordination *Although* the flight was long and cramped, the varied entertainment program made it bearable.

15 The Fourth C: Commit

Chapter 15 focuses on ways to be firm, colorful, and resolute, and to present a confident stance and a consistent tone.

15a Commit to a confident stance.

As you read your draft, ask yourself: Where am I in this draft? What will readers learn about what I want to say and what my reasons are for saying it? These questions lead you to language that shows your commitment to the point you want to make based on your knowledge and research findings. When you present your own opinions, do not overuse language that suggests ambivalence and indecisiveness, which is evident in words and phrases like *maybe, perhaps, might, it could be, it could happen, it might seem,* and *it would appear*—unless, of course, you are presenting tentative new concepts, hypotheses, and conclusions. Never apologize for lack of experience or knowledge, and, above all, make sure that what you give to readers is based on solid research and interpretation of your findings. Then you will turn to language that reflects accountability and commitment: *as a result, consequently, of course, believe, need, demand, think, should, must.* Remember, though, to use such language of commitment only after you have thoroughly researched your topic and have found the evidence convincing.

15b Commit to a consistent tone.

For most academic writing, commit resolutely to a neutral, serious tone (see 16b for how your word choice can alter your tone). Avoid sarcasm, colloquial language, name-calling, or pedantic words and structures, even in the name of variety. Make sure you dedicate a special reading of a draft to examining your tone; if you are reading along and a phrase or passage strikes you as unexpected or out of place, flag it for later revision. However, an appropriate and consistent tone for academic writing does not mean using long words and stuffy language. Pretentious language makes reading difficult, as the following example shows:

▶ **When a female of the species ascertains that a male with whom she is acquainted exhibits considerable desire to extend their acquaintance, that female customarily will first engage in protracted discussion with her close confidantes.**

Simplify your writing if you find sentences like those in your draft. Here are some words and phrases to watch out for:

Stuffy	Direct
ascertain	find out
commence	begin
deceased	dead
endeavor	try
finalize	finish
implement	carry out
optimal	best
prior to	before
purchase	buy
reside	live
terminate	end
utilize	use

Because tone is really a function of how you anticipate your audience's expectations, ask a tutor or friend to read your writing and note any lapses in consistency of tone.

16 The Fifth C: Choose Your Words Carefully

Appropriate word choice, or *diction,* contributes a great deal to the effect your writing has on your audience. Do not give readers puzzles to solve. As you read a draft, mark any words that strike you as too general, vague, informal, or exclusionary—and revise accordingly.

16a Choose vivid and specific words.

Choosing vivid words means avoiding clichés, sayings that have been heard and read too often, like *hit the nail on the head, crystal clear, better late than never,* and *easier said than done.* If you have a specific image in mind, use words that are vivid enough to describe it. Provide details that re-create visual images for your readers. General words such as *area, aspect, certain* ("a certain expression," for example), *circumstance, factor, kind, manner, nature, situation, nice,* and *thing* are too general and do not give a reader much information, so avoid them unless you have a special effect you want to achieve.

Vague	The girl in Kincaid's story, "Girl," did many *things* that are often regarded as women's jobs. [*Things* is a vague word.]
Specific	The girl in the story washed the clothes, cooked, swept, set the table, and cleared away dishes—all tasks seen as women's jobs.

16b Be cautious with slang, regionalisms, and jargon.

Slang In formal college essays, your tone and diction should consistently be formal rather than colloquial. Watch out especially for sudden switches to a chatty and conversational tone, as in "Nutrition plays a large part in whether people *hang on to* their own teeth as they age." (You would revise *hang on to,* changing it to *retain.*) Avoid slang and colloquial expressions, such as *folks, guy, OK, okay, pretty good, hassle, kind of interesting/nice, too big of a deal, a lot of, lots of,* and *a ways away.* Do not enclose a slang expression in quotation marks to signal to your readers that you know it is inappropriate. Instead, revise.

▶ The working conditions were "gross." disgusting.

▶ The jury returned the verdict that the guy was not guilty. defendant

Regional language Use regional and ethnic dialects in writing only when you are quoting someone directly: *"Your car needs fixed," he advised.* Otherwise, use Standard Academic English.

▶ I bought ~~me~~ *myself* a backpack.

▶ She used to ~~could~~ *be able to* run two miles, but now she's out of shape.

Jargon Most areas of specialized work and study have their own technical words that people outside those fields perceive as jargon. A sportswriter writing about baseball will, for instance, refer to *balks, ERAs, cutters,* and *brushbacks.* A linguist writing about language will use terms like *phonemics, kinesics,* and *suprasegmentals.* If you know that your audience is familiar with the technical vocabulary of the field, specialized language is expected, but try to avoid jargon when writing for a more general audience. If you must use technical terms, provide definitions that will make sense to your audience.

16c Avoid the dangers of biased and exclusionary language.

Do not use divisive terms that reinforce stereotypes or belittle other people. Do not emphasize differences by separating society into *we* to refer to people who are like you and *they* or *these people* to refer to people who are different from you. Use *we* only to be truly inclusive of yourself and all your readers. Be aware, too, of terms that are likely to offend. You don't have to be excessive in your zeal to be PC ("politically correct"), using *underachieve* for *fail,* or *vertically challenged* for *short,* but do your best to avoid alienating readers.

Gender The writer of the following sentence edited it to avoid gender bias in the perception of women's roles and achievements.

▶ ~~Mrs. John~~ *Andrea* Harrison, ~~married to a real estate tycoon and herself the bubbly, blonde~~ chief executive of a successful computer company, has expanded the business overseas.

Choice of words can reveal gender bias, too.

Avoid	Use
actress	actor
chairman	chairperson
female astronaut	astronaut
forefathers	ancestors
foreman	supervisor
mailman	mail carrier
man, mankind (meaning any human being)	person, people, our species, human beings, humanity
man-made	synthetic
policeman, policewoman	police officer
salesman	salesperson, sales representative, sales clerk
veterans and their wives	veterans and their spouses

With the use of pronouns, too, avoid the stereotyping that occurs by assigning gender roles to professions, such as *he* for a doctor or lawyer, and *she* for a nurse or secretary.

▶ **Before a surgeon can operate, he or she must know every detail of the patient's history.**

However, it is better to avoid the clumsy *he or she* phrase by recasting the sentence or using a plural noun or pronoun.

▶ **Before operating, a surgeon must know every detail of the patient's history.**

▶ **Before surgeons can operate, they must know every detail of the patient's history.**

See 23b and 23c for more on pronouns and gender.

Race and place   Name a person's race only when it is relevant.

▶ **Attending the meeting were three doctors and an** ~~Asian~~ **computer programmer.**

Use the names that people prefer for their racial or ethnic affiliation. Consider, for example, that *black* and *African American* are preferred terms; *American Indian* is now sometimes preferred to *Native American*, though this preference has swung back and forth; *Asian* is preferred to *Oriental*. Be careful, too, with the way you refer to countries and continents; the Americas include both North and South America. Avoid stereotyping people according to where they come from. Some British people may be stiff and formal, but not all are (one of the authors of this book is from London)! Not all Germans eat sausage and drink beer; not all North Americans carry cameras and chew gum.

Age Avoid derogatory, condescending, or disrespectful terms associated with age. Refer to a person's age or condition neutrally, if at all: not *well-preserved little old lady* but *woman in her eighties* or just *woman.*

Politics Words referring to politics are full of connotations—word associations—as distinct from a word's dictionary meaning, its *denotation.* The word *liberal,* for instance, has been used with positive and negative connotations in various election campaigns. Take care with words like *radical, left-wing, right-wing,* and *moderate.* Are you identifying with one group and implicitly criticizing other groups?

Religion One edition of an encyclopedia referred to "devout Catholics" and "fanatical Muslims." A newer edition refers to both Catholics and Muslims as "devout," thus eliminating biased language. Examine your use of words that sound derogatory or exclusionary, such as *cult* or *fundamentalist;* terms—such as *those people*—that emphasize difference; or even the word *we* when it implies that all of your readers share (or should share) your beliefs.

Health and abilities Avoid terms like *confined to a wheelchair* and *victim* (of a disease) so that you do not focus on difference and disability. Instead, write *someone who uses a wheelchair* and *person with* (a disease). However, do not draw unnecessary attention to a disability or an illness. In particular, avoid terms such as *retarded* or *handicapped.*

Sexual orientation Refer to a person's sexual orientation only if the information is necessary to your content. To say that someone was "defended by a gay lawyer" is gratuitous when describing a case of stock market fraud, but the information may be relevant in a case of discrimination against gays. You will not necessarily know your readers' sexual orientation, so do not assume it is the same as your own, and beware of using terms and making comments that might offend.

The word *normal* One word to be especially careful about using is *normal* when referring to your own health, ability, or sexual orientation. Some readers could justifiably find that offensive.

PART SIX

Common Sentence Problems

SOLVE

PURPOSE

- Where have you used sentence fragments, run-on sentences, or other confusing constructions that might obscure your purpose?
- If you have used intentional sentence fragments, do they serve a specific purpose in your text?

AUDIENCE

- Have you used any misplaced or dangling modifiers that might confuse your readers?
- How clear are each of your pronouns? Will your audience know to which antecedent each pronoun is referring?

VOICE

- Where do you see shifts in your verb tense? Are those shifts intentional and meaningful, or do you need to edit for consistency?
- Where do you use the passive voice, and would it make sense to revise to the active voice?

MEDIUM

- If you are working in a visual medium, are all items you have included in bulleted lists parallel in nature? Have you edited for consistency?
- If you are creating a presentation with multiple slides, have you checked that each pronoun has a clear antecedent on that same slide (not just on a previous slide)?

© 2016 Cengage Learning®

Set aside time for a separate reading of your draft in order to check for the common problem areas covered in part 6 and to make corrections. Do not rely solely on computer tools for editing. Spelling checkers and grammar-check programs are not sophisticated enough to understand your writing situation and cover all of the options. Spelling checkers will catch typographical errors, such as *teh* in place of *the*, but they will not catch missing -*s* or -*ed* endings, nor will they find a misspelled word that forms another word: *affect/effect, expect/except, then/than,* or *peek/peak/pique* for example (see part 9, Words to Watch For, page 243).

FAQs about Sentences

Questions	Short Answer	More Details
Can I begin a sentence with *and* or *but*?	Occasionally, yes	18c
Can I begin a sentence with *because*?	Yes	18b
Can I interchange *but* and *however*?	No: meanings are similar; usage and punctuation differ	19b
What are the errors called fragments, run-ons, and comma splices?	A fragment is an incomplete sentence; a run-on or a comma splice is written as one sentence but needs to be separated or rewritten.	18 and 19
Is it "The boss promoted Jack *and I*" or "Jack *and me*"?	Mentally use the "Drop the *and*" test: "The boss promoted *me*." Therefore, "The boss promoted Jack *and me*."	23a
When is it okay to use the phrase *he* or *she*?	Occasionally okay to use to refer to a singular noun phrase (such as "a teacher"). Consider changing the noun to its plural form, and then use *they*.	23c
When do I use *who, whom, which,* or *that*?	For people: *who, whom* For things: *which, that* There are many more considerations here, so turn to the sections in column 3.	23e, 26c

(continued)

(continued)

Questions	Short Answer	More Details
When do I use *good* or *well, bad* or *badly*?	Use *good* and *bad* to modify nouns. *Well* and *badly* modify verbs.	24a, 24b

18 Fixing a Sentence Fragment

A fragment is a group of words that is punctuated as a sentence but is grammatically incomplete.

18a What a sentence needs

Check that your sentences contain the following:

1. a capital letter at the beginning
2. an independent (main) clause—one that can stand alone—containing both a subject and a complete verb and not introduced by a word such as *when, because, although, which,* or *until* (such words, known as *subordinators* or *subordinating conjunctions,* introduce dependent clauses and are common culprits in fragments)
3. appropriate end punctuation: period, question mark, or exclamation point

   Most problems occur when what is presented as a sentence has no complete independent clause.

Not an independent clause:
no subject or verb

▶ He wanted to make a point. To prove his competence.

Not an independent clause (*because* connects to an idea in the previous sentence)

▶ The audience left. Because the film was too long and too confusing.

18b Ways to turn a fragment into a complete sentence

1. Connect the fragment (the second group of words in each example below) to what comes before or after:

   for
   ▶ The trip to the country was wonderful. For a change of scene.

▶ She had season tickets to the Brooklyn

   Cyclones/~~A~~ minor-league baseball team.
      , a

▶ The architect described her ~~plan. An~~ exciting plan
   to renovate the old paper mill.

▶ Roosevelt was stricken with polio/~~Which~~ is caused
   by a virus.
      , which

▶ The coronation had to be postponed/~~Because~~ of
   the king's illness.
      because

NOTE: It is a myth that a sentence should never begin
with *because*. A word like *because* at the beginning of a
sentence does not always signal a fragment. The following sentence is perfectly grammatical, beginning with
a dependent clause and ending with an independent
clause.

   ▶ Because the film was too long and too
      confusing, the audience left.

2. Complete the fragment:

   ▶ Nature held many attractions for Thoreau.
      Especially, the solitude in the countryside.
            he valued

   ▶ Many people resolve to improve their health. ~~Is~~ wise
      for them to avoid sugary snacks.
                                    It is

18c **Fixing a fragment beginning with *and*,
but, or *or***

Two separate sentences need two separate subjects. In Standard Academic English, one subject is enough for a compound
predicate (two verbs after the subject in the same sentence),
but it cannot do the work of a subject across two sentences.

FRAGMENT

▶ After an hour, the dancers changed partners. And
   ——————— fragment: no subject (Who adapted?) ———————
   easily adapted from rock and roll to the tango.

POSSIBLE REVISIONS

▶ After an hour, the dancers changed partners and easily
   adapted from rock and roll to the tango.

▶ After an hour, the dancers changed partners. They
   easily adapted from rock and roll to the tango.

▶ After an hour, the dancers changed partners, adapting easily from rock and roll to the tango.

▶ After an hour, the dancers changed partners. And they adapted easily from rock and roll to the tango.

NOTE: Occasionally, writers choose to start a sentence with *and* or *but*, either to attain the stylistic effect of emphasis or contrast or to make a close connection to the previous sentence:

▶ You can have wealth concentrated in the hands of a few, or democracy. But you cannot have both.

—Justice Louis Brandeis

This usage is found often in journalism, but the culture of academia is more conservative, and some readers may frown when they see *and* or *but* starting a sentence, especially if it happens often. Personal preference comes into play here, so check with your instructor.

18d Intentional fragments

Fragments are used frequently in advertisements to keep the text short. In academic writing, writers sometimes use a fragment intentionally for emphasis, after a question, as an exclamation, or at a point of transition.

▶ Did Virginia know that Tom was writing frequently at this time to Leonard asking for advice? Probably.

—Hermione Lee, *Virginia Woolf*

▶ Dylan [Thomas] lived twenty-four years after he began to be a poet. Twenty-four years of poetry, dwindling rapidly in the last decade.

—Donald Hall, *Remembering Poets*

In college essays, use intentional fragments sparingly.

19 Fixing a Run-on or Comma Splice

19a Identifying run-on (or *fused*) sentences and comma splices

A run-on or fused sentence consists of two independent clauses punctuated as one sentence instead of two. Readers expect two independent clauses to be separated—and by more than a comma alone.

Run-on
error

$\overline{\qquad\qquad\text{independent clause}\qquad\qquad}$

Blue jeans were originally made as tough work

$\overline{\qquad}\ulcorner\ \overline{\text{independent clause}\qquad}$

clothes they became a fashion statement

$\overline{\text{in the 1970s.}}$

Inserting a comma between the two clauses is no help. That would be a comma splice error.

Comma
splice
error

Blue jeans were originally made as tough work clothes, they became a fashion statement in the 1970s.

19b **Five options for correcting run-on sentences and comma splices**

KEY POINTS
Editing a Run-on or Comma Splice

1. When the two clauses are quite long, simply separate them.

   ▶ **Blue jeans were originally made as tough work clothes.** *They* **became a fashion statement in the 1970s.**

   ▶ **Blue jeans were originally made as tough work clothes;** *they* **became a fashion statement in the 1970s.**

2. Include a comma, but make sure it is followed by *and, but, or, nor, so, for,* or *yet.*

   ▶ **Blue jeans were originally made as tough work clothes,** *but* **they became a fashion statement in the 1970s.**

3. If you are switching direction or want to stress the second clause, separate the clauses with a period or a semicolon, followed by a transitional expression such as *however* or *therefore,* followed by a comma.

   ▶ **Blue jeans were originally made as tough work clothes;** *however,* **they became a fashion statement in the 1970s.**

4. Rewrite the sentences as one sentence by using, for example, *because, although,* or *when* to make one

(continued)

(continued)

clause introduce or set up the clause containing the important point.

▶ *Although* blue jeans were originally made as tough work clothes, they became a fashion statement in the 1970s.

5. Condense or restructure the sentence.

▶ Blue jeans, *originally* made as tough work clothes, became a fashion statement in the 1970s.

20 Untangling Sentence Snarls

Sentences with structural inconsistencies give readers trouble. Learn how to untangle snarls so that readers do not have to pause to work out your meaning.

20a Tangles: Mixed constructions, faulty comparisons, and convoluted syntax

Mixed constructions A mixed construction is a sentence with parts that do not match grammatically. The sentence begins one way and then veers off in an unexpected direction. Check to ensure that the subject and verb in a sentence are clear and work together, and note that a phrase beginning with *by* can never be the subject of a sentence. Do not use a pronoun to restate the subject (see 20h).

The
▶ ~~In the~~ novel *The Great Gatsby* has never been easy to
^adapt for the movies.

Running
▶ ~~By running~~ for president can place an enormous strain
^on a family.

▶ The teacher ~~she~~ was only three years older than her students.

When you start a sentence with a dependent adverbial clause (beginning with a word like *when, if, because,* and *since*), make sure you follow that clause with an independent clause. A dependent adverbial clause cannot serve as the subject of a verb.

Swimming
▶ ~~Because she swims~~ every day does not guarantee she
^ is healthy.

Trading
▶ ~~When~~ a baseball player ~~is traded~~ often causes family
^ problems.

Faulty comparisons When you make comparisons, readers need to know clearly what you are comparing. See also 23a for faulty comparisons with personal pronouns.

Faulty comparison	**Like Wallace Stevens, her job strikes readers as unexpected for a poet.** [Her job is not like the poet Wallace Stevens; her job is like his job.]
Revised	**Like Wallace Stevens, she holds a job that strikes readers as unexpected for a poet.**

Convoluted syntax Revise sentences that ramble on to such an extent that they become tangled. Make sure they have clear subjects, verbs, and connections between clauses.

Tangled	**The way I feel about getting what you want is that when there is a particular position or item that you want to try to get to do your best and not give up because if you give up you have probably missed your chance of succeeding.**
Possible revision	**To get what you want, keep trying.**

20b Misplaced modifiers

A modifier is a word or words describing a noun, verb, or clause. A misplaced modifier is a word, phrase, or clause that is wrongly placed so that it appears to modify the incorrect word or words.

Place a phrase or a clause close to the word it modifies.

Misplaced	**Bezmozgis notes that it takes three days to pickle a batch of cabbage *in his essay*.**
Revised	***In his essay*, Bezmozgis notes that it takes three days to pickle a batch of cabbage.**
Misplaced	**She shared the $5,000 *with her sister* that she won in the lottery.**
Revised	**She shared *with her sister* the $5,000 that she won in the lottery.**

Take care with modifiers such as *only* and *not*. Place a word such as *only, even, just, nearly, not, merely*, or *simply* immediately before the word it modifies. The meaning of a sentence can change significantly as the position of a modifier changes, so careful placement is important.

> Next year, everyone in the company will ~~not~~ get
> ^not^
>
> a raise. [The unrevised sentence says that nobody at all will get a raise. If you move *not*, the sentence now says that although not all workers will get a raise, some will.]

> *Only* the journalist began to investigate the incident. [no one else]

> The journalist *only* began to investigate the incident. [but didn't finish]

> The journalist began to investigate *only* the incident. [nothing else]

What you need to know about splitting an infinitive When you place a word or phrase between *to* and the verb (the infinitive), the result can be awkward. Avoid splitting an infinitive when the split is unnecessary or clumsy, as in the following:

> They waited for the sun ~~to brightly shine~~.
> ^to shine brightly^

> We want ~~to honestly and in confidence inform~~ you of
> ^to inform^
>
> our plans /
> ^honestly and in confidence.^

Traditionally, a split infinitive was frowned upon, but it is now acceptable, as in the *Star Trek* motto, "To boldly go where no man has gone before."

Sometimes, splitting an infinitive is not only a matter of sound and style but may be necessary to avoid ambiguity.

> We had *to stop* them from talking quickly. [Were they talking too quickly? Did we have to stop them quickly? The meaning is ambiguous.]

> We had *to quickly stop* them from talking. [The split infinitive clearly says that we were the ones who had to do something quickly.]

20c Dangling modifiers

A modifier beginning with *-ing* or *-ed* that is not grammatically connected to the noun or phrase it is intended to describe is said to *dangle*.

Dangling *Driving* across the desert, the saguaro *cactus* appeared eerily human. [Who or what was driving? the cactus?]

Usually you can fix a dangling modifier by either (1) making the modifier refer to the person or thing performing the action or (2) rewriting the modifier as a dependent clause.

Possible *Driving* across the desert, *the naturalists*
revisions thought the saguaro cactus appeared eerily human.

When the naturalists were driving across the desert, the saguaro cactus appeared eerily human.

20d Shifts

Do not shift abruptly from statements to commands.

> Consumers need to be more aggressive. ~~Demand~~ refunds for defective merchandise. _{They should demand}

(They should demand)

Do not shift from an indirect to a direct quotation, with or without quotation marks.

> The client told us that he wanted to sign the lease and ~~would we~~ prepare the papers.

(asked us to)

Do not shift your point of view. Be consistent in using pronouns such as *we, you*, and *one*. Avoid using *you* to refer to people generally (see 23d).

> We all need a high salary to live in a city because ~~you~~ have to spend so much on rent and transportation.

(we)

20e Logical sequence after the subject

Do not use a subject and predicate (the verb and its modifiers in the rest of the clause) that do not make logical sense together. Such juxtapositions may be called "faulty predication."

Building
▶ ~~The decision to build~~ an elaborate extension onto the
 ^
 train station made all the trains arrive late. [It was
 not the decision that delayed the trains; building the
 extension did.]

▶ According to the guidelines, ~~people in~~ dilapidated
 public housing will be demolished this year. [Surely
 the housing, not people, will be demolished!]

20f Parallel structures

Parallel structures are words, phrases, or clauses that use
similar grammatical form. Balance your sentences by
using similar grammatical constructions in each part.

Not parallel	The results of reform were that class size decreased, more multicultural courses, and being allowed to choose a pass/fail option.
Parallel clauses after *that*	The results of reform were that class size decreased, more multicultural courses were offered, and students were allowed to choose a pass/fail option.
Parallel noun phrases	The results of reform were a decrease in class size, an increase in the number of multicultural courses, and the introduction of a pass/fail option for students.

Use parallel structures in comparisons with *as* or *than*
and in lists.

Driving
▶ ~~To drive~~ to Cuernavaca is as expensive as taking the bus.
 ^

To drive
▶ ~~Driving~~ to Cuernavaca is as expensive as to take the bus.
 ^

Finding
▶ ~~To find~~ a life partner is infinitely more complex than
 ^
 choosing a new pair of shoes.

▶ Writing well demands the following: (1) planning
 revising,
 your time, (2) paying attention to details, (3) ~~the need~~
 ~~for revision~~, and (4) proofreading.   ^

20g **Definitions and reasons: *is when* and *the reason is because***

When you write a definition of a term, use parallel structure on either side of the verb *be*. Avoid using *is when* or *is where* (or *was when, was where*).

▶ A tiebreaker in tennis *is ~~when there's~~* a final game to decide a set.

   In giving reasons in both speech and writing, the expression *the reason is because* is becoming common. However, many readers of formal prose traditionally prefer *the reason is that* or simply *because* by itself. Decide what your readers may expect, and consider your options.

that

▶ *The reason* I was upset *is ~~because~~* the instructor gave me a D in the course.

▶ ~~*The reason*~~ I was upset *~~is~~ because* the instructor gave me a D in the course.

20h **Necessary and unnecessary words**

Necessary words in compound structures If you omit a verb form from a compound verb, the remaining verb form must fit into each part of the compound structure; otherwise, you must use the complete verb form.

tried

▶ He has always and will always try to preserve his father's good name in the community. [*Try* fits only with *will*, not with *has*.]

Necessary words in comparisons

as

▶ The debate team captain is as competitive or even more competitive than her teammates.

   Sometimes you create ambiguity for your readers if you omit the verb in the second part of a comparison. See also 20a on confusing comparisons.

does.

▶ He likes the parrot better than his wife. [Omitting *does* implies that he likes the parrot more than he likes his wife.]

Unnecessary pronoun Do not insert a pronoun to restate the subject.

▶ **The businessmen who supported the candidate** ~~they~~
subject

verb
felt betrayed when he lost the election. [The stated subject is "The businessmen."]

subject   verb
▶ **What may seem funny to some** ~~it~~ **can be deadly serious to others.** [The subject is the clause "What may seem funny to some."]

21 Using Verbs Correctly

A verb expresses what the subject of the sentence is or does. Verbs may change form according to person, number, and tense; can be regular or irregular; and may require auxiliary verbs (forms of *be, do,* or *have*) or modal verbs (*will, would, can, could, shall, should, may, might,* and *must*) to complete their meaning (see 21b).

21a Verb forms in Standard Academic English

Regular verbs follow a predictable pattern. From the base form—that is, the dictionary form—you can construct all of the forms.

Regular Verbs

Base	-s	*-ing* Present Participle	Past Tense	Past Participle
paint	paints	painting	painted	painted
smile	smiles	smiling	smiled	smiled

Irregular verbs have the *-s* and the present participle (*-ing* forms) but do not use *-ed* to form the past tense and the past participle. The list below shows some irregular verbs that can cause problems. (For *be, do,* and *have,* see 21b; for *rise, lie,* and *sit,* see 21c.) However, there are many more verbs, so always use a dictionary to check irregular past tense and past participle forms if you are unsure, and refer to 21b and 21d to decide which form to use in tenses after auxiliary verbs (such as *has swam* versus *has swum*—the latter is correct).

Examples of Irregular Verbs

Base Form	Past Tense	Past Participle
begin	began	begun
blow	blew	blown
break	broke	broken
choose	chose	chosen
come	came	come
drink	drank	drunk
drive	drove	driven
fall	fell	fallen
fly	flew	flown
forget	forgot	forgotten
give	gave	given
go	went	gone
ride	rode	ridden
ring	rang	rung
run	ran	run
see	saw	seen
speak	spoke	spoken
take	took	taken
wear	wore	worn
write	wrote	written

NOTE: Verbs such as *bet, burst, cost, cut, hit, hurt, let, put, quit, set, slit, split, spread,* and *upset* do not change in their past or past participle form.

21b Auxiliary verbs and the forms that follow

The auxiliary verbs *be, do,* and *have* can be used alone as an auxiliary verb before a main verb or with other auxiliaries (such as in "You should *have been* thinking"). The auxiliary verbs that express a meaning other than time are called "modal auxiliaries": *will, would, can, could, shall, should, may, might,* and *must.* They do not change form and are always followed by a base form of the main verb or another auxiliary, as in "The gecko *can climb* on vertical surfaces."

The forms of *be*, *do*, and *have*

Base	Present Tense Forms	*-ing*	Past	Past Participle
do	do, does	doing	did	done
have	have, has	having	had	had
be	am, is, are	being	was, were	been

Language and dialect variation with *be* In some languages (Chinese and Russian, for example), forms of *be* used as an auxiliary ("She *is* singing") or as a linking verb ("He *is* happy") can be omitted. In some spoken dialects of English (African American Vernacular, for example), subtle linguistic distinctions that are not possible in Standard Academic English can be achieved: the omission of a form of *be* and the use of the base form in place of an inflected form (a form that shows number, person, mood, or tense) signal entirely different meanings.

Vernacular	Standard
He busy. (temporarily)	He is busy now.
She be busy. (habitually)	She is busy all the time.

Standard Academic English always requires the inclusion of a form of *be*.

▶ Latecomers ^{are} always at a disadvantage.

Correct forms after auxiliary verbs An independent clause needs a complete verb. Verb forms such as the *-ing* form and the past participle are not complete because they do not show tense. They need auxiliary verbs to complete their meaning as a verb of a clause. See the following table.

Verb Forms that Follow Auxiliaries

Auxiliary Verbs	Forms that Follow
do, does, did	+ base form of verb
Modals: *will, would, can, could, shall, should, may, might, must*	*did work* *would try*
has, have, had	+ past participle *had written* *has gone*

(continued)

(continued)

Auxiliary Verbs	Forms that Follow
A form of *be*	+ *-ing* (active)
Note: The *-ing* form alone can never be a complete verb. Always use a *be* auxiliary before an *-ing* verb form.	*is teaching* *were singing*
A form of *be*	+ past participle (passive) *are taught* *was sung* *has been stolen*

21c Verbs commonly confused

Give special attention to verbs that are similar in form but different in meaning. Transitive verbs can be followed by a direct object; intransitive verbs cannot.

1. *rise*: to get up; ascend (intransitive, irregular)
   raise: to lift; to cause to rise (transitive, regular)

Base	-s	-ing	Past Tense	Past Participle
rise	rises	rising	rose	risen
raise	raises	raising	raised	raised

   ▶ The sun *rose* at 5:55 a.m. today.

   ▶ The historian *raised* the issue of accuracy. [The direct object answers the question "raised what?"]

2. *sit:* to occupy a seat (intransitive, irregular)
   set: to put or place (transitive, irregular)

Base	-s	-ing	Past Tense	Past Participle
sit	sits	sitting	sat	sat
set	sets	setting	set	set

   ▶ The audience *sat* on hard wooden seats.

   ▶ The artist *set* his "Squashed Clock" sculpture in the middle of the shelf.

3. *lie:* to recline (intransitive)
   lay: to put or place (transitive)

lie	lies	lying	lay	lain
lay	lays	laying	laid	laid

▶ She ~~laid~~ **lay** down for an hour after her oral presentation.

▶ She was ~~laying~~ **lying** down when you called.

▶ ~~Lie~~ **Lay** the map on the floor.

In addition, note the verb *lie* ("to say something untrue"), which is intransitive and regular.

| lie | lies | lying | lied | lied |

▶ He *lied* when he said he had won three trophies.

21d Verb tenses

Verbs indicate time, called "tense." Verbs change form to indicate present or past time, and auxiliary verbs (*be, do,* and *have*) are used with the main verb to convey aspects of those two versions of time: completed actions (perfect tense forms), actions in progress (progressive tense forms), and actions that are completed by some specified time or event and that emphasize the length of time in progress (perfect progressive tense forms).

Simple present Use the simple present tense for the following purposes:

1. to make a generalization

   ▶ Gardening *nourishes* the spirit.

2. to indicate a permanent or habitual activity

   ▶ The poet *uses* rhyme and meter in an innovative way.

   ▶ The directors *distribute* a financial report every six months.

3. to express future time in dependent clauses (clauses beginning with words such as *if, when, before, after, until, as soon as*) when *will* is used in the independent clause

   ▶ When the newt colony *dies* in the cold weather, building construction will begin.

4. to discuss literature and the arts (called the *literary present*) even if the work was written in the past or the author is no longer alive

   ▶ In *The Wealth of Nations,* Adam Smith *argues* that increased productivity is the sole source of a country's wealth.

However, when you write a narrative of your own, use the past tense to tell about past actions.

                    walked   kissed

▶ Then the candidate ~~walks~~ up to the crowd and ~~kisses~~ all the babies.

See citation style guidelines in Part 4 for possible variations.

Present progressive   Use the present progressive to indicate an action in progress at the moment of speaking or writing

▶ Publishers and writers *are getting* nervous about copyright issues.

However, do not use the progressive form with intransitive verbs such as *believe, know, like, prefer, want, smell, own, seem, appear,* and *contain.*

               believe

▶ Many people ~~are believing~~ that there may be life on other planets.

Present perfect and present perfect progressive   Use the present perfect (*has* or *have,* followed by a past participle) in the following instances:

1. to indicate that an action occurring at some unstated time in the past is related to present time

   ▶ They *have exhibited* here before, so they know the rules.

2. to indicate that an action beginning in the past continues to the present

   ▶ She *has played* basketball for three years.

   However, if you state the exact time when something occurred, use the simple past tense, not the present perfect.

   ▶ They ~~have~~ worked in Arizona four years ago.

3. to report research results in APA style

   ▶ Feynmann *has shown* that science can be fun.

   Use the present perfect progressive when you indicate the length of time that an action is in progress up to the present time.

▶ Researchers *have been searching* for a cure for arthritis for many years. [This sentence implies that they are still searching.]

Simple past   Use the simple past tense when you refer to an event in the past or when you illustrate a general principle with a specific incident in the past.

▶ World War I soldiers *suffered* in the trenches.

▶ Some bilingual schools offer intensive instruction in English. My sister *went* to a bilingual school where she *studied* English for two hours every day.

When the sequence of past events is indicated with words like *before* or *after,* use the simple past for both events.

▶ She *knew* how to write her name before she *went* to school.

Use the past tense in an indirect quotation (a reported quotation, not in quotation marks) that is introduced by a past tense verb.

▶ His chiropractor *told* him that the adjustments *were* over.

Past progressive Use the past progressive for an activity in progress over time or at a specified point in the past.

▶ Abraham Lincoln *was attending* the theater when he was assassinated.

▶ The Patriots *were winning* in the final quarter when Eli Manning threw for a touchdown for the New York Giants. [An event in progress—winning—was interrupted.]

Past perfect and past perfect progressive Use the past perfect or past perfect progressive when one past event was completed before another past event or stated past time.

▶ My sister announced that she *had joined* the Peace Corps. [She joined before she announced.]

▶ Ben *had cooked* the whole meal by the time Sam arrived. [Two events occurred: Ben cooked the meal; then Sam arrived.]

21e *-ed* forms (past tense and past participle)

With regular verbs, both the past tense form and the past participle form end in *-ed*. This ending can cause writers trouble, because in speech the ending is often dropped, particularly when it blends into the next sound. Standard Academic English requires the *-ed* ending in the following instances:

1. to form the past tense of a regular verb

▶ Her assistant ask_{ed} to take on more responsibility.

Pay attention to the verb used to express a past habit.

▶ George Clooney use_d to play a handsome doctor on *ER.*

2. to form the past participle of a regular verb for use with the auxiliary *has, have,* or *had* in the active voice or with

forms of be (*am, is, are, was, were, be, being, been*) in the passive voice (see 21g)

▶ She has work^ed^ for the city for a long time. [Active]

▶ The proposal will be finish^ed^ tomorrow. [Passive]

3. to form a past participle that is used as an adjective

▶ The nurses rushed to help the injure^d^ toddler.

▶ I was surprise^d^ to read how many awards he had won.

NOTE: The following -*ed* forms are used after forms of *be* or *get*: concerned, confused, depressed, divorced, embarrassed, married, prejudiced, satisfied, scared, supposed (to), surprised, used (to), worried. See also 21b.

▶ Americans are often confuse^d^ when they are driving around a rotary in England.

▶ They were suppose^d^ to call their parents.

Do not confuse the past tense and past participle forms of irregular verbs (21a). A past tense form occurs alone as a complete verb, and a past participle form must be used with a *have* or *be* auxiliary.

▶ He ~~drunk~~ **drank** the liquid before his medical tests.

▶ She ~~done~~ **did** her best to learn how to count in Japanese.

▶ The explorers could have ~~went~~ **gone** alone.

▶ A chime is ~~rang~~ **rung** to conclude the yoga session.

21f **Verbs in conditional sentences, wishes, requests, demands, and recommendations**

Conditional sentences When *if* or *unless* is used to introduce a dependent clause, the sentence expresses a condition. There are four types of conditional sentences; two refer to facts or possible predictions, and two refer to speculation and hypothetical situations.

KEY POINTS
Verb Tenses in Conditional Sentences

Meaning Expressed	*If* Clause	Independent Clause
1. Fact	Simple present	Simple present

▶ If mortgage rates *go* down, home sales *increase*.

2. Prediction/possibility	Simple present	*will, can, should, might* + base form

▶ If you *turn* left here, you *will reach* Mississippi.

▶ If I *were* you, I'd quit that job.
[But I'm not you.]

▶ If I *were* you, I'd ask the dean for a recommendation. [But I'm not you.]

3. Speculation about present or future	Simple past or *were* even with a singular subject (subjunctive; see page 188, below)	*would, could, should, might* + base form

▶ If he *had* an iPhone, he *would use* it all day long.
[But he does not have one.]

4. Speculation about the past	Past perfect (*had* + past participle)	*would have* *could have* *should have* *might have* } + past participle

▶ If they *had saved* the diaries, they *could have sold* them. [But they did not save them.]

Would in the *if* clause Do not use *would* in the conditional clause. However, you will hear *would* used frequently in the conditional clause in speech.

showed
▶ If the fish fry committee ~~would show~~ more initiative, more people might attend the events.

had
▶ If the speaker ~~would have~~ heard their criticisms, she would have been angry.

Wishes, requests, demands, and recommendations For a present wish—about something that has not happened and is therefore hypothetical and imaginary—use the past tense or *were* (see *subjunctive*, below) in place of *was* in the dependent clause. For a wish about the past, use the past perfect: *had* + past participle.

A WISH ABOUT THE PRESENT

▶ I wish I *had* your attitude.

▶ I wish that Shakespeare *were* still alive.

A WISH ABOUT THE PAST

▶ We all wish that the strike *had* never *happened.*

The subjunctive mood Verbs in the subjunctive mood (forms expressing conditions, wishes, and requests, not yet realized) use the base form of the verb (*try, go,* and so on) or the verb form *were* (not *was*), regardless of the person and number of the subject. The form *were* appears after *if* in speculations about the present or future or after a wish about the present, as shown in the examples above. In writing, verbs that look forward to a future action, such as *request, command, insist, demand, move* (meaning "propose"), *propose,* and *urge,* are followed by the subjunctive mood:

▶ The dean suggested that students *be* allowed to vote.

▶ He insisted that she *hand in* the report.

21g Active and passive voices

In the active voice, the grammatical subject is the doer of the action, and the sentence gives a straightforward display of "who is doing what." The passive voice tells what *is done to* the subject of the sentence. The person or thing doing the action may or may not be mentioned but is always implied: "My car was repaired" (by somebody at the garage).

ACTIVE

▶ Alice Walker wrote *The Color Purple.*

— subject — active voice verb (simple past) — direct object —

PASSIVE

▶ *The Color Purple* was written by Alice Walker.

— subject — passive voice verb (simple past) — doer or agent —

To form the passive voice, use an appropriate tense of the verb *be,* followed by a past participle. Do not overuse the passive voice. A general rule is to use the passive voice only when the doer in your sentence is unknown or unimportant or when you want to keep subjects consistent (see 14a).

▶ The pandas are rare. Two of them *will be returned* to the wild.

In scientific writing, the passive voice indicates objective experimental procedures: *The experiment* was conducted *in a computer lab.*

NOTE: Use the passive voice *only* with verbs that are transitive in English. Intransitive verbs such as *happen, occur,* and *try (to)* are not used in the passive voice.

▶ The ceremony ~~was~~ happened yesterday.

22 Making Subjects and Verbs Agree

22a Basic principles

The principle of agreement means that when you use the present tense, you must make the subject and verb agree in person (first, second, or third) and number (singular or plural). The ending *-s* can be added to both nouns and verbs but in very different contexts. The forms of *be* (see 21b) also change to agree with the subject: *am, is, are, was* or *were.*

KEY POINTS
Two Key Points about Agreement

1. Follow the *one -s rule* in the present tense. Generally, you can put an *-s* on a noun to make it plural, or you can put an *-s* on the verb to make it singular (note the irregular forms *is* and *has*). An *-s* on both subject and verb is not Standard Academic English.

No	The articles explains the controversy.
Possible revisions	The article explains the controversy. [one article]
	The articles explain the controversy. [more than one]

2. Do not omit a necessary *-s.*

   ▶ Whitehead's novel deal with issues of race and morality.
   (s)

   ▶ The report in the files describe the housing project in detail.
   (s)

22b **Words between the subject and verb**

When words separate the subject and the verb, find the verb and ask "Who?" or "What?" about it to determine exactly what the subject is. Ignore any intervening words.

▶ Her *collection* of baseball cards *is* increasing in value. [What is increasing in value? The subject, *collection*, is singular.]

▶ The government's *proposals* about preserving the environment *cause* controversy. [What things cause controversy? The subject, *proposals*, is plural.]

Do not be confused by intervening words ending in -*s,* such as *always* and *sometimes.* The -*s* ending still must appear on a present tense verb if the subject is singular.

▶ A school play always get the parents involved.
                          ^s

Phrases introduced by *as well as, along with, together with,* and *in addition to* that come between the subject and the verb do not determine the number of the verb.

▶ His daughter, as well as his two sons, want him to move nearby.
                                        ^s

22c **What to do when the subject follows the verb**

When the subject comes after the verb in the sentence, you must still make the subject and the verb agree.

1. **Questions** In a question, make the auxiliary verb agree with the subject, which follows the verb.

    ▶ *Does* the editor agree to the changes?

    ▶ *Do* the editor and the production manager [plural subject] agree to the changes?

2. **Initial *here* or *there*** When a sentence begins with *here* or *there*, make the verb agree with the subject, which follows the verb.

    ▶ There *is* a reason to rejoice.

    ▶ There *are* many reasons to rejoice.

    NOTE: The word *it* does not follow the same pattern as *here* and *there*. In sentences beginning with *it* (as the subject), always use a singular verb.

    ▶ It *is* hundreds of miles away.

3. **Inverted order**   Some sentences will begin not with the subject but with a phrase preceding the verb. (A phrase is a group of words with no subject or verb.) Make sure the verb still agrees with the subject, which follows it.

▶ In front of the library sit two stone lions.

(phrase — In front of the library; plural verb — sit; plural subject — two stone lions)

22d A list of eight tricky subjects with singular verbs

1. *Each* and *every*   *Each* and *every* may seem to indicate more than one, but grammatically they are singular words. Use them with a singular verb even if they are part of a compound subject (see 22f) using *and* or *or*.

   ▶ *Every change* in procedures *causes* problems.

   ▶ *Each* of the poems *employs* a different rhyme scheme.

   ▶ *Every* essay and quiz *counts* in the grade.

2. *-ing* subjects   With a subject noun formed from an *-ing* verb (called a *gerund*), always use a singular verb form.

   ▶ *Speaking* in public *causes* many people as much fear as death.

3. **Singular nouns ending in** *-s*   Some names of disciplines that end in *-s* (such as *economics, physics, politics, mathematics,* and *statistics*) are not plural. Use them and the noun *news* with a singular verb.

   ▶ Politics *is* dirty business.

4. **Phrases of time, money, and weight**   When the subject is regarded as one unit, use a singular verb.

   ▶ Five hundred dollars *seems* too much to pay.

5. **Uncountable nouns**   An uncountable noun (such as *furniture, money, equipment, food, advice, happiness, honesty, information,* and *knowledge*) encompasses all the items in its class. An uncountable noun does not have a plural form and is always followed by a singular verb (see also 34a).

   ▶ The information found in the newspapers *is* not always accurate.

6. **One of**   *One of* is followed by a plural noun and a singular verb form.

   ▶ *One* of the results *has* special significance.

7. **The number of**   The phrase "the number of" is followed by a plural noun (the object of the preposition *of*) and a singular verb form.

   ▶ The number of reasons *is* growing.

   However, with *a number of,* meaning "several," use a plural verb.

   ▶ A number of reasons *are* listed in the letter.

8. **The title of a work or a word referred to as the word itself**   Use a singular verb with a title of a long work or a word referred to as the word.

   ▶ *Cats was* based on a poem by T. S. Eliot.

   ▶ In her story, the word *dudes appears* five times.

22e   Agreement with a collective noun (*government, family,* and so on) as subject

A collective noun names a collection of people or things: *class, government, family, jury, committee, group, couple,* or *team.* If you refer to the group as a whole, use a singular verb.

▶ The family *returns* to Mexico every other year.

Use a plural verb if you wish to emphasize differences among the individuals or if members of the group are thought of as individuals.

▶ The jury *are* from every walk of life.

If that seems awkward to you, revise the sentence.

▶ The members of the jury *are* from every walk of life.

However, with the collective nouns *police, poor, elderly,* and *young,* always use plural verbs.

▶ The elderly *deserve* our respect.

22f   Subjects containing *and, or,* or *nor* (compound subjects)

A compound subject has two or more noun or pronoun parts. Always edit carefully to determine agreement with the verb.

With *and* When a subject has two or more parts joined by *and*, treat the subject as plural and use a plural verb form.

▶ His daughter and his son *want* him to move to Florida.

However, if the two joined parts refer to a single person or thing, use a singular verb.

▶ The restaurant's chef and owner *makes* good fajitas.

In addition, use a singular verb with a compound subject beginning with *each* or *every*.

▶ Every claim and conclusion *deserves* consideration.

With *or* or *nor* With compound subjects joined by *or* or *nor*, make the verb agree with the part of the subject nearer to it.

▶ Her sister or her *parents look* after her children every weekday.

▶ Neither her parents nor her *sister intends* to vote in the next election.

22g **Agreement with subjects such as *anyone, everybody, nobody* (indefinite pronouns)**

An indefinite pronoun, such as *anybody* or *something*, refers to a nonspecific person or object. Use a singular verb with an indefinite pronoun subject:

somance, somebody, something

anyone, anybody, anything

no one, nobody, nothing

everyone, everybody, everything

each, either, neither

▶ Nobody *knows* the answer.

▶ Everyone *agrees* on the filmmaker's motives.

▶ Both films are popular; neither *contains* gratuitous violence.

▶ Each of the chess games *promises* to be exciting.

22h **Agreement with words expressing quantity (*much, many, a few*, and so on)**

Words expressing quantity can be used alone or to modify a noun. Some are singular; some are plural; others can be used to indicate either singular or plural, depending on the noun they refer to.

Agreement with Quantity Words

With Singular Nouns and Verbs	With Plural Nouns and Verbs
much	many
(a) little	(a) few
a great deal (of)	several
a large amount (of)	a large number (of)
less	fewer
another	both

▶ Much *has* been accomplished.

▶ Much progress still *needs* to be made.

▶ Many *have* suffered in the recent economic decline.

▶ Fewer electronic gadgets *are* sold during a recession.

The following words that express quantity can be used with both singular and plural nouns and verbs: *all, any, half (of), more, most, neither, no, none, other, part (of), some.*

▶ You gave me *some* information. *More* is necessary.

▶ You gave me *some* facts. *More* are needed.

22i Agreement with *who, which,* or *that* in a relative clause

A dependent clause that begins with *who, which* or *that* is known as a relative clause; it relates to a noun or pronoun—its antecedent—in another clause. To determine whether to use a singular or plural verb in a relative clause, ask whether the word that *who, which,* or *that* refers to (its antecedent) is singular or plural.

▶ The book that *has* been at the top of the bestseller list for weeks gives advice about health. [*Book* is the antecedent of *that.*]

▶ The books that *have* been near the top of the bestseller list for a few weeks give advice about making money. [*Books* is the antecedent of that.]

For more on relative clauses and pronouns, see 23e.

23 Using Pronouns

A pronoun is a word that substitutes for a noun, a noun phrase, or another pronoun.

23a Which personal pronoun to use (*I* or *me, he* or *him, her* or *hers*?)

Personal pronouns change form to indicate person (first, second, or third) or number (singular or plural), and function in a clause as subject, object, or possessive (known as *case*). Use only the forms shown in the following Key Points box. Forms such as *himself, theirself,* and *they* used as a possessive are nonstandard.

KEY POINTS
Forms of Personal Pronouns

Person	Subject	Object	Possessive (+ Noun)	Possessive (Stands Alone)	Intensive and Reflexive
First person singular	I	me	my	mine	myself
Second person singular and plural	you	you	your	yours	yourself/ yourselves
Third person singular	he she it	him her it	his her its	his hers its (rare)	himself herself itself
First person plural	we	us	our	ours	ourselves
Third person plural	they	them	their	theirs	themselves

In a compound subject or object with *and*, mentally use the "Drop the *and*" test to decide which pronoun to use (*I* or *me, he* or *him*, for example).

▶ Jenny and ~~me~~ **I** volunteer in a soup kitchen. [Drop the words *Jenny and*. Then you will have *I volunteer*, not *me volunteer*. Here you need the subject form, *I*.]

▶ The librarian asked my brother and ~~I~~ **me** to show an ID. [If you drop the words *my brother and*, you will have *The librarian asked me to show an ID*. You need the object form, *me*. The form *myself* is used to refer to the subject: *I criticized myself*.]

▶ ~~Her~~ **She** and ~~me~~ **I** tried to solve the problem. [She tried. I tried.]

After a preposition, a word used before a noun or pronoun (such as *in, on, for, between, among*), always use an object form (*me, her, him, us, them*).

▶ Between you and ~~I,~~ **me,** the company is in serious trouble.

After a verb used with an infinitive (the dictionary form of the verb, preceded by the word *to*), use an object pronoun. When a sentence has only one object, this principle is easy to apply.

▶ The dean wanted *him* to lead the procession.

Difficulties occur with compound objects.

▶ The dean wanted ~~he and I~~ **him and me** to lead the procession. [The dean wanted *him* to lead. The dean wanted *me* to lead.]

In an appositive phrase including a pronoun and the word *and*, use the "Drop the *and*" test to determine whether the pronoun functions as a subject or an object. (An appositive phrase occurs next to and gives specific information about a noun.)

▶ The supervisor praised only two employees, Ramon and ~~I.~~ **me.** [She praised me.]

▶ Only two employees, Ramon and ~~me,~~ **I,** received a bonus. [I received a bonus.]

We or *us* before a noun? Decide whether the noun is the subject of the verb (*we*) or the direct object of a verb or preposition (*us*).

▶ ~~Us~~ **We** fans have decided to form a club.

▶ The singer waved to ~~we~~ **us** fans.

In comparisons with *than* and *as*, decide on the subject or object form of the pronoun by mentally completing the comparison.

▶ She is certainly not more intelligent than I. [. . . than I am.]

▶ Jack and Sally work together; Jack sees his boss more than she. [. . . more than she does.]

▶ Jack and Sally work together; Jack sees his boss more than her. [. . . more than he sees Sally.]

Before an *-ing* form (a form used as a noun, called a *gerund*), use a possessive.

▶ *Their* winning the marathon surprised us all.

▶ We appreciate *your* participating in the auction.

Sometimes, though, the pronoun itself rather than the noun *-ing* form is the direct object; in such a case, use the direct object form of the pronoun along with the present participle form (*-ing*).

▶ We saw *them* giving the runners foil wraps.

With possessive pronouns, use no apostrophe. Even though possessive in meaning, the pronouns *yours, ours, theirs, his,* and *hers* are never used with an apostrophe. For the distinction between *its* and *it's,* see 27d.

▶ Those conclusions were *ours*, too.

▶ That essay is *hers*.

Do not use the word *mines*. It is nonstandard.

▶ This hat is *mine*.

23b Making a pronoun refer to a specific antecedent

The noun, noun phrase, or pronoun that a pronoun refers to is known as its *antecedent*.

▶ Because the Canadian skater practiced daily, *she* won the championship. [The pronoun reference is clear: the antecedent of *she* is *skater*.]

State a specific antecedent. Avoid using a pronoun such as *they, this,* or *it* without an explicit antecedent.

No specific antecedent When Karen submitted her article, *they* told her they would publish it next week.

In the preface, *it* states that the author lives in Kenya.

Revisions When Karen gave her article to the newspaper editor, *he* told her he would publish it the following week.

The preface states that the author lives in Kenya.

Do not make a pronoun refer to a possessive noun or to a noun within a prepositional phrase.

George Orwell
▶ In ~~George Orwell's~~ "Shooting an Elephant," ~~he~~ reports an incident that shows the evil effects of imperialism.

Avoid an ambiguous reference. Your readers should never be left wondering which *this, they,* or *it* is being discussed.

Ambiguous reference He faced having to decide whether to move to California. This was not what he wanted to do. [We do not know what *this* refers to: having to decide? moving to California?]

Revision He faced having to decide whether to move to California. This decision was not one he wanted to make.

23c Making a pronoun agree with its antecedent

A plural antecedent needs a plural pronoun; a singular antecedent needs a singular pronoun.

▶ Listeners heard *they* could win free tickets. The ninth caller learned *she* was the winner.

NOTE: Demonstrative pronouns *this* and *that* are singular. *These* and *those* are the plural forms.

A generalized (generic) antecedent Generic nouns describe a class or type of person or object, such as a *student* meaning "all students." In academic writing, do not use *they* to refer to a singular generic noun, though this often occurs in speech, and make sure that you use *he* and *she* without gender bias (see 16c).

Faulty agreement	When *a student* writes well, *they* can go far in the business world.
Possible revision	When *a student* writes well, *he or she* can go far in the business world.
Better revision	When *students* write well, *they* can go far in the business world.
	Students who write well can go far in the business world.

Often, a plural noun is preferable because it avoids clumsy repetition of *he or she*.

▶ We should judge a person by who he or she is, not by the color of his or her skin.

*(edits: a person → **people**; he or she is, → **they are,**; his or her → **their**)*

A collective noun Refer to a collective noun such as *class, family, jury, committee, couple,* or *team* with a singular pronoun.

▶ The jury has not yet completed *its* task.

However, when the members of the group named by the collective noun are considered to be acting individually, use a plural pronoun.

▶ The jury began to cast *their* preliminary votes.

An indefinite pronoun Indefinite pronouns such as *one, each, either, neither, everyone, everybody, someone, somebody, something, anyone, anybody, anything, no one, nobody,* and *nothing* are generally singular in form (22g). A singular antecedent needs a singular pronoun to refer to it. For many years, the prescribed form in Standard Academic English was *he,* as in sentences such as *Everyone needs his privacy* or *Each person needs his privacy.* Now, however, such usage is regarded as biased; the alternative *he or she* is clumsy; and *they,* while used often in informal writing, is regarded by many as inaccurate. Use a plural noun and pronoun instead.

| Gender bias | *Everyone* picked up *his* marbles and went home. |
| Clumsy | *Everyone* picked up *his or her* marbles and went home. |

Informal usage	*Everyone* picked up *their* marbles and went home.
Revised	*The children* picked up *their marbles and went home.*

See 16c for more on gender bias with pronouns.

23d Appropriate use of *you*

In writing, do not use *you* to refer to "people" generally. Use *you* only to address the reader directly, as in "If you turn to the table on page 10, you will find. . . ."

▶ While growing up, ~~you~~ have arguments with
   teenagers

   ~~your~~ parents.
   their

23e Relative pronouns in relative clauses: *who, whom, which, that*

When to use *who, whom, which,* or *that* in a relative clause Use *who* (or *whom*) to refer to human beings; use *which* or *that* to refer to animals, objects, or concepts. Never use *what* as a relative pronoun.

▶ The teacher ~~which~~ taught me algebra was strict.
   who

See 22i for agreement with a verb in a relative clause.

When to use *who* or *whom, whoever* or *whomever* *Whom* is an object pronoun. You will often hear and read *who* in its place, but many readers prefer the standard form.

▶ *Whom* [informal *who*] were they describing?

Whom used as a relative pronoun can often be omitted.

▶ The players [*whom*] the team honored invited everyone to the party.

Never use *whom* in place of *who* in the subject position.

▶ They want to know ~~whom~~ we think *is in charge.*
   who

   [*Who* is the subject of *is.*]

▶ The manager will hire ~~whomever~~ *is qualified.*
   whoever

When to use *which/who/whom* or *that* Use *that* rather than *which, who,* or *whom* in a restrictive clause, one that provides necessary information (see 26c for more examples). When *that* is the object of its clause, you can omit it.

▶ **The book [*that*] you gave me is fascinating.** [*that you gave* me provides necessary information to identify which book is fascinating.]

Use *which/who/whom* when you provide additional information in a nonrestrictive clause, one that does not restrict the meaning of the subject in any way and is not essential to understanding the meaning. You will need to use *which, who,* or *whom* after proper nouns and nouns naming a specific person or thing.

▶ ***War and Peace, which* I read in college, is fascinating.** [*which I read in college* provides extra, not necessary, information. It does not restrict the meaning of *War and Peace.*]

▶ **The mayor's *deputy, who* represented him at the conference, gave a rousing speech.** [If you read *The mayor's deputy gave a rousing speech* you would not ask "Which deputy?" The relative clause provides information that is nonessential to the understanding of the sentence.]

See 25c for more on the punctuation of *who/whom/which* or *that* clauses.

24 Using Adjectives and Adverbs

Adjectives describe, or modify, nouns or pronouns. Do not add *-s* or change their form to reflect number or gender. Adverbs modify verbs, adjectives, and other adverbs, as well as whole clauses.

Adjective Mr. Lee tried three *different* approaches.

Adverb His new assistant settled down *comfortably*.

24a Forms of adjectives and adverbs

Check your dictionary for information on adjective and adverb forms that are not covered here.

Adverb: adjective + -ly Many adverbs are formed by adding *-ly* to an adjective: *intelligent/intelligently*. Sometimes when *-ly* is added, a spelling change occurs: *easy/easily*.

Adjectives ending in -ic To form an adverb from an adjective ending in *-ic,* add *-ally* (*basic, basically; artistic, artistically*), with the exception of *public,* whose adverb form is *publicly.*

Irregular adverb forms Several adjectives do not add *-ly* to form an adverb:

Adjective	Adverb
good	well
fast	fast
hard	hard

▶ He is a *good* cook.

▶ He cooks *well*.

NOTE: *Well* can also function as an adjective, meaning "healthy" or "satisfactory."

▶ A *well* baby smiles often.

▶ She feels *well* today.

24b When to use adjectives and adverbs

In speech, adjectives (particularly *good, bad,* and *real*) are often used to modify verbs, adjectives, or adverbs. This is nonstandard usage.

▶ She plays chess ~~bad.~~ badly.

▶ I sing ~~real good.~~ really well.

After verbs known as linking verbs—*be, seem, appear,* and *become*—use an adjective (known as a complement): She seems *pleasant.*

Certain verbs, such as *appear, look, feel, smell,* and *taste,* are sometimes followed by an adjective or an adverb. If the modifier tells about the subject of the clause, use an adjective. If the modifier tells about the action of the verb, not the subject, use an adverb.

| Adjective | She looks *confident* in her new job. |
| Adverb | She looks *confidently* at all her fellow employees. |

| Adjective | The steak smells *bad*. |
| Adverb | The chef smelled the lobster *appreciatively*. |

24c Hyphenated (compound) adjectives

A compound adjective needs hyphens to connect its parts. Note the form when a compound adjective is used: a hyphen, no noun plural ending, and an *-ed* ending where necessary (see 32b).

▶ They have a *five-year-old* daughter. [Their daughter is five years old.]

▶ He is a *left-handed* pitcher. [He pitches with his left hand.]

Many compound adjectives use the *-ed* form: *flat-footed, barrel-chested, broad-shouldered, old-fashioned, well-dressed, left-handed.*

24d Double negatives

Although some languages and dialects allow more than one negative to emphasize an idea, Standard Academic English uses only one negative in a clause. "I didn't say nothing" contains a double negative and is an error for "I didn't say anything." Note that words like *hardly, scarcely,* and *barely* are also considered negatives.

Double negative	We *don't* have *no* excuses.
Revised	We *don't* have *any* excuses.
	We have *no* excuses.

| Double negative | City residents *can't hardly* afford the sales tax. |
| Revised | City residents *can hardly* afford the sales tax. |

24e Comparative and superlative forms

Adjectives and adverbs have *comparative* and *superlative* forms that are used for comparisons. Use the comparative form when comparing two items, people, places, or ideas; use the superlative form when comparing more than two.

Short Adjectives

	Comparative (Comparing Two)	Superlative (Comparing More than Two)
short	shorter	shortest
pretty	prettier	prettiest
simple	simpler	simplest
fast	faster	fastest

Long Adjectives and -ly Adverbs

	Comparative	Superlative
intelligent	more intelligent	most intelligent
carefully	more carefully	most carefully

If you cannot decide whether to use an -er/-est form or *more/most,* consult a college dictionary. If there is an -er/-est form, the dictionary will say so.

NOTE: Do not use the -er form with *more* or the -est form with *most.*

▶ The first poem was ~~more~~ better than the second.

▶ Boris is the ~~most~~ fittest person I know.

Irregular Forms

	Comparative	Superlative
good	better	best
bad	worse	worst
much/many	more	most
well	better	best
badly	worse	worst

For more on not omitting necessary words in comparisons and on which pronouns to use in comparisons with *than* and *as,* see 20h and 23a, respectively.

PART SEVEN

Punctuation and Mechanics

EDIT	
PURPOSE	**AUDIENCE**
Failing to punctuate your sentences according to the conventions of Standard American English can work against your purpose in writing. • Are there common trouble spots that you should double-check in editing?	Punctuation creates signals for your audience. • Where in your writing are your points likely to be difficult to follow? Have you made the best use of punctuation to help your readers follow your points in those areas?
VOICE	**MEDIUM**
Overuse of some types of punctuation can have unintended effects on a writer's voice. • Are there paragraphs in which you have used many exclamation points, parenthetical phrases, or dashes, for instance? What effects do those marks create?	Some rules of punctuation and formatting vary according to the medium in which you are writing, especially if you are writing in a medium that does not give you access to italics, underlining, and other formatting features. • How can you show emphasis or indicate underlining and italics in a plain-text medium?

25 How Punctuation Shows Readers Your Intentions

Why do punctuation and mechanics matter? They matter because they chunk words into meaningful groups for readers and make proper nouns stand out. Try reading the following without the benefit of the signals that a reader usually expects.

When active viruses especially those transmitted by contact can spread easily within the world health organization hard working doctors are continually collaborating to find treatments for several infectious diseases sars avian flu and hepatitis.

Conventional punctuation and mechanics clarify the meaning:

When active, viruses—especially those transmitted by contact—can spread easily; within the World Health Organization, hard-working doctors are continually collaborating to find treatments for several infectious diseases: Ebola, avian flu, and hepatitis.

Punctuation: Signals for Your Readers

What Do You Want to Do?	Options
To end a sentence:	
To indicate the end of a sentence	Period, question mark, or exclamation point (. ? !) 29a
To make a close connection to the next sentence	Semicolon (;) 29b
To separate:	
To separate independent clauses only when a connecting word (*and, but, or, nor, so, for,* or *yet*) is used	Comma (,) 26a, item 1
To separate an introductory word(s), a phrase, or a clause from an independent clause	Comma (,) 26a, item 2
To separate coordinate adjectives (where *and* can be used)	Comma (,) 26a, item 6

To separate items in a list that contains internal commas (*x, x; y, y;* and *z*)	Semicolon (;) 29b
To separate a verb from a quoted statement that follows or precedes it	Comma (,) 26a, item 7
To separate lines of poetry written as running text	Slash (/) 29d
To insert:	
To insert a word, words, or a phrase or clause containing "extra information"	Commas (, ,) 26c, item 3
To give more emphasis to the insert	Dashes (—) 29d
To insert a change within a quotation	Square brackets [ ] 29d
To insert explanatory information	Parentheses ( ) 29d
To delete:	
To indicate material deleted from a quotation	Ellipsis dots (. . .) 29e
To anticipate:	
To indicate an explanation or a list that follows an independent clause	Colon (:) 29c
To quote:	
To quote exact words or to give the title of a story, a poem, or an article	Quotation marks (" ") 28a
To enclose a quotation within another quotation	Single quotation marks (' ') 28c
To indicate possession:	
For most words	Apostrophe + -*s*('*s*) 27a
For nouns forming the plural with -*s*	Apostrophe after the *s* (*s*') 27a, 27b

26 Commas

A comma separates parts of a sentence; it does not separate one sentence from another.

26a Comma: Yes

Use the following guidelines, but note that variations can occur. Blue shading = note the comma

---

KEY POINTS
Comma: Yes

1. between two independent clauses connected by a coordinating conjunction: *and, but, or, nor, so, for,* or *yet*

   ▶ The talks failed, but the union leaders held their ground.

   A comma is optional if the clauses are short.

   ▶ He offered to help and he did.

2. after most introductory words, phrases, or clauses

   ▶ While the guests were eating, a mouse ran across the floor. [Omitting the comma here can lead to a misreading.]

3. to set off extra (nonrestrictive) information included in a sentence ("extra commas with extra information"—see 26c)

   ▶ My friend, a realtor, works on weekends.

4. to set off a transitional expression such as *however, therefore, for example,* and *in fact*

   ▶ The ending of the film, however, is disappointing. In fact, it is totally predictable.

5. to separate three or more items in a series

   ▶ The robot vacuums, makes toast, and plays chess.

6. between adjectives that can be reversed and connected with *and* (coordinate adjectives)

   ▶ When people move, they often discard their worn, dilapidated furniture.

7. before or after a quotation

   ▶ "I intend to win the marathon," she announced. He replied, "So do I."

26b Comma: No

(= no comma here)

🔑 KEY POINTS
Comma: No

1. not between subject and verb

   ▶ **Conversations with students helped the dean understand the need for more career counselors.**

   NOTE: Use paired commas, however, to set off any extra material inserted between the subject and the verb. See 26c.

   ▶ **The fund manager, a billionaire, has been married five times.**

2. not before the word *and* that connects two verbs to the same subject

   ▶ **Amy Tan has written novels and adapted them for the screen.**

3. not *after* a coordinating conjunction (*and, but, or, nor, so, for, yet*) connecting two independent clauses, but *before* it

   ▶ **The movie tried to be engaging, but it failed miserably.**

4. not between two independent clauses without any coordinating conjunction, such as *and* or *but* (use either a period or a semicolon)

   ▶ **The writing had faded; it was hard to decipher.**

5. not between an independent clause and a following dependent clause introduced by *after, before, because, if, since, unless, until,* or *when* (no comma either before or after the subordinating conjunction)

   ▶ **Test results tend to be good when students study in groups.**

6. not before a clause beginning with *that*

   ▶ **The dean warned the students that the speech would be long.**

(continued)

(continued)

7. not before and after essential, restrictive information (see 26c)

   ▶ **The player who scored the goal became a hero.**
   [Here the information "who scored the goal" is essential. Without it, "The player became a hero" leads to the question, "Which player?" The clause "who scored the goal" restricts the meaning.]

8. not between a verb and its object or complement

   ▶ **The best gifts for college students are food and clothes.**

9. not after *such as*

   ▶ **Popular fast-food items, such as hamburgers and hot dogs, tend to be high in cholesterol.**

10. not separating cumulative adjectives (adjectives that cannot be connected by *and* and whose order cannot be reversed)

    ▶ **the little old stone house**

26c Commas with extra (nonrestrictive) elements

Use commas to set off a phrase or a clause that provides extra, nonrestrictive information (26a). Such information may be included almost as an aside or "by the way." If the insertion comes in midsentence, think of the commas as handles that can lift the information out without leaving your reader baffled.

▶ **His dog, a big Labrador retriever, is afraid of thunder.**
[If you read "His dog is afraid of thunder," you would not necessarily need to know what type of dog he owns to understand the point of the sentence. The insert provides additional information that is not necessary for understanding the meaning.]

▶ **She loves her car, a red Toyota.** [The insert after the comma provides additional information about her car.]

▶ **The firm's financial analyst, who is only twenty-five, has been promoted.** [The independent clause "The firm's financial analyst has been promoted" does not lead the reader to ask, "Which analyst?" The relative clause merely adds interesting information; it does not define or restrict the noun *analyst*.]

However, do not use commas to set off essential (restrictive) information.

▶ **The people who live in the apartment above mine make too much noise.** [If you read only "The people make too much noise," you would ask, "Which people?" The relative clause here restricts "the people" to a subgroup: not all people make too much noise; those in the apartment above do.]

26d Special uses of commas

To set off a phrase that modifies the whole sentence (an absolute phrase)

▶ **The audience looking on in amusement, the valedictorian blew kisses to all her favorite instructors.**

To set off an inserted idea, a contrast, or a conversational tag (such as *yes, no, well*, or a direct address)

▶ **Yes, the author has again written a probing analysis.**

▶ **The show dwelt on tasteless, not educational, details.**

▶ **Whatever you build here, Mr. Trump, will cause controversy.**

To separate the day from the year in a date

▶ **On May 14, 1998, the legendary singer Frank Sinatra died.**

NOTE: No comma is used before the year in the alternative style for dates when the day precedes the month: 14 May 1998

To divide numbers into thousands or millions

▶ 1,200 ▶ 515,000 ▶ 34,000,000

NOTE: No commas are necessary in years (1999), numbers in addresses (3501 East 10th Street), or page numbers (page 1002).

To set off a person's title or degree (31b)

▶ **Stephen L. Carter, PhD, gave the commencement speech.**

To separate the parts of an address

▶ **Alice Walker was born in Eatonton, Georgia, in 1944.**

NOTE: Do not use a comma before a ZIP code: Berkeley, CA 94704.

Apostrophes

Apostrophes show a possessive relationship (*the government's plans*—the plans of the government, belonging to the government). They also signal omitted letters in contractions (see item 3, below).

27a Apostrophe: Yes and no

> **KEY POINTS**
> Apostrophe: Yes

1. Use -*'s* for the possessive form of all nouns except those already ending in plural -*s*: *student's, reporter's, women's, boss's*.

2. Use an apostrophe alone for the possessive form of plural nouns that end with -*s*: *students', bosses'* (27b).

3. Use an apostrophe to indicate omitted letters in contractions formed by omitting part of a word, such *as not, is, are, us, am, would,* or *will,* as in *wasn't, it's, they're, let's, I'm, he'd,* or *we'll*. However, some readers of formal academic writing may object to such contractions.

NOTE: If you do use a contraction, use *it's* only to stand for "it is" or "it has": *It's a good idea; it's been a long time* (see 27d).

> **KEY POINTS**
> Apostrophe: No

1. Do not use an apostrophe to form plurals of nouns: *big bargains, coming attractions*. See 27c for rare exceptions.

2. Never use an apostrophe before an -*s* ending on a verb: *She likes him*.

3. Do not use an apostrophe with possessive pronouns *hers, its, ours, yours, theirs: The house lost its roof*.

4. MLA, APA, and *Chicago* styles recommend that you not use an apostrophe to form the plurals of names (*the Browns*), abbreviations (*VCRs*), and decades (*the 1990s*).

5. With inanimate objects and concepts, *of* is often preferred to an apostrophe: *the end of the garden, the back of the desk, the cost of the service*.

27b Special instances of the apostrophe to show possession

More than one noun When you want to indicate separate ownership for two nouns in a sentence, make each one possessive.

▶ Vargas Llosa's and Roth's recent works have received glowing reviews.

For joint ownership, use only one apostrophe: *Sam and Pat's house.*

Compound nouns Add the *-'s* to the last part of a compound noun.

▶ The taxi driver borrowed his brother-in-law's car.

Singular words ending in *-s* Add *-'s* for the possessive.

▶ Dylan Thomas's imagery conjures up the Welsh landscape.

NOTE: When a singular word ending in *-s* has a *-z* pronunciation, an apostrophe alone can also be used: *Moses' law.*

Plural nouns If a plural noun does not end in *-s*, add *-'s* to form the possessive: *the women's* tasks. Add an apostrophe alone to a noun forming its plural with an *-s: the students' suggestions.*

27c *-'s* for a plural form: Two exceptions

1. Use *-'s* for the plural form of letters of the alphabet. Italicize only the letter, not the plural ending.

   ▶ Georges Perec wrote a novel with no *e*'s in it at all.

2. Use *-'s* for the plural form of a word used to refer to the word itself. Italicize the word used as a word, but do not italicize the *-'s* ending.

   ▶ You have used too many *but*'s in that sentence.

27d *It's* and *its*

When deciding whether to use *its* or *it's,* think about meaning. *It's* means *it is* or *it has. Its* means "belonging to it." Use the apostrophe only if you intend *it is* or *it has.*

▶ It's a good idea.   ▶ The committee took its time.

Many writers slip up with these forms. Use your spelling checker to search your entire document for instances of both *its* and *it's,* and check each one with the "Am I saying *it is* or *it has*?" test. If the answer is yes, use *it's* (or *it is*). If the answer is no, use *its.*

28 Quotation Marks

28a How to use quotation marks

Double quotation marks indicate the beginning and end of a short quotation—the exact words that someone said, thought, or wrote.

▶ **"The world is a stage, but the play is badly cast."**

—Oscar Wilde in "Lord Arthur Savile's Crime"

(For more on changing or omitting parts of quotations and on using long quotations, see 8c. For indirect quotations, see 28e and 37c.)

Quoting a complete sentence   After an introductory verb such as *says,* use a comma and a capital letter. Put the sentence period inside the quotation marks at the end.

▶ **Calvin Trillin says, "As far as I'm concerned, *whom* is a word that was invented to make everyone sound like a butler."**

—In "Whom Says So?"

After a complete sentence introducing a quotation, use a colon and a capital letter.

▶ **Nora Ephron always made us laugh even about depressing truths: "When your children are teenagers, it's important to have a dog so that someone in the house is happy to see you."**

—In I Feel Bad about My Neck: And Other
Thoughts on Being a Woman

Quoting part of a sentence   When you integrate the words of a quote into the structure of your own sentence, use no special introductory punctuation other than the quotation marks.

▶ **To Hendrik Hertzberg at age nine, President Truman was "like an elderly pediatrician."**

—In Politics

Placing periods and commas   Always put periods and commas inside quotation marks, even if the period or comma does not appear in the original quotation.

► When Rosovsky characterizes Bloom's idea as "mind-boggling," he is not offering praise.

—In *The University*

NOTE: In a documented paper in MLA style, put the period after a parenthetical citation, not before the closing quotation marks. See 8c for long quotations.

► Geoffrey Wolff observes that when his father died, there was nothing "to suggest that he had ever known another human being" (11).

—In *The Duke of Deception*

Placing question marks and exclamation points When question marks and exclamation points are part of the original source, put them inside the quotation marks. When your own sentence is a statement, do not use a comma or period in addition to a question mark or exclamation point.

► She asked, "Where's my mama?"

When a question mark or exclamation point belongs to your own sentence, put it outside the closing quotation marks.

► This paper answers the question: What was "the Contract with America"?

Placing semicolons and colons Put semicolons and colons outside the quotation marks if they are part of your sentence and not part of the quotation.

► Abigail Adams asked her husband to "remember the ladies"; however, the Constitution did not include rights for women.

28b **Quotation marks in dialogue**

Do not add closing quotation marks until the speaker changes or you interrupt the quotation. Begin each new speaker's words on a new line.

► "I'm not going to work today," he announced to his son. "Why should I? My boss is away on vacation. And I have a headache."

   "Honey, your boss is on the phone," his wife called from the bedroom.

If a quotation from one speaker continues for more than one paragraph, place closing quotation marks at the end of only the *final* paragraph. However, place opening quotation marks at the beginning of every paragraph so that readers realize that the quotation is continuing.

28c Double and single quotation marks

Use single quotation marks to enclose a quotation or a short title within a quotation that uses double quotation marks. (British usage is different, with single quotation marks for the original quotation and double quotation marks for an enclosed quotation.)

▶ Joan announced, "I read most of 'Travels in Siberia' this weekend."

▶ To our surprise, the lecturer boasted, "Several scholars have said that I am 'brilliant and original.'"

NOTE: Put a comma or a final sentence period inside both single and double quotation marks.

28d How to handle titles, definitions, and translations

KEY POINTS
How to Handle Titles

1. Use quotation marks with the title of an article, short story, poem, song, or chapter: "Richard Corey"; "Lucy in the Sky with Diamonds"; "I Stand Here Ironing"; "America: The Multinational Society."

2. Use italics (or underlining in handwritten material) with the title of a book, journal, magazine, newspaper, film, play, or long poem published alone: *Finishing the Hat, Newsweek, The Hours, The Iliad.*

For more on capital letters with titles, see 31a.

Enclose definitions and translations in quotation marks.

▶ The abbreviation *p.m.* is short for "post meridiem," which means "afternoon."

28e When not to use quotation marks

Not around indirect quotations

▶ One student reported that he couldn't get any of his first-choice classes.

Not around clichés, slang, or trite expressions Instead, revise (see 16b).

> to be involved.
> ► All they want is ~~"a piece of the action."~~
>   ^

Not at the beginning and end of long indented quotations In academic writing, when you use MLA style to quote more than three lines of poetry or four typed lines of prose, indent the whole passage one inch (or ten spaces) from the left margin. Indent five spaces in APA or *Chicago* style. Do not enclose the quoted passage in quotation marks, but retain any internal quotation marks (see an example in 8c).

Not around your own essay title Use quotation marks in your title only when your title includes a quotation or the title of a short work, as in the following example. In addition, do not underline or italicize your own title:

> ► Alice Walker's "Everyday Use" and the Issue of Heritage

29 Other Punctuation Marks

29a Periods, question marks, and exclamation points

Periods, question marks, and exclamation points end a sentence. The Modern Language Association (MLA), in its list of Frequently Asked Questions at <http://www.mla.org>, recommends leaving one space after a punctuation mark at the end of a sentence, but it also sees "nothing wrong with using two spaces after concluding punctuation marks." (Consult your instructor.) In a list of works cited, however, whether you are using MLA, APA, or other styles, leave only one space after each period in an entry.

Period (.) Use a period to end a sentence or to signal an abbreviation: *Mr., Dr., a.m.,* and so forth (see 31b). Do not use a period with a name of a government agency or organization indicated by initials, in an acronym (an abbreviation pronounced as a word), or in Internet abbreviations indicated by initials: *ACLU, IRS, NOW, URL.*

Question mark (?) Use a question mark to signal a direct question.

► When will the troops come home?

Do not use a question mark with an indirect question (see 37c).

▶ **The interviewer asked when the troops would come home**

Exclamation point (!) An exclamation point at the end of a sentence tells the reader that the writer considers the statement surprising, extraordinary, or worthy of emphasis.

NOTE: Avoid exclamation points in academic writing, which tends to favor a restrained, understated style. Instead, let your words convey the points you want to emphasize.

29b Semicolons

> **KEY POINTS**
> Semicolon: Yes

1. between closely connected independent clauses with no *and, but, or, nor, so, for* or *yet* connecting them.

   ▶ **Biography tells us about the subject; biographers also tell us about themselves.**

   NOTE: Do not overuse semicolons in this way. They are more effective when used sparingly. Save them for when you need to emphasize the close connection between independent clauses. Do not use a capital letter to begin a clause after a semicolon.

2. between independent clauses connected with a transitional expression, such as *however, moreover, in fact, nevertheless, above all,* or *therefore* (see the list in 14b)

   ▶ **The results of the study support the hypothesis; however, further research with a variety of tasks is necessary.**

3. to separate items in a list containing internal commas

   ▶ **When I cleaned out the refrigerator, I found a chocolate cake, half-eaten; some canned tomato paste, which had a blue fungus growing on the top; and some possibly edible meat loaf.**

Do not use semicolons interchangeably with colons. Section 29c shows when to use colons.

29c Colons

A colon (:) signals anticipation. It follows an independent clause and introduces information that readers will need. A colon tells readers, "What comes next will define, illustrate, expand, or explain what you have just read."

▶ Ellsworth Kelly has produced a variety of works of art: drawings, paintings, prints, and sculptures.

🔑 KEY POINTS
Colon: Yes

1. after an independent clause to introduce a list

   ▶ The students included three pieces of writing in their portfolios: a narrative, an argument, and a documented paper.

2. after an independent clause to introduce an explanation, expansion, or elaboration

   ▶ After an alarming cancer diagnosis and years of treatment, Lance Armstrong was victorious: he won the Tour de France seven times.

   Some writers prefer to use a capital letter after a colon introducing an independent clause. Be consistent in your usage.

3. to introduce a rule or principle, which may begin with a capital letter

   ▶ The main principle of public speaking is simple: Look at the audience.

4. to introduce a quotation that is not integrated into your sentence and not introduced by a verb such as *say*

   ▶ Oscar Wilde makes the point well: "The real schools should be the streets."

   a colon also introduces a long quotation set off from your text (see 8c).

5. in salutations, precise time notations, biblical citations, and within titles

   Dear Chancellor Witkin: 7:20 p.m.

   To: The Chancellor   Genesis 37:31–35

   Isamu Noguchi: A Sculptor's World [book title and subtitle]

Do not use a colon directly after a verb (such as a form of *be* or *include*); after expressions such as *for example, especially*, and *such as*; or after a preposition.

▶ The book includes a preface, an introduction, an appendix, and an index.

▶ They packed many foods for the picnic, such as tortilla chips, salsa, and three-bean salad.

▶ His taste is so varied that he furnishes his living room with antiques, modern art, and art deco lighting fixtures.

29d Dashes, parentheses, slashes, and brackets

Dashes (—) set off material that is inserted into a sentence. Type a dash or two hyphens with no extra space before, after, or between them. (Software will automatically convert two hyphens to a dash as you type.)

▶ Armed with one weapon—his wit—he set off.

Commas can sometimes be used to set off inserted material, too, but when the insertion itself contains commas, dashes are preferable.

▶ The contents of his closet—torn jeans, frayed jackets, and suits shiny on the seat and elbows—made him reassess his priorities.

Parentheses ( ) mark an aside or some supplementary information.

▶ Everyone admired Chuck Yeager's feat (breaking the sound barrier in level flight in 1947).

At the end of a sentence, place the period inside the last parenthesis only when a complete new sentence is enclosed.

▶ Competition in the aerospace industry followed Chuck Yeager's feat. (In 1947, Yeager broke the sound barier in level flight.)

Slashes (/) separate lines of poetry quoted within your own text. Insert a space before and after a slash. For quoting four or more lines of poetry, see 8c.

▶ Elizabeth Barrett Browning writes of loss and enduring presence: "Go from me. Yet I feel that I shall stand / Henceforward in thy shadow."

Slashes are also used to designate word options such as *and/or* and *he/she*. Do not overuse these expressions.

Square brackets ([ ]) indicate inserted or changed material within a quotation. Insert only words or parts of words that help the quotation fit into your sentence grammatically or that offer necessary explanation.

▶ According to Ridley, information is "the key to both of these features of life [the ability to reproduce and to create order]."

Use [sic], meaning "thus," to indicate that an error in what you are quoting appears in the original source and is not your own error.

Angle brackets (< >) enclose e-mail addresses and URLs when they are required in an MLA paper or works-cited list (see items 49–51 in 9g).

29e Ellipsis dots

Use an ellipsis mark, or three dots with a space between each dot (. . .), when you omit material from the middle of a quotation. Do not use ellipsis dots at the beginning or end of a quotation unless the omission of part of a sentence occurs at the beginning or end of your own sentence. See also 8d.

▶ Ruth Sidel reports that the women in her interviews "have a commitment to career . . . and to independence" (27).

When the omitted material falls at the end of a quoted sentence, put a period before the three ellipsis dots, making four dots in all.

▶ Ruth Sidel reports that some women "have a commitment to career, to material well-being, to success, and to independence. . . . In short, they want their piece of the American Dream" (27).

To omit material at the end of a quoted sentence when the omission coincides with the end of your own sentence, use three dots, and place the sentence period after the parenthetical reference to the source.

▶ Ruth Sidel reports that some women "have a commitment to career . . . " (27).

When you omit a complete sentence, use three ellipsis dots after the period. To omit one line or more of poetry from a long, indented quotation, indicate the omission with a line of dots.

▶ Forlorn! The very word is like a bell
 To toll me back from thee to my sole self!
 . . . .
 Was it a vision, or a waking dream?
 Fled is that music:—Do I wake or sleep?

30 Italics and Underlining

Use italics or underlining to highlight a word, phrase, or title. Word processing programs offer italic type, and current MLA guidelines recommend italics in place of underlining. However, underlining can be useful in annotating rough drafts because it is more distinctive. When writing online, use italics because underlining is used for links.

30a Italicize titles of long, whole works

Italicize the titles of books, magazines, newspapers, plays, films, television and radio series, long poems, musical compositions, software programs, works of art, and Web sites.

▶ *The Sun Also Rises*

▶ *Newsweek*

▶ *The Daily Show*

See 28d and 28e for more on how to handle the title of a short work or the title of your own essay.

NOTE: Do not italicize the names of sacred works such as the Bible, books of the Bible (Genesis, Psalms), and the Koran (Qur'an) or the names of documents such as the Declaration of Independence and the Constitution.

30b Italicize letters, figures, words used as words, named transportation, and words from other languages not yet adopted in English

▶ *Mayflower*   ▶ *Columbia*

▶ a lowercase *r*   ▶ a big gold *5*

▶ *Zarf* is a useful word for some board games.

▶ The author's *Weltanschauung* promotes gloom.

30c Underlining and italics online

In an online source, URLs are hyperlinked and therefore appear as underlined on the screen. When you write for publication on the Web, always use italics to indicate titles and other usually underlined expressions.

However, some plain-text e-mail providers may not support text features such as italics or underlining. In such cases, use single underscore marks to indicate underlining (James Joyce's _Ulysses_) and asterisks for emphasis (They were *noticeably* antagonistic).

31 Capitals, Abbreviations, and Numbers

31a Capitals

Use capital letters in the following instances.

For the pronoun *I* and the first word of a sentence

Although some people do not capitalize the pronoun *I* or the first word of a sentence when writing emails, it is important to do so when writing to your instructor or supervisor.

With specific names (proper nouns):

Albert Einstein	March
Spaniards, the Navajo	Wednesday
Spain, Greece	the Fourth of July
the Adirondacks	Buddhism, Buddhists
Golden Gate Park	the Bible, biblical
the Roosevelt Memorial	the Koran (or the Qur'an)
University of Texas	the Civil War
Department of English	the USS *Kearsarge*
the Red Cross	the Milky Way
the Renaissance	Kleenex, Xerox

Use internal capitals when appropriate for online names such as *YouTube* and *eBay*.

NOTE: Do not capitalize general classes or types of people, places, things, or ideas: *government, jury, mall, prairie, utopia, traffic, court, the twentieth century, goodness, reason.*

With a title before a person's name

▶ The reporter interviewed Senator Feingold.

Do not use a capital when a title does not precede a person's name.

▶ **Each state elects two senators.**

For major words in titles In titles of published books, journals, magazines, essays, articles, films, poems, and songs, use a capital letter for all words except articles (*the, a, an*), coordinating conjunctions (*and, but, or, nor, so, for, yet*), *to* in an infinitive (*to stay*), and prepositions unless they begin or end a title or subtitle.

▶ **"Wrestling with the Angel: A Memoir"**

For the first word of a quoted sentence

▶ **Quindlen says, "This is a story about a name," and thus tells us the topic of her article.**

However, do not capitalize when you merge a quotation into your own sentence:

▶ **When Quindlen says that she is writing "a story about a name," she is announcing her topic.**

For capital letters after colons, see 29c, item 2.

NOTE: Avoid the prolonged use of capital letters in online communications. Readers may perceive it as shouting.

31b Abbreviations

Do not abbreviate words to save time and space. For example, write *through*, not *thru; night*, not *nite; chapter*, not *chap; pound* not *lb*.

In general, use a name *(Spock)* with no title when you refer to a person in an essay. Omit any abbreviated titles: *Mr., Ms., Mrs., Prof., Dr., Gen.,* and *Sen*. Some abbreviated titles, however, appear after names: *Sr., Jr., PhD, MD, BA,* and *DDS*. Never use a title both before and after a name; choose one or the other.

▶ **Dr. Spock**   ▶ Benjamin Spock, MD

Sometimes titles such as *MD* appear with periods: *M.D.;* however, both MLA and *The Chicago Manual of Style* prefer not to include periods. Whichever form you use, be consistent. Do not abbreviate a title that is not attached to a name.

doctor
▶ **He went to the ~~dr.~~ twice last week.**
                    ^

Use common and familiar abbreviations, such as FBI, IRS, UCLA, YMCA, SAT, CD-ROM. If you use a specialized abbreviation, first use the term in full with the abbreviation in parentheses; then use the abbreviation. See 29a for more on periods and abbreviations.

▶ The Graduate Record Examination (GRE) is required by many graduate schools. GRE preparation is therefore big business.

For the plural of an abbreviation, just add -s: VCRs; CDs; SUVs.

Abbreviate terms used with times and numbers. Use the abbreviations *BC, AD, AM* (or *a.m.*), *PM* (or *p.m.*), *$, mph, wpm, mg, kg,* and other units of measure only when they occur with specific numbers. Do not abbreviate days of the week or months in your text; in MLA works-cited lists, however, use abbreviations for all months, except May, June, and July.

▶ **35 BC** [meaning "before Christ," now often replaced with BCE, "before the common era"]

▶ **AD 1776** [*anno domini,* "in the year of the Lord," now often replaced with CE, "common era," used after the date: 1776 CE]

▶ **2:00 AM, 2:00 A.M., or 2:00 a.m.** [*ante meridiem,* Latin for "before midday"; always use periods with the lowercase letters *a.m.* and *p.m.*]

Do not use these abbreviations when no number is attached to them.

▶ They arrived late in the p.m. afternoon.

Abbreviate common Latin terms. Use *etc., e.g.,* and *NB,* but only in notes, parentheses, and source citations, not in the body of your text.

31c Numbers

Spell out numbers at the beginning of a sentence.

▶ One hundred twenty-five members voted for the new bylaws.

▶ Thirty thousand people attended the rally.

Even after plural numbers, use the singular form of *hundred, thousand,* and *million.* Add a plural *-s* only when there is no preceding number: Hundreds *of books were damaged in the flood.* Five hundred *books were damaged in the flood.*

In the humanities and in business letters

- Use words for numbers consisting of not more than two words and for fractions (*nineteen, fifty-six, two hundred, one-half*).
- Use a combination of words and numerals for numbers over a million (*45 million*).
- Use the numeral and symbol for percentages and money (*75%, $24.67*), or spell out the expression if it is fewer than four words (*seventy-five percent, twenty-four dollars*).
- Use numerals for longer numbers (*326; 5,625*).
- Use numerals in the following instances:

  Time and dates: *6 p.m. on 31 July 2010*

  Decimals: *20.89*

  Statistics: *median score 35*

  Addresses: *16 East 93rd Street*

  Chapters, pages, scenes, lines: *Chapter 5, page 97*

  Abbreviations or symbols: *6°C (temperature Celsius), 6´7˝ (feet and inches)*

  Scores: *The Giants won the World Series 4–1.*

In scientific and technical writing

- Write all numbers above nine as numerals.
- Write numbers below ten as numerals only when they show precise measurement, such as when they are grouped and compared with other larger numbers (*5 of the 39 participants*), or when they precede a unit of measurement (*6 cm*), indicate a mathematical function (*8%; 0.4*), or represent a specific time, date, age, score, or number in a series.
- Write fractions as words: *two-thirds.*

NOTE: For the plural form of numerals, do not use an apostrophe. Use *-s,* not *-'s: in the 1980s, 700s in the SATs.*

32 Hyphens

32a Hyphens with prefixes

Many words with a prefix (element attached to the beginning of a word) are spelled without hyphens: *cooperate, multilingual, unnatural.* Others are hyphenated: *all-inclusive, self-indulgent.* Always use a hyphen when the main word is a number or a proper noun: *post-2000, all-American.* If you are unsure about whether to insert a hyphen, check a dictionary.

If you omit the second part of a hyphenated adjective, follow the hyphen with a space: *a one- to two-year commitment.*

32b Hyphens in compound words

Some compound nouns are written as one word (*toothbrush*), others as two words (*coffee shop*), and still others with one or more hyphens (*role-playing, father-in-law*). Always check an up-to-date dictionary for compound nouns and compound verbs (*cross-examine, baby-sit*).

NOTE: Take care also when using an apostrophe with a compound noun:

possessive apostrophe
▶ Her sister-in-law's children have good manners.

Hyphenate a compound adjective preceding a noun: *a well-organized party, a law-abiding citizen, a ten-page essay.* However, use no hyphen when the modifier follows the noun: *The party was well organized. Most citizens try to be law abiding. The essay was ten pages long.*

Do not insert a hyphen between an *-ly* adverb and an adjective or after an adjective in its comparative (*-er*) or superlative (*-est*) form: *a tightly fitting suit, a sweeter sounding melody.*

32c Hyphens in spelled-out numbers

Use hyphens when spelling out two-word numbers from twenty-one to ninety-nine (see 31c). Also use a hyphen in spelled-out fractions: *two-thirds of a cup.*

32d End-of-line hyphens

Most word processors either automatically hyphenate words or automatically wrap words around to the next line.

Choose the latter option to avoid the strange and unaccept-able word division that sometimes appears with automatic hyphenation.

Never insert a hyphen into a URL to split it across lines (34a). If a URL includes a hyphen, do not break the line after the hyphen—a reader may not know whether the hyphen is part of the address. Different documentation styles have additional guidelines for splitting URLs. See 9g, 10f, and 11f for specific instructions.

PART EIGHT

Writing across Languages and Cultures

GO GLOBAL

PURPOSE

Revising writing to match expectations of Standard Academic English can help you achieve your purpose more effectively.

- Are there elements of your written English—such as sentence structure, word order, pronoun usage—that you can focus on revising to clarify your purpose?

AUDIENCE

When reaching an audience across cultures and languages, it might be helpful to use more than one method for communicating the same message. For example, when delivering a message orally, you will increase your chances of being understood if you provide notes or other text in writing as well.

- What are some additional ways you can deliver your message?

VOICE

Most writers speak a variety of English that varies from Standard Academic English, sometimes in significant ways.

- At times, it might be appropriate to use vernacular language in an academic text for a specific purpose, but where can you carefully revise your writing to follow expectations of Standard Academic English consistently?

MEDIUM

Many writing technologies offer tools that will help you revise your writing to follow features of Standard Academic English.

- What tools can you use to find linguistic features of your own writing that you need to revise?

33 Diversity, Standard Academic English, and Multilingual Writers

College students in North America are a linguistically diverse group: monolingual English-speaking students who have no experience with other cultures and who may speak a local version of English; students who have grown up in North America among family and friends with their own languages and cultures; students who have learned English in formal or informal situations, either in their own countries or after they immigrated; students who speak several languages fluently; and various mixes and remixes of these categories. Use chapters 33–36 to help you with the particular language issues that concern you as you write.

33a Cultures and Englishes

While travel and the Internet make us more aware of diversity and other countries' languages and cultures, we are also experiencing a spread in the use of English. According to language scholar David Crystal, non-native speakers of English outnumber native speakers of English three to one (2003). More than 400 million people speak English as their native language, and more than one billion use English as a common language for special communicative, educational, and business purposes within their own communities. And by 2017, the estimated number of people speaking English will be about three billion—that is, half the world.

But languages are not fixed and static, and the users of English in their various locations adapt the language for their own use. The concept of one English or a "standard" language is becoming more fluid, more focused on the situation and the readers of any particular piece of writing rather than on one set of rules. Consequently, the English that is regarded as standard in North America is not necessarily standard in Australia, the United Kingdom, Hong Kong, Singapore, Indonesia, India, or Pakistan. Scholars see Englishes—varieties of English—in place of one monolithic language, and these Englishes claim their own names, such as Spanglish, Singlish, Hindlish, and Taglish.

Despite the complexity and fluidity of the varieties of English, with all their quirks, irregularities, rules, and exceptions, the conventions of Standard Academic English remain relatively constant in grammar, syntax, and vocabulary (though not in spelling), with only subtle variations from country to country and region to region. Whether you are monolingual—familiar only with American English—or are multilingual or learned English formally or informally as an ESL (English as a Second Language) student, in everyday life you, too, constantly switch the Englishes you use, depending on whether you are texting a friend, writing a report for a supervisor, or writing a research paper in college. In all instances, it is *you* in the writing but different *voices* of you. The academic voice is the one to use in academic contexts.

33b Brief editing guide: Spoken varieties and Standard Academic English

The following table shows some of the common features used by speakers of local varieties of English in North America (such as African American Vernacular English—AAVE—and many other local varieties) and other English-speaking countries when they move between their home culture and academia. Many of you who learned English as a second language with exposure to neighborhoods, friends, and local conditions will find these features familiar. Add your own examples to the table.

Spoken Vernaculars and Standard Academic English

Linguistic Feature of the Vernacular	Example (Nonstandard)	Edited for Standard Academic English
Omitted form of *be*	Maxine studying.	Maxine *is* studying.
Use of *be* for habitual action	Ray be working at home.	Ray *usually works* at home.
Use of *been* without *have*	I been looking for you.	*I have* (*I've*) been looking for you.
Omitted -ed	The books arrive this morning.	The books *arrived* this morning.
No -s ending for third person singular present tense verb	That book have a lot of pictures.	That book *has* a lot of pictures.
No plural form after a plural number	Jake own two dog.	Jake *owns* two *dogs*.

(continued)

(continued)

Linguistic Feature of the Vernacular	Example (Nonstandard)	Edited for Standard Academic English
Verb inversion before indefinite pronoun subject	Can't nobody do that.	*Nobody can* do that.
They instead of possessive *their*	The singers took they seats.	The singers took *their* seats.
Hisself instead of *himself*	That musician promote hisself too much.	That musician promotes *himself* too much.
Personal pronoun restates subject	His views, they too extreme.	His views *are* too extreme.
No apostrophe + *-s* for possessive	She my brother wife.	*She is* (*She's*) my *brother's* wife.
It used in place of *there*	It's a gate at the entrance.	*There is* (*There's*) a gate at the entrance.
Double negative	You don't know nothing.	You do*n't* know *anything*. / You *know nothing*.

34 Nouns and Articles (*a*, *an*, and *the*)

The articles *a, an, the,* or a zero article are used before nouns. To decide whether to use an article (*a, an,* or *the*) or no article at all before a noun, first you need to recognize the type of noun it is: proper or common, countable or uncountable. Some languages do not use articles or use them according to a different system, so if you had to learn English later in life rather than during childhood, you may still find articles troublesome.

34a Differentiating types of nouns

Nouns fall into two categories: proper nouns and common nouns.

Proper nouns　A proper noun names a unique person, place, or thing and begins with a capital letter: *Virginia Woolf, Indian Ocean, Grand Canyon, Museum of Contemporary Art.*

Common nouns   A common noun does not name a unique person, place, thing, or idea: *bicycle, furniture, plan, daughter, home, happiness.* Common nouns can be further categorized into two types, countable and uncountable, a distinction that does not apply in languages such as Japanese and Spanish:

- A *countable noun* can have a number before it (*one, two,* and so on), and it has a plural form. Countable nouns frequently add -*s* to indicate the plural: *picture, pictures; plan, plans.* Singular countable nouns can be used after *a, an, the, this, that, each, every.* Plural countable nouns can be used after *the, these, those, many, a few, both, all, some, several.*

- An *uncountable noun* has no plural form: *furniture, equipment, advice, information, scenery, happiness.* Uncountable nouns can be used after *the, this, that, much, some, any, no, a little, a great deal of,* or a possessive such as *my* or *their.* They can never be used after a number or a plural quantity word such as *several* or *many.* Never use an uncountable noun after *a* or *an.*

  ▶ My country has ~~a~~ lovely scenery.

Some nouns can be countable in one context and uncountable in another.

▶ **He loves** *chocolate.* [All chocolate, applies to the class: uncountable]

▶ **She gave him** *a chocolate.* [One piece of candy from a box: countable]

NOTE: You can use an uncountable noun in a countable sense—that is, indicate a quantity of it—by adding a word or phrase that indicates quantity, but the noun itself always remains singular: three pieces of *furniture,* two bits of *information,* many pieces of *advice.*

34b   Basic rules for *a*, *an*, and *the*

1. Use *the* whenever a reference to a common noun is specific and unique for the writer and reader (see 34c).

   ▶ **He loves (the) museum that Rem Koolhaas designed.**

2. Do not use *a/an* with plural countable nouns.

   ▶ **They cited ~~a~~ reliable surveys.**

3. Do not use *a* or *an* with uncountable nouns.

   ▶ He gave ~~a~~ helpful advice.

4. Use *a* before a consonant sound: *a bird, a sonnet, a house, a ukulele.* Use *an* before a vowel sound: *an ostrich, an hour, an ugly vase.*

5. To make a generalization about a countable noun, do one of the following:

   • Use the plural form: *Lions are majestic.*

   • Use the singular with *a/an: A lion is a majestic animal.*

   • Use the singular with *the* to denote a classification: *The lion is a majestic animal.*

6. Make sure that a countable singular noun is preceded by an article or by a demonstrative pronoun (*this, that*), a numeral, a singular word expressing quantity (22h), or a possessive.

   A (Every, That, One, Her) nurse
   ▶ ~~Nurse~~ has a difficult job.
   ^

7. In general, although there are many exceptions, use no article with a singular proper noun (*Mount Everest*), and use *the* with a plural proper noun (*the Himalayas*).

34c *The* for a specific reference

When you use a common noun that both you and the reader know refers to one or more specific persons, places, things, or concepts, use the article *the*. The reference can be specific in two ways: outside the text or inside it.

Specific reference outside the text

▶ I study *the* earth, *the* sun, and *the* moon. [the ones in our solar system]

▶ She closed *the* door. [of the room she was in]

▶ Her husband took *the* baby to the doctor. [the baby belonging to the couple]

Specific reference inside the text

▶ *The* kitten that her daughter brought home had a distinctive black patch above one eye. [a specific kitten—one that was brought home]

▶ Her daughter found a kitten. When they were writing a lost-and-found ad that night, they realized that *the* kitten had a distinctive black patch above one eye.

[The second mention is of a specific kitten identified earlier—the one her daughter had found.]

The with a superlative

▶ She chose *the most expensive* dessert on the menu.

34d Four questions to ask about articles

Ask four basic questions about a noun to decide whether to use an article and, if so, which article to use.

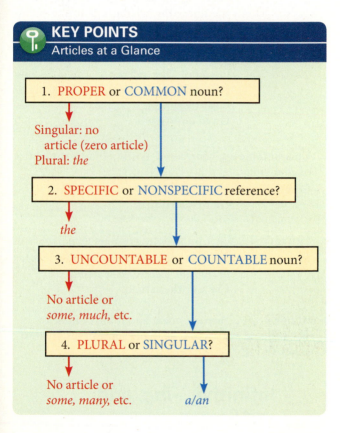

KEY POINTS
Articles at a Glance

1. PROPER or COMMON noun?

Singular: no
article (zero article)
Plural: *the*

2. SPECIFIC or NONSPECIFIC reference?

the

3. UNCOUNTABLE or COUNTABLE noun?

No article or
some, much, etc.

4. PLURAL or SINGULAR?

No article or
some, many, etc.   *a/an*

You can use the questions in the Key Points box to decide which article, if any, to use with the noun *poem* as you consider the following sentence:

▶ Milton wrote ___?___ moving poem about the blindness that afflicted him before he wrote some of his greatest works.

1. **Proper or common?** Is the noun *poem* a proper noun or a common noun?

   Common   It can be used after *a*.
   Go to question 2.

2. **Specific or nonspecific?** Does the common noun refer to a specific person, place, thing, or idea known to both the writer and the reader as unique, or is the reference nonspecific?

   Nonspecific   The word *poem* is not identified to the reader in the same way that *blindness* is. We know the reference is to the blindness that afflicted Milton before he wrote some of his greatest works. However, there is more than one "moving poem" in literature. The reference would be specific only if the poem had been previously discussed.
   Go to question 3.

3. **Uncountable or countable?** Is the noun uncountable or countable?

   Countable   We can say *one poem, two poems*.
   Go to question 4.

4. **Plural or singular?** Is the noun plural or singular?

   Singular   The first letter in the noun phrase *moving poem* is *m*, a consonant sound.
   Use *a* as the article.

▶ Milton wrote *a* moving poem about the blindness that afflicted him before he wrote some of his greatest works.

35 Infinitive, *-ing*, and *-ed* Forms

35a Verb followed by an infinitive

Some verbs are followed by an infinitive (*to* + base form): *His father wanted to rule the family.* Verbs commonly followed by an infinitive include the following:

agree	beg	choose	decide	fail
ask	bother	claim	expect	hope

manage	offer	pretend	refuse	want
need	plan	promise	venture	wish

Note any differences between English and any other language you know. In Spanish, for example, the word for *refuse* is followed by the equivalent of an -*ing* form.

► He refused ~~criticizing~~ the system.
  ^{to criticize}

Some verbs, such as *advise, allow, ask, cause, command, convince, encourage, expect, force, need, order, persuade, remind, require, tell, urge, want,* and *warn* are followed by a noun or pronoun and then an infinitive.

► The librarian *advised them to use* a better database.

Spanish and Russian use a *that* clause after verbs like *want.* In English, however, *want* is followed by an infinitive, not by a *that* clause.

► Rose *wanted* ~~that her son would~~ become a doctor.
  ^{her son to}

Infinitive with a negative When you use an infinitive, take care where you place a negative word. The position can create a difference in meaning.

► He did *not decide* to buy a new car. His wife did.

► He *decided not to* buy a new car. His wife was disappointed.

Make, let,* and *have After these verbs, use a noun or pronoun and a base form of the verb (without *to*).

► He *made his son practice* for an hour.

► They *let us leave* early.

► She *had her son-in-law wash* the car.

35b Verb followed by -*ing* (gerund)

► I can't help *laughing* at Jon Stewart.

The verbs that are systematically followed by an -*ing* form (known as a *gerund*) make up a relatively short and learnable list:

admit	avoid	can't help	delay	discuss
appreciate	be worth	consider	deny	dislike

enjoy	keep	practice	resist	suggest
finish	miss	recall	risk	tolerate
imagine	postpone			

▶ We considered ~~to invite~~ **inviting** his parents.

▶ Most people dislike ~~to hear~~ **hearing** cell phones at concerts.

Note that a negation comes between the verb and the -*ing* form.

▶ During their vacation, they enjoy *not* getting up early every day.

35c Preposition + -*ing*

After a preposition, use the -*ing* form that functions as a noun (the gerund).

▶ They congratulated him *on winning* the prize.

▶ He ran three miles *without stopping*.

▶ The cheese is the right consistency *for spreading*.

NOTE: Take care with the word *to*. *To* can work as part of a verb infinitive or as a preposition.

▶ They want *to adopt* a child. [verb infinitive]

▶ They are looking forward *to going* to the country this weekend. [preposition + -*ing* as noun]

Check the usage by seeing if you can substitute a noun phrase for the -*ing* form, as in *They are looking forward to the weekend.* See part 9, Words to Watch For: A Glossary of Usage, for forms used after *used to* and *get used to*.

35d Verb followed by an infinitive or –*ing*

Some verbs can be followed by either an infinitive or an -*ing* form (a gerund) with almost no discernible difference in meaning: *begin, continue, hate, like, love, start.*

▶ She continued *reading.*   ▶ She continued *to read.*

With a few verbs (*forget, remember, try, stop*), however, the infinitive and the -*ing* form signal different meanings.

▶ He *remembered to call* his parents. [intention]

▶ He *remembered calling* his parents. [past act]

35e   *-ing* and *-ed* forms as adjectives

Adjectives can be formed from both the present participle *-ing* form and the past participle form of verbs (*-ed* ending for regular verbs). Each form has a different meaning: The *-ing* adjective indicates that the word modified produces an effect; the past participle adjective indicates that the word modified has an effect produced on it.

▶ The **boring** cook served **baked** beans yet again.
  [The cook produces boredom. Everyone is tired of baked beans.]

▶ The **bored** cook yawned as she scrambled eggs.
  [The cook felt the emotion of boredom as she did the cooking, but the eggs could still be appreciated.]

Produces an Effect	Has an Effect Produced on It
amazing	amazed
amusing	amused
annoying	annoyed
confusing	confused
depressing	depressed
disappointing	disappointed
embarrassing	embarrassed
exciting	excited
interesting	interested
satisfying	satisfied
shocking	shocked
worrying	worried

NOTE: Do not drop the *-ed* ending from a past participle. Sometimes in speech it blends with a following *t* or *d* sound, but in writing the *-ed* ending must be included.

▶ I was surprise^d^ to see her wild outfit.

▶ The researchers were ~~worry~~ worried that the results were contaminated.

36 Sentence Structure and Word Order

36a Basic rules of order

- Always include the subject of a clause, even a filler subject like *it* or *there*.

  > The critics hated the movie because was ^it^
  > too sentimental.

  > When the company lost money, were immediate ^there^
  > effects on share prices.

- Do not put an adverb or a phrase between the verb and its object.

  > The quiz show host congratulated ~~many times~~
  > the winner/ ^many times.^

- Position a long descriptive phrase after, not before, the noun it modifies.

  > I would go to ~~known only to me~~ places/ ^known only to me.^

- Stick to the order of subject–verb–direct object.

  > ~~Good grades received~~ every student in the class/ ^E^ ^received good grades.^

- Do not use a pronoun to restate the subject.

  > Visitors to the Statue of Liberty ~~they~~ have worn the steps down.

- Do not include a pronoun that a relative pronoun has replaced.

  > The house that I lived in ~~it~~ for ten years has been sold.

36b Direct and indirect objects

Some verbs can be followed by both a direct object (DO) and an indirect object (IO). (The indirect object is the person or thing to whom or to what, or for whom or for what, something is done.) *Give, send, show, tell, teach, find, sell, ask, offer, pay, pass,* and *hand* are some verbs that take indirect objects. The indirect object follows the verb and precedes the direct object.

▶ He gave his mother some flowers.

▶ He gave her some flowers.

An indirect object can also be replaced with a prepositional phrase that *follows* the direct object.

▶ He gave some flowers to his mother.

NOTE: Some verbs—such as *explain, describe, say, mention,* and *open*—are never followed by an indirect object. However, they can be followed by a direct object and a prepositional phrase with *to* or *for.*

▶ She explained ~~me~~ the election process. to me.

36c Direct and indirect questions

A direct question ends with a question mark. When a direct question is reported, the indirect question then loses the quotation marks, the word order of a question, and the question mark. Sometimes changes in tense are also necessary after an introductory verb in the past tense.

Direct question   The buyer asked, "*Are the goods ready to be shipped?*"

Indirect question   The buyer asked *if the goods were ready to be shipped*

Use only a question word or *if* or *whether* to introduce an indirect question. Do not also use *that.*

▶ My boss wondered ~~that~~ why I had left early.

Avoid shifts between direct and indirect quotations (see 20d).

36d *Although* and *because* clauses

In some languages, a subordinating conjunction (such as *although* or *because*) can be used along with a coordinating conjunction (*but, so*) or a transitional expression (*however, therefore*) in the same sentence. In English, only one is used.

▶ *Although* he loved his father, ~~*but*~~ he did not visit him.

▶ ~~*Because*~~ **She**~~ she~~ loved children, *therefore* she became a teacher.

See 26a and 29b for punctuation with *therefore* and other transitional expressions.

PART NINE

Words to Watch For

37 A Glossary of Usage

Listed in this glossary are words that are often confused (*affect/effect, elicit/illicit*) or misspelled (*it's/its*). Also listed are nonstandard words (*irregardless, theirself*) and colloquial expressions (*OK*) that should be avoided in formal writing.

a, an Use *an* before words that begin with a vowel sound (the vowels are *a, e, i, o,* and *u*): *an apple, an hour* (silent *h*). Use *a* before words that begin with a consonant sound: *a planet, a yam, a ukelele, a house* (pronounced *h*).

accept, except, expect *Accept* is a verb: *She accepted the job offer. Except* is usually a preposition: *Everyone has gone to the party except me. Expect* is a verb: *They expect to see us when they come to town.*

adapt, adopt *Adapt* means "to adjust" and is used with the preposition *to*: *It takes people some time to adapt to the work routine after college. Adopt* means "to take into a family" or "to take up and follow": *The couple adopted a three-year-old child. The company adopted a more aggressive policy.*

adverse, averse *Adverse* is an adjective describing something as hostile, unfavorable, or difficult. *Averse* indicates opposition to something and usually takes the preposition *to*. *My training partner was averse to running in adverse conditions.*

advice, advise *Advice* is a noun: *Take my advice and don't start smoking. Advise* is a verb: *He advised his brother to stop smoking.*

affect, effect In their most common uses, *affect* is a verb, and *effect* is a noun. To *affect* is to have an *effect* on something: *Pesticides can affect health. Pesticides have a bad effect on health. Effect* can also be used as a verb meaning "to bring about": *The administration hopes to effect new environmental legislation. Affect* can also be used as a noun in psychology, meaning "a feeling or emotion."

aisle, isle You'll find an *aisle* in a supermarket or a church. An *isle* is an island.

all ready, already *All ready* means "totally prepared": *She is all ready for her final examination. Already* is an adverb meaning "by this time": *He has already written the report.*

all right, alright *All right* (meaning "satisfactory") is standard, especially in formal writing. *Alright* is an informal usage and is used in popular culture to mean "wonderful."

all together, altogether *All together* is used to describe acting simultaneously: *As soon as the boss had presented the plan, the managers spoke up all together. Altogether* is an adverb meaning "totally," often used before an adjective: *His presentation was altogether impressive.*

allude, elude *Allude* means "to refer to": *She alluded to his height. Elude* means "to avoid": *He eluded her criticism by leaving the room.*

allusion, illusion The noun *allusion* means "reference to": *Her allusion to my weight made me uncomfortable.* The noun *illusion* means "false idea": *He had no illusions about being a great cook.*

almost, most Do not use *most* to mean *almost: Almost* [not *Most*] *all my friends are computer literate.*

alot, a lot of, lots of *Alot* is nonstandard. *A lot of* and *lots of* are regarded by some as informal for *many* or *a great deal of: They have performed many* [not *lots of*] *research studies.*

aloud, allowed *Aloud* is an adverb meaning "out loud": *She read her critique aloud. Allowed* is a form of the verb *allow: The audience is not allowed backstage.*

ambiguous, ambivalent *Ambiguous* is used to describe a phrase or act with more than one meaning: *The ending of the movie is ambiguous; we don't know if the butler really committed the murder. Ambivalent* describes uncertainty and the coexistence of opposing attitudes and feelings: *The committee is ambivalent about the new design.*

among, between Use *between* for two items, *among* for three or more: *I couldn't decide between red or blue. I couldn't decide among red, blue, or green.*

amoral, immoral *Amoral* can mean "neither moral nor immoral" or "not caring about right or wrong," whereas *immoral* means "morally wrong": *Some consider vegetarianism an amoral issue, but others believe eating meat is immoral.*

amount, number *Amount* is used with uncountable expressions: *a large amount of money, work, or effort. Number* is used with countable plural expressions: *a large number of people, a number of attempts.* See 22h.

an See *a.*

ante-, anti- *Ante-* is a prefix meaning "before," as in *anteroom. Anti* means "against" or "opposite," as in *antiseptic* or *antifreeze.*

anyone, any one *Anyone* is a singular indefinite pronoun meaning "anybody": *Can anyone help me? Any one* refers to one from a group and is usually followed by *of* + plural noun: *Any one* [as opposed to any two] *of the suggestions will be considered acceptable.*

anyplace The standard *anywhere* is preferable.

anyway, anywhere, nowhere; anyways, anywheres, nowheres *Anyway, anywhere,* and *nowhere* are standard forms. The others, ending in *-s,* are not.

apart, a part *Apart* is an adverb: *The old book fell apart. A part* is a noun phrase: *I'd like to be a part of that project.*

as, as if, like See *like.*

as regards See *in regard to.*

assure, ensure, insure *Assure* means "to make confident": *She assured him that the children were safe. Ensure* means "to make sure something happens": *She ensured that the children were safe. Insure* means "to issue an insurance policy": *She insured her car.*

awful Avoid using *awful* to mean "bad" or "extremely": not *He's awful late* but *He's extremely late.*

a while, awhile *A while* is a noun phrase: *a while ago; for a while. Awhile* is an adverb meaning "for some time": *They lived awhile in the wilderness.*

bad, badly *Bad* is an adjective, and *badly* is an adverb. Use *bad* after linking verbs (such as *am, is, become, seem*): *They felt bad after losing the match.* Use *badly* to modify a verb: *They played badly.*

bare, bear *Bare* is an adjective meaning "naked": the *bare* facts, a *bare*faced lie. *Bear* is a noun (the animal) or a verb meaning "to carry" or "to endure": *He could not bear to watch the end of the game.*

barely Avoid creating a double negative (such as *can't barely type*). *Barely* should always take a positive verb: *She can barely type. They could barely keep their eyes open.* See *hardly.*

because, because of *Because* is a subordinating conjunction used to introduce a dependent clause: *Because it was raining, we left early. Because of* is a two-word preposition: *We left early because of the rain.*

being as, being that Avoid. Use *because* instead: *Because* [not *Being as*] *I love the opera, I bought season tickets.*

belief, believe *Belief* is a noun: *She has radical beliefs. Believe* is a verb: *He believes in an afterlife.*

beside, besides *Beside* is a preposition meaning "next to": *Sit beside me. Besides* is a preposition meaning "except for": *He has no relatives besides us. Besides* is also an adverb meaning "in addition": *I hate horror movies. Besides, there's a long line.*

better See *had better.*

between See *among.*

breath, breathe The first word is a noun, and the second is a verb: *Take three deep breaths. Breathe in deeply.*

can't hardly This expression is nonstandard. See *hardly.*

censor, censure The verb *censor* refers to editing or removing from public view. *Censure* means to criticize harshly. *The new film was censored for graphic content, and the director was censured by critics for his irresponsibility.*

cite, site, sight *Cite* means "to quote or mention"; *site* is a noun meaning "location"; *sight* is a noun meaning "view": *She cited the page number in her paper. They visited the original site of the abbey. The sight of him in his cap and gown made her cry.*

complement, compliment As verbs, *complement* means "to complete or add to something," and *compliment* means "to make a flattering comment about someone or something": *The wine complemented the meal. The guests complimented the hostess on the fine dinner.* As nouns, the words have meanings associated with the verbs: *The wine was a fine complement to the meal. The guests paid the hostess a compliment.*

compose, comprise *Compose* means "to make up"; *comprise* means "to include." *The conference center is composed of twenty-five rooms. The conference center comprises twenty-five rooms.*

conscience, conscious *Conscience* is a noun meaning "awareness of right and wrong." *Conscious* is an adjective meaning "awake" or "aware." *Her conscience troubled her after the accident. The victim was still not conscious.*

continual, continuous *Continual* implies repetition; *continuous* implies lack of a pause. *The continual interruptions made the fans restless. Continuous rain stopped the game for two hours.*

could care less This expression is often used but is regarded by some as nonstandard. In formal English, use it only with a negative: *They could not care less about their work.*

credible, creditable, credulous *Credible* means "believable": *The jury found the accused's alibi to be credible and so acquitted her. Creditable* means "deserving of credit": *A B+ grade attests to a creditable performance. Credulous* means "easily taken in or deceived": *Only a child would be so credulous as to believe that the streets are paved with gold.* See also *incredible, incredulous.*

custom, customs, costume All three words are nouns. *Custom* means "habitual practice or tradition": *a family custom. Customs* refers to taxes on imports or to the procedures for inspecting items entering a country: *go through customs at the airport.* A *costume* is "a style of dress": *a Halloween costume.*

decease, disease *Decease* is a verb or noun meaning "die" or "death." *Disease* is an illness: *The disease caused an early decease.*

decent, descent, dissent *Decent* is an adjective meaning "good" or "respectable": *decent clothes, a decent salary. Descent* is a noun meaning "way down" or "lineage": *She is of Scottish descent. Dissent,* used both as a noun and a verb, refers to disagreement: *Dissent over the Vietnam War led to protests in the streets.*

desert, dessert *Desert* can be pronounced two ways. It can be a noun with the stress on the first syllable (*the Mojave Desert*) or on the second as in the expression derived from the verb "to deserve" (*They got their just deserts*). It can also be a verb with the stress on the second syllable meaning "to abandon" (*He deserted his family*). *Dessert* (with the stress on the second syllable) is the sweet course at the end of a meal.

differ from, differ with To *differ from* means "to be unlike": *Lions differ from tigers in several ways, despite being closely related.* To *differ with* means to "disagree with": *They differ with each other on many topics but are still good friends.*

discreet, discrete *Discreet* means "tactful": *Be discreet when you talk about your boss.* *Discrete* means "separate": *He writes on five discrete topics.*

disease See *decease.*

disinterested, uninterested *Disinterested* means "impartial or unbiased": *The mediator was hired to make a disinterested settlement.* *Uninterested* means "lacking in interest": *He seemed uninterested in his job.*

dissent See *decent.*

do, due *Do* is a verb. Do not write "*Do* to his absences, he lost his job"; instead use the two-word preposition *due to* or *because of.*

drag, dragged Use *dragged* for the past tense of the verb *drag. Drug* is nonstandard when used as a verb.

drown, drowned The past tense of the verb *drown* is *drowned; drownded* is not a word: *He almost drowned yesterday.*

due to the fact that, owing to the fact that Wordy. Use *because* instead: *They stopped the game because* [not *due to the fact that*] *it was raining.*

each, every These are singular pronouns; use them with a singular verb. See also 22d and 22g.

each other, one another Use *each other* with two; use *one another* with more than two: *The twins love each other. The triplets all love one another.*

effect See *affect.*

e.g. In the body of your paper, use *for example* or *for instance* in place of this Latin abbreviation.

elicit, illicit *Elicit* means "to get or draw out": *The police tried in vain to elicit information from the suspect's accomplice.*

Illicit is an adjective meaning "illegal": *Their illicit deals landed them in prison.*

elude See *allude.*

emigrate, immigrate *Emigrate from* means "to leave a country"; *immigrate to* means "to move to another country": *They emigrated from Ukraine and immigrated to the United States.* The noun forms *emigrant* and *immigrant* are derived from the verbs.

eminent, imminent *Eminent* means "well known and noteworthy": *an eminent lawyer. Imminent* means "about to happen": *an imminent disaster.*

ensure See *assure.*

etc. This abbreviation for the Latin *et cetera* means "and so on." Do not let a list trail off with *etc.* Rather than *They took a tent, a sleeping bag, etc.,* write *They took a tent, a sleeping bag, cooking utensils, and a stove.*

every, each See *each.*

everyday, every day *Everyday* (one word) is an adjective meaning "usual": *Their everyday routine is to break for lunch at 12:30. Every day* (two words) is an adverbial expression of frequency: *I get up at 6:00 every day.*

except, expect See *accept.*

explicit, implicit *Explicit* means "clear and direct": *She gave explicit instructions. Implicit* means "implied": *A tax increase is implicit in the proposal.*

farther, further Both words can refer to distance: *She lives farther (further) from the campus than I do. Further* also means "additional" or "additionally": *The management offered further incentives. Further, the union proposed new work rules.*

female, male Use these words as adjectives, not as nouns in place of *man* and *woman: There are only three women* [not *females*] *in my class. We are discussing female conversational traits.*

few, a few *Few* means "hardly any": *She feels depressed because she has few helpful colleagues. A few* means "some"; it has more positive connotations than *few: She feels fortunate because she has a few helpful colleagues.*

fewer, less Formal usage demands *fewer* with plural countable nouns (*fewer holidays*), *less* with uncountable nouns (*less sunshine*). However, in informal usage, *less* with plural nouns commonly occurs, especially with *than: less than six* *items, less than ten miles, fifty words or less.* In formal usage, *fewer* is preferred.

first, firstly Avoid *firstly, secondly,* and so on, when listing reasons or examples. Instead, use *first, second,* and so on.

flaunt, flout *Flaunt* means "to show [something] off" or "to display in a proud or boastful manner." *Flout* means "to defy or to show scorn for." *When she flaunted her jewels, she flouted good taste.*

former, latter These terms should be used only in reference to a list of two people or things: *We bought lasagna and rhubarb, the former for dinner and the latter for dessert.* For more than two items, use *first* and *last: I had some pasta, a salad, and rhubarb; though the first was very filling, I still had room for the last.*

get married to, marry These expressions can be used interchangeably: *He will get married to his fiancée next week. She will marry her childhood friend next month.* The noun form is *marriage: Their marriage has lasted thirty years.*

go, say Avoid replacing the verb *say* with *go* because this is nonstandard usage: *Jane says* [not *goes*], *"I'm tired of this game."*

good, well *Good* is an adjective; *well* is an adverb: *If you want to write well, you must use good grammar.* See 24a.

had better Include *had* in Standard English, although it is often omitted in advertising and in speech: *You had better* [not *You better*] *try harder.*

hardly This is a negative word. Do not use it with another negative: not *He couldn't hardly walk* but *He could hardly walk.*

have, of Use *have,* not *of,* after *should, could, might,* and *must: They should have* [not *should of*] *appealed.*

hisself Nonstandard; instead, use the reflexive pronoun *himself,* and other standard forms of reflexive pronouns, such as *ourselves* and *themselves.*

I, me Do not confuse *I* and *me.* Use *I* only in the subject position, and use *me* only in the object position. See 23a for examples.

illicit See *elicit.*

illusion See *allusion.*

immigrate See *emigrate.*

imminent See *eminent.*

implicit See *explicit.*

imply, infer *Imply* means "to suggest in an indirect way": *He implied that further layoffs were unlikely. Infer* means "to guess" or "to draw a conclusion": *I inferred that the company was doing well.*

incredible, incredulous *Incredible* means "difficult to believe": *The violence of the storm was incredible. Incredulous* means "skeptical, unable to believe": *They were incredulous when he told them he had finished the marathon in three hours.*

infamous *Infamous* is an adjective meaning "notorious": *Blackbeard's many exploits as a pirate made him infamous along the American coast.* Avoid using it as a synonym for "not famous."

in regard to, as regards Use one or the other. Do not use the nonstandard *in regards to.*

insure See *assure.*

irregardless Nonstandard; instead use *regardless: He selected a major regardless of the preparation it would give him for a career.*

it's, its The apostrophe in *it's* signals not a possessive but a contraction of *it is* or *it has. Its* is the possessive form of the pronoun *it: The city government agency has produced its final report. It's available upon request.* See also 27d.

kind, sort, type In the singular, use each of these nouns with *this* and a singular noun: *this type of book.* Use in the plural with *these* and a plural noun: *these kinds of books.*

kind of, sort of Do not use these to mean "somewhat" or "a little." *The pace of the play was somewhat* [not *kind of*] *slow.*

knew, new *Knew* is the past tense of the verb *know. New* is an adjective meaning "not old." Don't confuse them in writing.

lend, loan *Lend* is a verb, and *loan* is ordinarily used as a noun: *Our cousins offered to lend us some money, but we refused the loan.*

less See *fewer.*

lie, lay Be sure not to confuse these verbs. *Lie* does not take a direct object; *lay* does. See 21c.

like, as, as if In formal usage, *as* and *as if* are subordinating conjunctions and introduce dependent clauses: *She walks as her father does. She looks as if she could eat a big meal. Like* is a preposition and is followed by a noun or pronoun, not by a clause: *She looks like her father.* In speech, however, and increasingly in writing, *like* is often used where formal usage dictates *as* or *as if*: *She walks like her father does. He looks like he needs a new suit.* Know your audience's expectations.

likely, liable *Likely* means "probably going to," while *liable* means "at risk of" and is generally used to describe something negative: *Eddie plays the guitar so well he's likely to start a band. If he keeps playing that way, he's liable to break a string. Liable* also means "responsible": *The guitar manufacturer cannot be held liable.*

literally Avoid overuse: *literally* is an adverb meaning "actually" or "word for word" and should not be used in conjunction with figurative expressions such as *my jaw literally hit the floor* or *he was literally bouncing off the walls. Literally* should be used only when the words describe exactly what is happening: *He was so scared his face literally went white.*

loan See *lend.*

loose, lose *Loose* is an adjective meaning "not tight": *This jacket is comfortable because it is so loose. Lose* is a verb (the past tense form and past participle are *lost*): *Many people lose their jobs in a recession.*

lots of See *alot.*

man, mankind Avoid using these terms because they are gender-specific. Instead, use *people, human beings, humankind, humanity,* or *men and women.*

may be, maybe *May be* consists of a modal verb followed by the base form of the verb *be*; *maybe* is an adverb meaning "perhaps." If you can replace the expression with *perhaps,* make it one word: *They may be there already, or maybe they got caught in traffic.*

me, I See *I.*

most See *almost.*

myself Use only as a reflexive pronoun (*I told them myself*) or as an intensive pronoun (*I myself told them*). Do not use *myself* as a subject pronoun: not *My sister and myself won* but *My sister and I won.*

no, not *No* modifies a noun: *The author has no intention of deceiving the reader. Not* modifies a verb, adjective, or adverb: *She is not wealthy. He does not intend to deceive.*

nowadays All one word. Be sure to include the final *-s.*

nowhere, nowheres See *anyway.*

number See *amount.*

off, off of Use only *off,* not *off of: She drove the car off* [not *off of*] *the road.*

oftentimes Do not use. Use *often.*

OK, O.K., okay Reserve these forms for informal speech and writing. Choose another word in a formal context: not *Her performance was OK* but *Her performance was satisfactory.*

one another See *each other.*

owing to the fact that See *due to the fact that.*

passed, past *Passed* is a past tense verb form: *They passed the deli on the way to work. He passed his exam. Past* can be a noun (*in the past*), an adjective (*in past times*), or a preposition (*She walked past the bakery*).

peak, peek, pique *Peak* is the top of a summit: *She has reached the peak of her performance. Peek* (noun or verb) means "glance": *A peek through the window is enough. Pique* (also a noun or a verb) has to do with feeling indignation: *Feeling insulted, he stormed out in a fit of pique.*

personal, personnel *Personal* is an adjective meaning "individual," while *personnel* is a noun referring to employees or staff: *It is my personal belief that a company's personnel should be treated like family.*

plus Do not use *plus* as a coordinating conjunction or a transitional expression. Use *and* or *moreover* instead: *He was promoted, and* [not *plus*] *he received a bonus.* Use *plus* as a preposition meaning "in addition to": *His salary plus his dividends placed him in a high tax bracket.*

pore, pour To *pore* is to read carefully or to ponder: *I saw him poring over the want ads before he poured himself a drink.*

precede, proceed *Precede* means "to go or occur before": *The Roaring Twenties preceded the Great Depression. Proceed* means "to go ahead": *After you pay the fee, proceed to the examination room.*

pretty Avoid using *pretty* as an intensifying adverb. Use *really, very, rather,* or *quite: The stew tastes very* [not *pretty*] *good.* Often, however, the best solution is to avoid using any adverb: *The stew tastes good.*

principal, principle *Principal* is a noun (*the principal of a school*) or an adjective meaning "main" or "most important": *His principal motive was monetary gain. Principle* is a noun meaning "standard or rule": *He always acts on his principles.*

quite, quiet Do not confuse the adverb *quite,* meaning "very," with the adjective *quiet* ("still" or "silent"): *We were all quite relieved when the audience became quiet.*

quote, quotation *Quote* is a verb. Do not use it as a noun; use *quotation: The quotation* [not *quote*] *from Walker tells the reader a great deal.*

real, really *Real* is an adjective; *really* is an adverb. Do not use *real* as an intensifying adverb: *She acted really* [not *real*] *well.*

regardless See *irregardless.*

respectable, respectful, respective *Respectable* means "presentable, worthy of respect": *Wear some respectable shoes to your interview. Respectful* means "polite or deferential": *Parents want their children to be respectful to adults. Respective* means "particular" or "individual": *The friends of the bride and the groom sat in their respective seats in the church.*

respectfully, respectively *Respectfully* means "showing respect": *He bowed respectfully when the queen entered. Respectively* refers to items in a list and means "in the order mentioned": *Horses and birds gallop and fly, respectively.*

rise, raise *Rise* is an intransitive verb: *She rises early every day. Raise* is a transitive verb: *We raised alfalfa last summer.* See 21c.

should (could, might) of Nonstandard; instead use *should have: You should have paid the bill.*

since Use this subordinating conjunction only when time or reason is clear: *Since you insist on helping, I'll let you paint this bookcase.* Unclear: *Since he got a new job, he has been happy.*

site, sight See *cite.*

sometimes, sometime, some time The adverb *sometimes* means "occasionally": *He sometimes prefers to eat lunch at* *his desk.* The adverb *sometime* means "at an indefinite time": *I read that book sometime last year.* The noun phrase *some time* consists of the noun *time* modified by the quantity word *some: After working for Honda, I spent some time in Brazil.*

sort, type See *kind.*

sort of See *kind of.*

stationary, stationery *Stationary* is an adjective meaning "not moving" (*a stationary vehicle*); *stationery* is a noun referring to writing paper.

supposedly Use *supposedly,* not *supposably: She is supposedly a great athlete.*

taught, thought Do not confuse these verb forms—a spelling checker won't catch the error. *Taught* is the past tense and past participle form of *teach; thought* is the past tense and past participle form of *think: The students thought that their professor had not taught essay organization.*

than, then *Then* is a time word; *than* must be preceded by a comparative form: *bigger than, more interesting than.*

their, there, they're *Their* is a pronoun indicating possession; *there* indicates place or is used as a filler in the subject position in a sentence; *they're* is the contracted form of *they are: They're over there, guarding their luggage.*

theirself, theirselves, themself Nonstandard; instead, use *themselves.*

threat, treat These words have different meanings, so be careful: *She gave the children some cookies as a treat. The threat of an earthquake was alarming.*

to, too, two Do not confuse these words. *To* is a sign of the infinitive and a common preposition; *too* is an adverb meaning *also; two* is the number: *She is too smart to agree to report to two bosses.*

uninterested See *disinterested.*

unique The adjective *unique* means "the only one of its kind" and therefore should not be used with qualifying adjectives like *very* or *most: His recipe for chowder is unique* [not *most unique* or *quite unique*].

used to, get (become) used to "Used to" tells about a past habit that no longer exists; it is followed by the base form of a verb: *He used to wear his hair long.* (Note that after *not,* the

form is *use to: He did not use to have a beard.*) The expression *get (become) used to,* meaning "get accustomed to," is followed by a noun or an *-ing* verb form: *She couldn't get used to driving on the left when she was in England.*

wear, were, we're *Wear* is a verb meaning "to have on" as clothes (*He always wears black*); *were* is a past tense form of *be; we're* is a contraction for *we are.*

weather, whether *Weather* is a noun; *whether* is a conjunction: *The weather will determine whether we go on the picnic.*

whose, who's *Whose* is a possessive: *Whose goal was that? Who's* is a contraction of *who is* or *who has: Who's the player whose pass was caught? Who's got the ball?*

your, you're *Your* is a pronoun used to show possession. *You're* is a contraction for *you are: You're wearing your new shoes today, aren't you?*

Text Credits

15: Susan Sontag, *On Photography*. New York: Farrar, Print. **15:** David Halle, "The Family Photograph." *Art Journal* 46.3 (1987): 217–25. *JSTOR*. Web. 15 Sept. 2010. **15:** Richard Chalfen, *Snapshot Versions of Life*. Bowling Green, OH: Popular-Bowling Green State UP, 1987. Print. **16:** Hiawatha Bray, "Polaroid Shutting Two Mass. Facilities, Laying off 150." Boston.com. *New York Times*, 8 Feb. 2008. Web. 14 Sept. 2010. **19:** Nicola Döring and Axel Gundolf. "Your Life in Snapshots: Mobile Weblogs." *Knowledge, Technology, and Policy* 19:1 (2006): 80–90. MasterFILE Premier. Web. 16 Sept. 2010. **19:** Sandra Boxer, "Prospecting for Gold among the Photo Blogs." *New York Times*, 25 May 2003. Web. 15 Sept. 2010. **19:** Meredith Badger, "Visual Blogs." *Into the Blogosphere: Rhetoric, Community, and Culture of Weblogs*. Ed. Laura J. Gurak, Smiljana Antonijevic, Laurie Johnson, Clancy Ratliff, and Jessica Reyman. U of Minnesota P, 2004. Web. 16 Sept. 2010. **20:** Shawn Michelle Smith, "Family Photographs and Kelly McKaig's Dreamworlds." *Frontiers: A Journal of Women Studies* 19.3 (1998): 98–111. *JSTOR*. Web. 17 Sept. 2010. **55:** Carlin Flora, "The Beauty Paradox." *Psychology Today* 47.1 (2014): 36–37. *Academic Search Complete*. Web. 4 Apr. 2014. **67:** Paul Fussell, *Uniforms: Why We Are What We Wear*. Boston: Houghton Mifflin, 2002. Print. **69:** Terence Des Pres, "Poetry and Politics." *The Writer in Our World*. Ed. Reginald Gibbons. Boston: Atlantic Monthly Press, 1986. 20. **69:** Ross Douthat, "The Truth about Harvard." *Atlantic*. Mar. 2005: 95–99. Print. **70:** *The Chicago Manual of Style*. 16th ed. Chicago: U of Chicago P, 2010. Print. **71:** Sarah Hatchuel, "Leading the Gaze: From Showing to Telling in Kenneth Branagh's Henry V and Hamlet." **108:** C. Bruck, "The Art of the Billionaire." *The New Yorker*. 6 Dec. 2010. 50–61. Print. **111:** W. J. Baumol, R. E. Litan, and C. J. Schramm, *Good Capitalism, Bad Capitalism, and the Economics of Growth and Prosperity*. New Haven, CT: Yale University Press, 2007. Print. **134:** R. J. Sternberg, *Psychology*. 4th ed. Toronto, Canada: Wadsworth, 2004. Print. **134:** D. A. Treffert and G. L. Wallace, "Islands of Genius." *Scientific American Mind* (January 2004). Retrieved from http://scientificamerican.com. **135:** L. Osborne, "Savant for a Day." *The New York Times Magazine* 22 June 2003. Retrieved from http://www.nytimes.com. **135:** A. Snyder, H. Bahramali, T. Hawker, and D. J. Mitchell, "Savant-like Numerosity Skills Revealed in Normal People by Magnetic Impulses." *Perception* 35 (2006): 837–845. doi:10.1068/p5539. **144:** Margaret Crompton, *George Eliot: The Woman*. London: Cox and Wyman, 1960. Print. **171:** Hermione Lee, *Virginia Woolf*. **171:** Donald Hall, *Remembering Poets*. **214:** Oscar Wilde, "Lord Arthur Savile's Crime." **214:** Calvin Trillin, "Whom Says So?" **214:** Nora Ephron, *I Feel Bad about My Neck: And Other Thoughts on Being a Woman*. **214:** David Remnick, Introduction. *Politics*. By Hendrik Hertzberg. New York: Penguin, 2004. xvii–xxiv. Print. **215:** Geoffrey Wolff, *The Duke of Deception*. **217:** The Modern Language Association (MLA), Frequently Asked Questions at http://www.mla.org.

Index

An asterisk (*) points to the page number on which you can find a definition, explanation, and/or example of the indexed term.

Planning Notes Using the Critical Thinking Framework

You may find it helpful to take notes on your purpose, audience, voice, and medium as you think about a specific writing project.

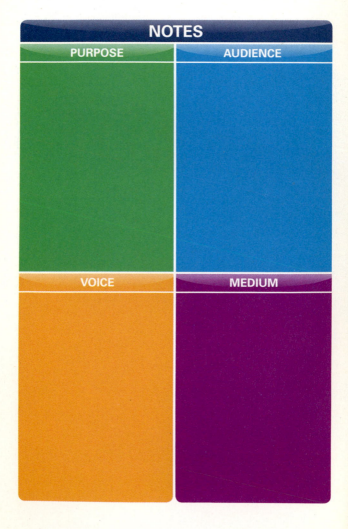

NOTES

PURPOSE

AUDIENCE

VOICE

MEDIUM

NOTES

PURPOSE	AUDIENCE

VOICE	MEDIUM

NOTES

PURPOSE

AUDIENCE

VOICE

MEDIUM

NOTES

PURPOSE	AUDIENCE

VOICE	MEDIUM

NOTES

PURPOSE	AUDIENCE

VOICE	MEDIUM

Common Correction and Editing Marks

Note: Numbers refer to sections in the book.

Abbreviation	Meaning
ab or abbr	abbreviation **31b**
adj	adjective **24**
adv	adverb **24**
agr	agreement **22, 23c**
art	article **34**
awk	awkward **13, 14, 20**
bias	biased language **16c, 23c**
case	pronoun case **23a**
cap (tom)	use a capital letter **31a**
comp	comparison **20a, 20h, 23a, 25e**
coord	coordination **14c, 26a**
cs	comma splice **19**
dic	diction **16**
db neg	double negative **24d**
dm	dangling modifier **20c**
doc	documentation **9–11**
-ed	error in *-ed* ending **21e**
frag	sentence fragment **18**
fs	fused sentence **19**
hyph	hyphenation **32**
ind quot	indirect quotation **20d, 36c**
-ing	*-ing* error **35**
ital	italics/underlining **30**
jar	jargon **16b**
lc (Me)	use lowercase, not capital **31a**
mix or mixed	mixed construction **20a**
mm	misplaced modifier **20b**
ms	manuscript form **4a, 4b, Model papers 1–4**
num	faulty use of numbers **31c**
p	punctuation **25–29**

Abbreviation	Meaning
pass	ineffective passive **13c, 21g**
pron	pronoun error **23**
quot	quotation error **8d**
ref	pronoun reference **23b, 23c**
rel cl	relative clause **23e, 26c**
rep	repetitive **12a**
r-o	run-on sentence **19**
-s	error in *-s* ending **22**
shift	needless shift **20d**
sp	spelling **1e**
s/pl	singular/plural **22, 34a**
sub	subordination **14c, 26b, 36d**
sup	superlative **24e**
s-v agr	subject-verb agreement **22**
trans	transition **14b, 19b**
und	use underlining or italics **30**
use	usage error **37**
vb	verb error **21**
vt	verb tense error **21d**
wdy	wordy **12**
wo	word order **36**
ww	wrong word **16, 37**

Symbol	Meaning
??	unclear
¶ or par	new paragraph
no ¶	no new paragraph
//	parallelism
⌒	close up space
#	add space
^	insert
ℓ	delete
∽	transpose
×	obvious error
⊙	needs a period
^stet	do not change

Research Paper Dos and Don'ts

- **DO start early and plan.** Gather the tools and materials you will need, and allot yourself time to complete your tasks by the assignment deadline.
- **DON'T be afraid to ask questions.** There are no "silly questions." Make sure you understand the assignment.
- **DO assemble your copy of the assignment,** your purpose statement and thesis statement, all your copies of your sources, your notebook and your notes, your working bibliography, and your proposal or outline.
- **DON'T panic at the beginning.** Take a deep breath, and give yourself a block of time to get started.
- **DO turn off your cell phone, log off** *Facebook,* close the door, and promise yourself you won't emerge before you have written several pages.
- **DON'T worry about perfection.** A draft is something you are going to edit, revise, and rework repeatedly. For now, just get something down on paper.
- **DON'T necessarily start at the beginning.**
- **DO write the parts you know most about first.**
- **DON'T constantly imagine your instructor's response to what you write.**
- **DO write as much as you can, as fast as you can.** Just keep writing and don't worry about gaps. Write at least something on each one of the points in your outline. Write until you feel you have expressed all your main points.

When revising, make an outline of what you have written and ask these questions:

- Have I covered the most important points?
- When I read my paper aloud, where do I hesitate to sort out the meaning?
- Do I come across as someone with ideas on this topic?
- Have I cited my sources accurately and responsibly?
- Where do I need to provide more evidence?

On the next page is a sample block schedule. Copy it, fill it out, and put your schedule in a place where you can look at it every day. In practice, you will find that several tasks overlap and the divisions are not so neat. If you finish a block before its deadline, move on and give yourself more time for the later blocks.